PS
3525
I 5156
Z52

Arthur Miller : new perspectives / edited and with an introduction by Robert A. Martin. — Englewood Cliffs, N.J. : Prentice-Hall, c1982.

x, 223 p. ; 21 cm. — (Twentieth century views)

"A Spectrum book."
Bibliography: p. 205-219.
Includes index.
ISBN 0-13-048801-1

1. Miller, Arthur, 1915-   —Criticism and interpretation—Addresses, essays, lectures.   I. Martin, Robert A.   II. Series.

PS3525.I5156Z52   812'.52—dc19   81-15752
                                                     AACR 2   MARC

Library of Congress

TWENTIETH CENTURY VIEWS

The aim of this series is to present the best in contemporary critical opinion on major authors, providing a twentieth century perspective on their changing status in an era of profound revaluation.

Maynard Mack, *Series Editor*
Yale University

ARTHUR MILLER

NEW PERSPECTIVES

Edited and
with an Introduction by
Robert A. Martin

Prentice-Hall, Inc. Englewood Cliffs, N.J. 07632

Library of Congress Cataloging in Publication Data
Main entry under title:

Arthur Miller: new perspectives.

"A Spectrum Book."
(Twentieth Century Interpretations)
Bibliography: p.
Includes index.
1. Miller, Arthur, 1915–   –Criticism and inter-
pretation–Addresses, essays, lectures. I. Martin,
Robert A.
PS3525.I5156Z52   812'.52   81–15752
                                       AACR2

ISBN 0-13-048801-1

ISBN 0-13-048793-7 (PBK.)

Editorial/production supervision by Donald Chanfrau
Manufacturing buyer: Barbara A. Frick

© 1982 by Prentice-Hall, Inc., Englewood Cliffs, New Jersey 07632

A SPECTRUM BOOK

10   9   8   7   6   5   4   3   2   1

Printed in the United States of America

PRENTICE-HALL INTERNATIONAL, INC., London
PRENTICE-HALL OF AUSTRALIA PTY. LIMITED, Sydney
PRENTICE-HALL OF CANADA, LTD., Toronto
PRENTICE-HALL OF INDIA PRIVATE LIMTED, New Delhi
PRENTICE-HALL OF JAPAN, INC., Tokyo
PRENTICE-HALL OF SOUTHEAST ASIA PTE. LTD., Singapore
WHITEHALL BOOKS LIMITED, Wellington, New Zealand

For John, Doug, Carole, and Christy Martin

Contents

Acknowledgments

I would like to thank Arthur Miller for permission to use quoted material; Harriet C. Jameson and Margaret Berg of the Rare Book Room at the University of Michigan for their invaluable assistance and courtesy; Ellen Dunlap of the Humanities Research Center Manuscript Collection at the University of Texas; and Viking Penguin, Inc., for permission to reprint excerpts from the following:

Arthur Miller's Collected Plays, © 1957 by Arthur Miller.
All My Sons, © 1947 by Arthur Miller.
Death of a Salesman, © 1949, renewed 1977 by Arthur Miller.
The Crucible, © 1953 by Arthur Miller.
A View from the Bridge, © 1955 by Arthur Miller.
After the Fall, © 1964 by Arthur Miller.
A Memory of Two Mondays, © 1955 by Arthur Miller.
Incident at Vichy, © 1964, 1965 by Arthur Miller.
The Price, © 1968 by Arthur Miller and Ingeborg M. Miller, Trustee.

Also, I would like to credit the following sources for secondary permissions:

Quotations from *The American Theater Today* edited by Alan S. Downer. Copyright © 1967 by Basic Books, Inc., Publishers, New York. Reprinted by permission.

Quotations from *What is Theatre* by Eric Bentley. Copyright © 1968 by Eric Bentley. Reprinted with the permission of Atheneum Publishers.

Quotations from "After the Silence" by Arthur Ganz in *Drama Survey,* 3 (Spring–Summer 1964). Reprinted with permission of the Editor, *Drama Survey.*

Quotations from *"Anti-Semite and Jew"* by Jean-Paul Sartre, trans. by George J. Becker. Copyright © 1948 by Schocken Books, Inc. Copyright renewed © 1976 by Schocken Books, Inc.

Quotations from *Six Plays of Henrik Ibsen* by Henrik Ibsen, trans. by Eva Le Gallienne (New York: Modern Library, 1932, pp. 254–55. Copyright © 1932 by Random House, Inc.

Excerpt from *The Affluent Society* by John Kenneth Galbraith. Copyright © 1958, 1969, 1976 by John Kenneth Galbraith. Reprinted by permission of Houghton Mifflin Company and André Deutsch Ltd.

ARTHUR MILLER

Introduction

by Robert A. Martin

I

Arthur Miller has occupied a central place in the American theater for more than three decades, ever since *Death of a Salesman* opened at the Morosco Theatre in New York City on February 10, 1949. Since that time, new plays by Miller have appeared at regular intervals, along with books of fiction, essays, reportage, and screenplays. This collection of essays undertakes to bring into public view the current state of Miller criticism and to assess his development as a playwright.

Miller's rapid rise to prominence suggests that he himself is "the man who had all the luck"—this, ironically, being the title of his first Broadway play, which closed after four performances in 1944. Most Miller plays have been better received, although a few, such as *The Creation of the World* and *The Archbishop's Ceiling,* have yet to find an audience. When *A View from the Bridge* reopened in its revised and expanded two-act form in 1956, Miller wrote in his Introduction to the published text:

> A play is rarely given a second chance. Unlike a novel, which may be received intially with less than enthusiasm, and then as time goes by hailed by a large public, a play usually makes its mark right off or it vanishes into oblivion. Two of mine, *The Crucible* and *A View from the Bridge,* failed to find large audiences with their original Broadway productions. Both were regarded as rather cold plays at first. However, after a couple of years *The Crucible* was produced again Off-Broadway and ran two years, without a line being changed from the original.

Although none of Miller's plays has "vanished into oblivion," most of his work before *All My Sons* in 1947 is unknown to theater audiences and readers. Between his graduation from the University of Michigan in 1938 and *The Man Who Had All the Luck* in 1944, he had written "perhaps a dozen plays, none of which I could truly believe were finished. I had written many scenes but not a play. A play, I saw then, was an organism of which I had fashioned only certain parts. The decision formed to write one more, and if again it turned out to be unrealizable, I would go into another line of work." During the two years Miller spent on *All My Sons,* the variety of themes and subjects he had experimented with previously appeared to him to be "tangential to the secret drama its author was quite unconsciously trying to write." It was not until he recognized that the "secret drama" involved an exploration of family relationships, specifically "of the father-son relationship and of the son's search for his relatedness," that his most characteristic theme emerged in *All My Sons,* quickly followed in two years by *Death of a Salesman.* Although Miller apparently did not recognize in the family theme the matrix of his earlier work, it is clear that, dramatically, home ground has always been for him the primal family unit before and after the economic "fall," which is to say, before and after external social pressures have disrupted the essential family peace and unity.

Miller's first play, *No Villain,* was written in 1936 while he was a student at the University of Michigan. As Kenneth Rowe establishes in his essay, "Shadows Cast Before," most of Miller's themes and thematic inversions on the subject of family relationships appear in early form in *No Villain* and in its subsequent revisions as *They Too Arise* and *The Grass Still Grows.* In each of these plays, Miller portrayed the disruption brought to a middle-class Jewish family by economic forces causing the collapse of the father's business and the creation of tensions within the group—tensions further complicated by philosophical differences about social injustice and the family's best interests for the future. There are, to be sure, echoes of Clifford Odets in these plays, but Miller's emphasis is quite clearly on social and economic forces in general (presented as symbolic of the social order within which the individual and the family must work out their respective destinies) rather than the specific circumstances of the Depression of the 1930s. Altogether, Miller wrote four plays and had partially completed a fifth before his graduation in 1938, all but one of them involving families or members of families engaged in a losing struggle with such forces. *Honors at Dawn* is basically a social protest play in the manner of the 1930s. It has, nevertheless, as its central characters two brothers, "caught," as Miller has described it, "on either side of radicalism in a university." Taken with his recognition while working on *The Man Who Had All the Luck* ("that two of the characters, who had been friends in the previous drafts, were logically brothers and had the same father"), the early plays establish beyond doubt the significance for Miller of the family theme.

II

Miller's major family plays—*All My Sons* (1947), *Death of a Salesman* (1949), *The Crucible* (1953), *A View from the Bridge* (1955, 1956), *After the Fall* (1964), *The Price* (1968), *The Creation of the World* (1972), and *The American Clock* (1980)—have for their central focus, as every theatergoer knows, the family in crisis, trapped in moments of stress and conflict resulting from past or present actions that threaten to destroy its members individually or collectively. It is as though Miller is viewing them under a microscope with revolving lenses, bringing into focus the father, the mother, the uncle, the aunt, and then one of the sons or the niece to project a succession of different points of view into the consciousness of the audience. This is perhaps why *Death of a Salesman* has consistently evoked such a strong sense of identification among different spectators. Miller cites examples in the Introduction to his *Collected Plays*:

> I received visits from men over sixty from as far away as California who had come across the country to have me write the stories of their lives, because the story of Willy Loman was exactly like theirs. The letters from women made it clear that the central character of the play was Linda; sons saw the entire action revolving around Biff or Happy, and fathers wanted advice, in effect, on how to avoid parricide.

With *All My Sons* and after, there begins a change in the family situation. In the early plays, the father is a decent, hard-working man devoted to establishing a business for his sons and to earning a comfortable living for his family. Given to idealistic speech and behavior, he is also innocent of doing harm to preserve his business. His sons, more like Chris in *All My Sons* than Biff and Happy in *Salesman,* although they have a highly developed sense of social justice, do not have to choose in these plays between their father and their father's values.

Beginning with *All My Sons,* Miller neatly complicates this scene: now the father becomes flawed morally to such an extent that the outside forces function as reflections or testimonies of the essential inner weakness. Thus, Joe Keller allows defective airplane parts to be shipped out, ruins his business partner's life and family, and is responsible for the deaths of twenty-one pilots. His own family, whose welfare he is supposedly trying to protect, suffers the loss of one son by suicide when he learns of his father's actions and is torn apart by divided loyalty to a father, on the one hand, and to honorable behavior on the other. Nothing can be done; Joe Keller also commits suicide (as if this could undo the mischief!), and the harm to the family becomes irreversible. Miller's revised approach allows him to probe the interior failure while retaining sympathy for a man who acts out of misguided but instinctive values for the preservation of his family. In this way, Miller discovered in the "secret drama" a method by which he could explore social issues within a family context, and thus examine an entire society in its most fundamental assumptions.

In *Death of a Salesman* and *The Crucible*, Miller focuses again on the primal family unit of mother, father, and sons; Proctor, however, is less directly concerned with his sons' relationship to himself than Joe Keller or Willy Loman. Unlike Keller, who knows who the enemy is—"I'm in business, a man is in business. . . . You got a process, the process don't work, you're out of business; you don't know how to operate, your stuff is no good; they close you up, they tear up your contracts, what the hell's it to them?"—Willy Loman can't precisely identify his opposition. To Willy, everything is possible, and even if he can't find the secret to the American Dream of material wealth that he is so obviously searching for, some connection somewhere is likely to turn up if one is well liked and keeps looking. But Willy seeks a short cut to success by establishing a sexual relationship with a woman buyer in Boston, where he is unhappily discovered by Biff in a hotel room, a place symbolically antithetical to the image of home and family. Thus, Willy, the disciple of Horatio Alger, Brother Ben, and Madison Avenue, becomes his son's destroyer while attempting to improve his family's economic position—having ultimately failed (as Ruby Cohn points out in her informative essay) "as salesman, gardener, mechanic, husband, father." The tragedy of Willy Loman is that he destroys himself, his son, and his family through the guilt that economic failure in a highly material culture inflicts.

John Proctor's initial inability to identify his enemy in *The Crucible* springs also from an overwhelming sense of guilt, the consequence of an adulterous affair somewhat differently presented than Willy Loman's in *Salesman*. Proctor does not believe in witchcraft and cannot believe that the Salem judges will condemn him for something that does not exist. He and his wife are estranged, not by the charge of witchcraft, but because he has committed adultery and has lied to protect his family name and conscience. His insistence on his good name and integrity is directly related to his concern for his family since one of the main reasons for his refusing to sign an exculpating confession that he has already made is his anxiety about his children: "How may I teach them to walk like men in the world, and* I sold my friends?" This cry of anguish is only a more dramatic version of the question Miller has posed to all of us in his essay, "The Family in Modern Drama":

> How may a man make of the outside world a home? How and in what ways must he struggle, what must he strive to change and overcome within himself if he is to find the safety, the surroundings of love, the ease of soul, the sense of identity and honor which, evidently, all men have connected in their memories with the idea of family?

Proctor's dilemma is not unlike Willy Loman's, and structurally the two plays rest squarely on the unforeseen and destructive consequences of a moral lapse. By expanding the issues in *The Crucible* to include a broader social engagement between personal integrity and bureaucratic injustice, Miller achieves a finer balance between private guilt and public conscience. Dramatically, the issues in *The Crucible* are greater than Willy Loman's private struggle to maintain his role as father-god-hero to his sons, while at the same time struggling with insurance payments, broken refrigerator belts, and buyers who don't know him anymore. The tragedy in both plays, however, and in *All My Sons*, is partially redeemed through the character of the mother as when, in *Salesman,* Linda says:

> Forgive me, dear. I can't cry. I don't know what it is, but I can't cry. I don't understand it. Why did you ever do that? Help me, Willy, I can't cry. It seems to me that you're just on another trip. I keep expecting you. Willy, dear, I can't cry. Why did you do it? I search and search and I search, and I can't understand it, Willy.

By giving the last word in each play to the wife and mother, Miller returns our attention to the family, emphasizing forgiveness for the past, courage and endurance for the future. Although Linda says

---

*Editor's note: "And" is a printer's error in the *Collected Plays* for "an," in the Elizabethan sense or meaning of "if."

again and again that she can't cry and doesn't understand Willy's suicide, she and her sons must walk away from Willy's grave into their own lives. Similarly, in *All My Sons,* Kate Keller tells Chris, "Don't take it on yourself. Forget now. Live," almost immediately after Joe has shot himself, but "begins sobbing" as she moves toward the house to confront the rest of her life. In *The Crucible*, it is Elizabeth Proctor who cries out in the final moment of the play even as Proctor is being hanged, "He have his goodness now. God forbid I take it from him!" As the final drum-roll crashes, and the Reverend Mr. Hale weeps in frantic prayer, Miller symbolizes her faith and endurance by a simple and strikingly effective stage direction: *"The new sun is pouring in upon her face, and the drums rattle like dry bones."* As an image of strength and renewed life, the sun expresses Elizabeth's endurance in the past and her ability to continue into the future, lighting up the figure of the mother-wife who contains both past and present of the family and carries it forward past the moment of the husband-father's defeat.

In *A View from the Bridge*, Miller altered his family relationships somewhat, but retained the basic situation of a flawed protagonist, Eddie Carbone, who is torn between his sexual desire for his niece, Catherine, and the universal taboo against incest. The threat from the outside world arrives in the form of two of his wife's relatives, Marco and Rodolpho, both illegal immigrants. Rodolpho and Catherine fall in love, and Eddie is faced with the problem of ridding himself of this new impediment to the relationship between himself and Catherine as uncle and niece, platonic lover and coy mistress. Short of surrendering Catherine to Rodolpho, however, nothing can be done, and Eddie betrays his relatives to the immigration authorities.

Unlike the guilty act in Miller's previous plays, no "crime" has yet been committed when the play opens, although Eddie is in conflict with his inarticulate self and has become emotionally estranged from his wife, Beatrice. As the play moves forward to its resolution, the emphasis on the family as a self-contained unit dissolves into sub-themes of incest, betrayal, homosexuality, identity, and guilt. These themes, however, are contingent upon the establishment of Eddie, Beatrice, and Catherine as the primal family unit in whose relationships departures and arrivals to and from the outside world can produce shattering alterations. When Eddie dies in a fight with Marco, he dies with the knowledge that his public insistence on his name and self-respect is actually a cloak for his misplaced passion and for his guilt at the destruction of his marriage. Although Eddie's requiem is conducted by Alfieri, the lawyer-narrator of the play, it is significant that Miller once again gives the final stage action of the play to the wife-mother-aunt figure of Beatrice, who dominates it through her unspoken act of forgiveness and protectiveness both during and immediately after Eddie's death.

> *Eddie lunges with the knife. Marco grabs his arm, turning the blade inward and pressing it home as the women and Louis and Mike rush in and separate them, and Eddie, the knife still in his hand, falls to his knees before Marco. The two women support him for a moment, calling his name again and again.*

Catherine. Eddie, I never meant to do nothing bad to you.
Eddie. Then why—Oh, B.!
Beatrice. Yes, yes!
Eddie. My B.!

> *He dies in her arms, and Beatrice covers him with her body. Alfieri, who is in the crowd, turns to the audience. The lights have gone down, leaving him in a glow, while behind him the dull prayers of the people and the keening of the women continue.*

III

A View from the Bridge is the last family play by Miller that relies on a seriously flawed protagonist for dramatic conflict. Eddie, and his counterparts in *All My Sons, Death of a Salesman,* and *The Crucible,* are to a considerable extent reconcilable as tragic heroes with Aristotle's view that the proper hero for tragedy is "a man who is not eminently good and just, yet whose misfortune is brought about not by vice or depravity, but by some error or frailty." In the plays following *A View from the Bridge—After the Fall, The Price, The Creation of the World,* and *The American Clock*—Miller turns slightly away from the primal family of mother, father, and sons. None of the fathers in these later plays has committed an act that endangers the well-being of his family. They are guilty only of economic failures and appear almost as secondary figures in a retrospective view of the past through their sons' memories of them as fathers. In *After the Fall* (and here we assume that "the fall" is from a state of economic security as well as from childhood innocence), Quentin's struggle to come to terms with his present life is shown through his nearly traumatic family experiences in the past. The tone of his entire conversation with the Listener is established within the first few minutes when he says, "God, I wrote you about *that*, didn't I? Maybe I dream those letters. . . . Mother

died. Oh, it's four, five months ago, now. Yes, quite suddenly." Soon
after, he abruptly returns to his mother's death once again: "It's like
my mother's funeral; I still hear her voice in the street sometimes,
loud and real, calling my name. She's under the ground but she's not
impressively dead to me." Thereupon, immediately a scene with his
father in the hospital materializes in which Quentin and his brother,
Dan, attempt to tell their father that their mother has died. It is a
strong scene, impressively understated, dramatically moving, and
reminiscent of those episodes in earlier plays depicting a husband's
reliance on his wife for moral and spiritual support. After telling his
father that his mother has died of a heart attack, Quentin, with Dan's
help, attempts to console him.

Dan. Now look, Dad, you're a hell of a fella. Dad, listen—
Father. God damn it! I couldn't take care of myself, I knew she was
   working too hard!
Quentin. Dad, it's not your fault, that can happen to anyone.
Father. But she was sitting right here. She was . . . she was right here!

*Now he weeps uncontrollably into his hands. Quentin puts an awkward arm
around him.*

Father. Oh, boys—she was my right hand!

A third scene in Act One takes Quentin back to childhood, his
mother telling him that when she married his father he could not
even read a menu in a restaurant, but she loved him nevertheless and
in spite of the fact that theirs was an arranged marriage. Yet, the
image that stays in Quentin's mind is of his father's economic
mismanagement. When the mother learns that their entire fortune—
money, bonds, stocks, and insurance—has all gone to sustain his
failing business and their high standard of living, she turns on him.

All right, then—we'll get rid of my bonds. Do it tomorrow. . . . What do
   you mean? Well you get them back. I've got ninety-one thousand
   dollars in bonds you gave me. Those are my bonds. I've got bonds. . . .

   Breaks off; open horror on her face and now a growing contempt.

You mean you saw everything going down and you throw good money
   after bad? Are you some kind of moron?
Father. You don't walk away from a business; I came to this country with a
   tag around my neck like a package in the bottom of the boat!
Mother. I should have run the day I met you!
Father, as though stabbed. Rose!

   He sits, closing his eyes, his neck bent.

Mother. I should have done what my sisters did, tell my parents to go to hell and thought of myself for once! I should have run for my life!
Father. Sssh, I hear the kids.

A sharp shaft of light opens a few yards away and he glances toward it.

Mother. I ought to get a divorce!
Father. Rose, the college men are jumping out of windows!
Mother. But your last dollar? *Bending over, into his face:* You are an idiot!

Her nearness forces him to stand; they look at each other, strangers.

As Quentin's mind turns from one event to another throughout the play, the mother figure appears and reappears calling the father "an idiot," his brother Dan appears and reappears to reassure him that "wherever you are this family's behind you," and memories recur repeatedly of missing a family outing to Atlantic City: "They sent me for a walk with the maid. When I came back the house was empty for a week. God, why is betrayal the only truth that sticks! . . . Yes! *He almost laughs.* 'Love everybody!' And I can't even mourn my own mother. It's monstrous." The truth that Quentin discovers is that the seeds of disaster are permanently sown in the primal family unit, even though they do not flower equally for everyone.

In *The Price*, Miller brings two brothers together after sixteen years of estrangement to dispose of some old furniture in the attic of their dead parents' home and to face the past through conversation about their separate lives, both unsatisfactory. One brother, Walter, has become a surgeon, the other, Victor, a policeman. Their lives as estranged brothers were determined by their father's refusal to loan Victor money to go to college. Victor, unlike Walter, assuming his father was financially ruined, chose to support him at the expense of his own career. Gradually, the play strips away each brother's defense for the action taken in abandoning or supporting his father. When Victor learns that his father was not broken financially, he continues to justify his life by recreating the past as he believes it was. When Walter tells him their father took Victor's money while sitting on $4,000 of his own, Victor remains adamant in his father's defense.

Victor. What does that change! I know I'm talking like a fool, but what does that change? He couldn't believe in anybody any more, and it was unbearable to me! *The unlooked for return of his old feelings seems to anger him. Of Walter:* He'd kicked him in the face; my mother—*he glances toward Walter as he speaks; there is hardly a pause*—the night he told us he was bankrupt, my mother . . . It was right here on this couch. She was all dressed up—for some affair, I think. Her hair was piled up, and long earrings? And he had his tuxedo on . . . and made all of us sit down; and he told us it was all gone. And she vomited. *Slight pause. His horror and pity twist in his voice.* All over his arms. His hands. Just kept on vomiting, like thirty-five years coming up. And he sat there. Stinking like a sewer. And a look came onto his face. I'd never seen a man look like that. He was sitting there, letting it dry on his hands.

Victor's account of his father's economic collapse is a moving and realistic re-creation of the Depression atmosphere, and carries itself from beginning to end, without a break in emotional intensity or objectivity. Compared with the scene in *After the Fall* where the mother calls the father "an idiot," its dramatic impact is stronger, the effect on the family more sharply etched in the audience's mind. Victor doesn't have to add anything: the story he is telling is obviously one of the central moments in his life, and everything he has done since leads from it. It is his key point in the play and depends for its meaning on the audience's identification with Victor as the betrayed son who refuses to accept the betrayal as a fact in his life.

Walter, who is a disillusioned realist, counters now with his defense. In addition to his testimony that his father had money available all during the time when Victor claims, "we were eating garbage here," he demolishes Victor's notion of having prevented the family from "falling apart."

Is it really that something fell apart? Were we brought up to believe in one another? We were brought up to succeed, weren't we? Why else would he respect me so and not you! What fell apart? What was here to fall apart? Was there ever any love here? When he needed her, she vomited. And when you needed him, he laughed. What was unbearable is not that it all fell apart, it was that there was never anything here.

The Price is the first play in which Miller sets brother against brother. Each brother tries to tell the other that something that happened to him yesterday has made his life today what it should not have been. "But here is what really happened," one brother says. "No, it didn't happen that way," the other replies, and both are left grappling with the ghost of a dead father amid the remnants of another life. It is all very much like O'Neill's *Long Day's Journey Into Night*, with the father in *The Price* combining the worst qualities of both the father and mother in the Tyrone family. Also like O'Neill, Miller resolves the action of his play with the implication that no resolution is possible. At the end Walter and Victor simply part company, unable to face their past or their father or each other with more than a minimum of understanding or forgiveness. Thematically, *The Price* might well have taken its departure from Mary Tyrone's lines in *Long Day's Journey*: "None of us can help the things life has done to us. They're done before you realize it, and once they're done they make you do other things until at last everything comes between you and what you'd like to be, and you've lost your true self forever."

IV

Miller's continuing exploration of the family extends into *The Creation of the World* and *The American Clock*. These plays are not considered in the essays here because neither has yet received major attention. On the surface, *The Creation of the World* seems to represent the mythical core of all Miller's plays involving a father and sons and to be the source of sources to which he has returned in play after play. This movement back to biblical home ground may account for its cool reception by critics such as Richard Watts of the *New York Post*, who wrote in his review of December 1, 1972 that it appeared "uncertain of the viewpoint it was driving at and far from clear about its aim. It is an intelligent and inventive comedy of ideas but not a very satisfying one." Miller later transformed the play into a musical comedy, *Up From Paradise,* which may indeed be its most natural form. Miller himself seems to think so. After months of work on the adaptation and after writing twenty-six lyrics for music by Stanley Silverman, he is said to have commented during a rehearsal, "Now I know why I wrote *The Creation of the World*."

The American Clock, Miller's most recent play, has been called by Miller, "a mural for the theater," using a documentary approach of many short scenes to suggest the political and social atmosphere of the Depression years. "I've attempted a play," Miller told Studs Terkel in an interview for *Saturday Review*, September 1980, "about more than just a family, about forces bigger than simply overheard voices in the dark. It's a story of the United States talking to itself." The focus of the play gradually narrows to one family—mother, father, and son—living in Brooklyn. The story is familiar: a father, Moe Baum, loses everything in the crash and goes into a decline; the mother, Rose, played by Miller's sister, Joan Copeland, although a woman of courage and endurance, is driven toward a nervous breakdown by economic losses she can neither accept nor understand.

The son, Lee, as in *A Memory of Two Mondays*, postpones his plans to attend college and goes to work to save money for a future enrollment. All this is authentic Miller, whose obsessive subject— and his best one—has always been the American Dream, its failures and successes, its economic and spiritual impact on the lives of those who, like Fitzgerald's Gatsby, believe in "the orgiastic future that year by year recedes before us," and whose disillusionment with the Dream is dramatically centered in the family.

V

The essays in this volume are divided into Overviews (essays tracing Miller's use of theme, form, character, or language through several plays) and Views (essays on a specific play). Of the fourteen essays, four are chapters from books, four are reprinted from scholarly journals, and six are new essays written especially for this collection. In addition, Charles A. Carpenter has contributed an international bibliography of Miller criticism since 1966, which appears in print for the first time in this volume.

Shadows Cast Before

by Kenneth Rowe

I

The image of Arthur Miller as a student at the University of Michigan that recurs most frequently and vividly to my mind comes from the spring of 1938, his senior year, and followed upon weekly meetings through the greater part of two academic years. I was in my office at my desk. My office was a cubicle built into a buttress that closes one end of a three-story colonnade on the front of Angell Hall. A bronze door opens onto three steps from the colonnade floor up to the office floor. (This rather special office assignment was for the convenience of association between me and my dog Nym.) There was a knock on the door, slightly ajar for the spring weather, and I called, "Come in." The door swung open, Arthur stepped inside and stopped at the foot of the steps, looking up, eyes glowing and face alight; and that is the picture that is in my mind, the moment before he announced, "Professor Rowe, I've made a discovery!"

Sitting straight, as usual, in the big Morris chair across from the desk, he explained that the discovery was a new method for revision. He was working on the third draft of *The Great Disobedience*, his major project of the year. The end of the second act worried him, and he couldn't put his finger on the trouble, except that the right rhythm of intensity, the wave movement to a crest, wasn't there. He felt sure he had the material for climax, and the climax didn't come off. He marked off that last section of the act into, as he put it, its "indivisible dramatic units." Then he numbered a card for each unit and wrote on the card what happened, the function, and the emotional effect. He laid the cards out on a table in order as in the play and studied them, concentrating especially on the emotional effect. He had been

"Shadows Cast Before" by Kenneth T. Rowe appears in print for the first time in this volume, with the author's permission.

counting for his climax on the material of the third card, I think it was, from the last, but found the material of the fifth card had potentially more intensity. The effect of card five killed that of three, but was itself not adequately led up to. He found he could switch five and three, with three becoming part of the buildup to five as the climax. The procedure had worked so well that he was eager for me to tell my other students about it so they could use it, too.

The quick concern for the playwriting of other students was characteristic. In the playwriting class, which met as a seminar around a big table, Arthur habitually sat straight but inclined a little over the table, his face intent on a student's play being read, or on each speaker in turn in class discussion. His own participation was positive in effect whether adverse, questioning, or applauding; not, it seemed to me, by anything so self-conscious as mere courtesy or consideration, but by dramatic imagination, the intuitive penetration of another consciousness. It was always the aim in the course that comments and suggestions should start from trying to see the author's objective and help toward its attainment, with avoidance of the impulse toward vicarious playwriting. The desired state so generally characterized the class discussions after a few weeks that anyone who slipped was more likely than not pulled up by other students.

I was excited by Arthur's discovery for what it revealed of his progressive relation to playwriting. He was among the talented students whose drive and eagerness to get to the writing impels them to resist spending time on preliminaries. He wrote three full drafts of *The Great Disobedience* without scenarios, but the method of revision by which he reordered the latter part of the second act was essentially an *ex post facto* adaptation of one form of scenario to a detail of his own structure. He had taken possession of the function of scenarios in revision on his own terms. As John Keats once wrote in a letter, "Axioms of philosophy are not axioms until they are proved upon our pulses." Arthur was on his way to the eclectic approach by which most practicing playwrights develop individual working methods. He may or may not have applied his discovery again directly. Either way, it was good training for his subconscious. Perception and respect and downright enthusiasm for dramatic structure were also there, and a commitment to making a perfect job of a play. All this another signal flag going up of a new playwright.

The Great Disobedience was the fourth play in the first two years of Arthur's playwriting. The first play, as he stated in an interview, was undertaken as a "lark" and written during the six days of spring vacation in 1936, his sophomore year. He entered the play in the Avery Hopwood Awards competition in creative writing at the University of Michigan that spring and received a Minor Award of $250 (sophomores were not eligible for the Major Awards). The play, entitled *No Villain*, gave rise directly to two other plays: *They Too Arise*, the next play, written from October 1936 to February 1937; and—after two intervening plays—*The Grass Still Grows*, written from April 1938 to March 1939. While Arthur has referred to each of these plays as a revision of the preceding, each is an entity with its own character. At the same time they constitute a closely related group. I find it not only convenient but, somehow, pleasant to think of them as *The Abe Simon Family Trilogy*.

The Simon family consists of Abe, his wife Esther, older son Ben, who left college after two years to help in his father's business, younger son Arnold, hitchhiking his way home from his first year at the University of Michigan, thirteen-year-old daughter Maxine, and Grandfather Barnett.

No Villain opens in the parlor of the Simon's small six-room house in a suburb of New York City, which alternates for subsequent scenes with the office, workroom, and showroom of the Simon Coat and Suit Company in the city. The time is late in a spring evening. The family is waiting for the arrival of Arnold. Esther is worrying that he is so late, parrying all efforts at reassurance with fresh possibilities, ranging from expulsion for those Communist friends and books he reads to maybe he's on the road with no money to buy himself something to eat.

Abe's business is in trouble. The time throughout the *Trilogy* presumably is the depression years of the 1930s. The word *depression*, however, does not occur. There is reference to bad times in each play, but only a scattering of explicit remarks. The most distinguishing is from Esther to Ben in *They Too Arise*. "Years ago you'd have a couple bad years and you'd come back stronger than ever. Now it seems you just lay on the bottom. . . . 'n you lay there."

Not to worry Esther, Abe and Ben say little about the failing business and money lacking at home, so she worries because no one tells her anything. She does know, however, about a loan from the bank that is due for repayment in two days. The first act is a getting-acquainted scene with only foreshadowings of the plot, no movement. When Arnold arrives and the tumult has subsided, and after a quieter interval of family exchanges, the act comes to a beautiful ending in a glimpse of the dining room where the grandfather is lighting two candles, their flames illuminating the highboy and his head and shoulders. He begins a rhythmic swaying to the murmur of his voice. The family has started for the dining room and is arrested in the doorway, standing silent as with swifter rhythm and greater volume the grandfather rises to a crescendo. With his body tense and arms outstretched, "he cries, 'Odonoi Ellohaynu!' his call to the Lord." This is the culmination and curtain of Act One, a tableau of family unity in the grandfather's prayer of gratitude for the safe return of a son.

The first play is structured not obviously or conventionally, but imaginatively. In the first act the audience is identified with the family and home. There are low-keyed suggestions of a threat from outside. The threat comes from the shop and the business. The second act opens at the shop the next morning, and the threat is developed with intensifying effect until at the end we know that the business is doomed.

Abe cannot meet the note at the bank. The shipping clerks are striking for higher wages and stopping deliveries from going through the picket line. If Abe could achieve delivery of an order and a receipt—evidence of doing business—he could get an extension. Without it, his business will be closed.

Sam Roth, an old friend of Abe's, has developed a million-dollar business by ruthless methods that Abe would not pursue, taking his work to scab shops by which he can undersell clothing businesses that try to be fair to labor. Roth has no son to whom to hand on the business, but he has a daughter, Helen. He wants to retire and enjoy himself, and has proposed to Ben that he marry Helen and take over the business. Ben, however, is not ready to marry, considers Helen dumb, although a college girl, and does not like her father. The present crisis puts the question in a different light. Abe's business could be saved by the alliance.

Ben is too deeply imbedded to get out of the business even though he hates it for its dog-eat-dog ethic. He is determined that Arnold, who wants to write, should stay away from the business and have his chance. At college Arnold has become imbued with sympathy for labor. He has a principle against scabbing and sees deliveries through the picket line as scabbing. He learns that Ben, too, has read Marx. Ben tells him that this knowledge only makes it "more tragic" because he "knows what it is that moves us about so." When he joins the other manufacturers in paying for strikebreakers, he knows it is evil. Later, when it becomes apparent that Ben alone cannot get the delivery through on which the survival of Abe's business hangs, Arnold's principle against scabbing is put in a different light.

With two twenty-four-hour reprieves for delivery, there begins a two-day action of successive and unavailing attempts at delivery and of fruitless efforts to obtain a further extension of time. In each of four scenes, three at home and one at the shop, the stress and tensions from the business world severely jar one of the family relationships of affection and unity. The stress between Esther's singleminded principle—when a father needs a son's help, a son gives it—and Arnold's dilemma of loyalty to his father as against loyalty to his principles on scabbing produces a climactic scene; the same stress between Arnold and Ben produces another. In view of the shortage of household money, Abe unreasonably protests at the burden of the grandfather, and says he should go to work. Esther's shocked response is interrupted by the grandfather's collapse from a critical heart attack. Under accumulating frustrations next day at the office, Abe breaks into an irrational berating of Ben for the failures of delivery. The scene ends with a telephone call from home saying that Grandfather Barnett is dead, while a process server drops a folded paper in Abe's lap.

All the elements are there for the functioning of the final scene. It is a remarkable scene for any playwright to have written at any time, yet this is a first play by a young man of twenty-one in his second year at the university; moreover, a young man who, although he had read plays, had seen on stage only two—in local Harlem theaters before coming to the University of Michigan. The scene is more in panto-mime than in speech, and all but three of the speeches are confined to a single line. Every posture, movement, and word is conceived not as something to be staged, but as a scene observed and heard within a stage and recorded.

The scene is the parlor late that same night. A plain black coffin on four pillars is at the center of the room. A tall candelabrum with four lighted tapers is at each end. They are the sole lights. The head of the coffin cover is folded back. Five bearded old men in black, standing behind the coffin facing front, sway and murmur softly. Ben stands leaning on the radio, hat on, gazing at the floor. Esther, in bathrobe and slippers, enters slowly from the doorway on the left supported by Abe, who seats her in a chair at the left beside the doorway. Ben goes across through the doorway and returns with a wooden kitchen chair, which he places on Esther's right. He motions to Abe, but the latter indicates that he will stand. "Esther looks blankly at the candle flames as they flicker, their shadows playing on her upturned face."

Abe. Esther can I get you anything?
Esther (turning her face up to him): No, Abe . . . . Why don't you sit down, Abe? Come, sit down. (*He comes slowly around in front of her and sits on the chair.*)

The simplicity of the exchange between Abe and Esther is complete. The movement in the stage directions, the moments of silence indicated by the nine-point ellipsis, and the words are a forgiveness to Abe for his harsh words of the grandfather. The scene continues without a spare word, with every significant movement provided for in the stage directions, everything shaped spatially to the dimensions of the stage and the organization of its furnishings, with movement and speech coordinated.

In the flickering candlelight, and with the background of swaying bodies and murmuring voices, the scene unfolds in slow motion as in a dream. The doorbell rings. Ben admits Roth in black suit and pearl-gray hat and Helen in silver fox collar and black coat. They offer condolence. Roth goes to Ben and with a prologue of, "I know it ain't the time to talk about such things . . . . but . . . . ," says he doesn't want Ben to worry about the financial part . . . . he heard they closed in on them. Before he can repeat his invitation to marry Helen and take over the business, Ben interrupts: "I'm sorry, Mr. Roth . . . ." He is interrupted by Esther's, "Ben!"

One of the old men lifts his hand to call for silence and inadvertently tips the opened section of the coffin. It falls with a thud. The man starts to open it. Ben rushes past Roth and slaps his hand on it. "Leave it!" The man protests. Ben reiterates, "Leave it shut!" After another attempt to open the lid, all the old men talking at once in protest, Ben, speaking calmly, tells them to get out. Under his surveillance the old men file out, looking at him and mumbling. Roth starts to protest and Ben dismisses him and Helen. Esther is sobbing; Roth and Helen leave. Arnold is standing by the right wall. Abe says, "So now?" His brief "So now?" once Ben has cleared the stage down to the family unit, is at once a submission and a challenge—you have the floor; what do you propose?

The trajectory of the scene reflects, by plan or intuition, an effective application of the varied forces present. With the sudden sharp sound of Ben's hand on the coffin lid, the voices go into staccato, the tempo accelerates, and the direction of the scene does a rightabout. It continues to the curtain with Ben's reply to Abe's "So now?"

> Ben (calmly and very slowly). So now? (Looking intently at his parents.) For us it begins, Arny and I . . . For us there begins not work toward a business, but just a . . . . . . sort of a battle . . . . sort of a fight . . . . so that you'll know that this, (covers the scene with an arc motion of his hand) this will never be in our lives. We'll never have to sit like you sit there now for the reasons you are sitting there . . . . Dad, now we not only are working people . . . . we know we are. Maybe I'm afraid . . . . . . I don't know. But I couldn't start this thing over again. I've got to build something bigger . . . . . . Something that'll change this deeply . . . . to the bottom . . . . . . It's the only way, Dad . . . . it's the only way.

Ben's speech is so unassumingly undogmatic and undoctrinaire as to be almost as enigmatic as Abe's two words. I think it is clear, however, that he is not withdrawing from saving his father's business to avoid a distasteful marriage, but to avoid perpetuating something that can absorb his whole life and come to nothing—a compromise of conscience and humanity in the name of survival. In the background of *The Abe Simon Family Trilogy,* stressed in each play, there is a sharp and strongly felt division in social status between the owner of a business and everyone else who works for a salary or wage.

Arthur's fine sense of timing appears in *No Villain* only in the last scene, where it is suddenly, astonishingly, complete. It is as though he discovered timing on the sixth day of creation. His sense of theater, stage, and audience as a three-dimensional physical fact is also fully present in the last scene of *No Villain*. But the scene of the grandfather's prayer, beautifully conceived, would not be in view for a great part of the audience without some modification of the stage set. The set for the Simon Coat and Suit Company is likewise impractical, with half the stage from left to right occupied by the shop (where no drama occurs), furnished with sixteen sewing machines in two rows of eight each, one facing the audience, the other away, a man bending over each machine, the machines whirring. The other half of the stage is a showroom with a cubicle office partitioned off in one corner. In *They Two Arise,* the showroom occupies the entire stage, and a door to the shop takes care of the necessary interaction.

It is irrelevant to note the flaws and limitations of *No Villain* except as doing so reveals the wonder of what happened in six days. It is as though there was a stage in Arthur's head uncovered progressively during the process of writing. Whatever its faults, the play is as full of good things as Jack Horner's Christmas pie, and it casts long shadows, as far as *Death of a Salesman*, and beyond.

II

With a good takeoff in *No Villain,* Arthur arrived back at the university in the fall of 1936 wound up for rewriting. He strengthened and enriched the character of Abe and added new dramatically strong characters and scenes. The first act home-scene of *They Too Arise* introduces the family as before, but with a major difference—the grandfather is newly created. Grandfather Barnett was simply a dignified and smiling elderly gentleman. His prayer tableau was an effective close to the first act; otherwise, we see and hear little of him. In *They Too Arise,* however, Grandpa Isaac Stein is the kind of man of whom people say "He's a character!" He is of medium height, but with majestic carriage. When he sits, it is with care for the crease in his trousers. The involutions of his Germanic sentences are sometimes bewildering and continuously comic. Abe has a semihumorous appreciation of his idiosyncracies and maintains a humorous tolerance of what could easily be Grandpa Stein's most annoying habit of offering advice on every problem. Since he had been in the cloak business himself, he seizes on every opening with "Now my advice is," and pontificates on the principle, particularly irrelevant in the current state of Abe's business: "To sell, you have to have a big stock, offer lots of choice."

While Grandpa Stein is actually reconceived, Ben and Arnold are developed. Arnold becomes a more positive character, more likeable, more active and vigorous for his principles. He does not merely not scab, but helps the strikers print handbills. The new version of the Manufacturers Association meeting gives scope beyond that in *No Villain* for strength and ability to be evidenced by Ben. The greatest development, however, is in Abe, to a warmer, richer, stronger character. In both plays, the two Esthers are the least distinguished. Esther I is softer than Esther II and is the better worrier; Esther II the better lamenter. Both are loving and lovable, family-centered, amusingly naive, and sometimes exasperatingly single-minded.

In *They Too Arise,* plot lines and lines of stress that are held until later in *No Villain* are introduced in the first act. Now there is a strike impending in the morning that will bring tension between Abe's need of Arnold to help with deliveries and Arnold's hostility to scabbing. The introduction of the strike brings with it one of Esther's best speeches. For her the picket line presents no problem, ethical or practical, to Arnold's delivery of coats: "That ain't scabbing. Poppa's his father. He ain't the United States Steel Company. If they stop him, he'll say he's helping his father, 'n that's all." Moreover, the discussion of the Roth business-and-marriage proposal is precipitated and enlivened in the revised play by the brief appearance of Helen Roth, which validates Ben's objection in *No Villain* that she is dumb.

In the second act of *They Too Arise,* Arnold goes to the shop in the morning without knowing about the strike, and Abe gives him boxes of coats to deliver. He returns shortly with the boxes—he can't scab. He tells his father that small manufacturers like him are closer to the workers than to the big manufacturers. Ben's attempts to deliver the order that would save Abe's business also fail. Abe says there is one person to whom he could apply for a loan—Roth. But help from Roth will depend on Ben's taking Helen and the management of Roth's business off his hands. Abe hates to do this to Ben; he knows Ben doesn't like Helen or her father. Ben says it's all right, to call Roth. Abe says he can't do it and asks Ben to call. Ben does so, gets Roth, and arranges to call on him later in the day. Abe stands with his back turned, his shoulders shaking, and as Ben hangs up, rushes through the door to the shop sobbing. The curtain falls.

Before calling Roth, Ben tells Abe that a meeting of the Manufacturers Association has been called for that evening for a vote on bringing in strikebreakers. Just before Ben tells Abe of the meeting, a contractor, Liebowitz, a shrivelled old man with back bent from years over a sewing machine, enters. Liebowitz tells them he got an order for three hundred coats from Schaft, the biggest man in the cloak business. But when Schaft paid the bill, he took off fifty dollars, his kickback. When Liebowitz protested, Schaft hired two gangsters to break his hand. Liebowitz shows them his right hand, which he has held in his coat pocket; Abe and Ben are shocked. The episode is movingly well composed and a telling preparation for the next scene, the meeting.

A group of men representing opposed positions on a controversial matter, seated at a long table, seems to provide effective theater as consistently as a courtroom. The introduction of the scene was a masterstroke of rewriting. The vote is on assigning money from the Association treasury to hire strikebreakers. Ben and Abe point out there are two kinds of men present: those worth $75,000, and those with a business of $5,000 or less, and $5,000 is nearer zero than it is to $75,000. The owners of the $5,000 businesses are closer to the workers than the $75,000 men are. Four of the men present are in the poorer group—Rosen, Levy, Abe, and Ben—and seven are in the richer. Some of the latter, Ben points out, have obviously planned to railroad a vote through for strikebreakers without opportunity for dissent.

Then Abe gains the floor. He has always believed in majority rule, but he wants them all to know he will *not* vote to hire gangsters. He concludes with: "I say maybe it's honest for the steel companies to work this way, but it ain't the way for Jewish men to act . . . . Jewish men in the cloak business. That's all I gotta say. But I hope, so that I can keep my respect for all of you . . . . I hope you ain't gonna do this . . . . (He sits)." It is a beautiful speech, a dramatic revelation of the heart of Abe Simon, as he turns inward for the identity that is his vantage point on conduct; and it foreshadows those powerful phrasings fixed in memory by a rhythmic turn of repetition with variation that characterize Arthur's later plays.

The meeting gets tumultuous. Finally, on a majority agreement to close debate the vote is taken: seven are for hiring strikebreakers, four against. The scene ends with Ben shouting, ". . . . Murderers!" and Abe with his head bowed. Abe and Ben both gain stature from the Manufacturers Association meeting.

The next scene, the third of Act Two, is a new scene growing out of the new meeting scene and the essentially new character of Grandpa Stein. Abe and Ben arrive home late, tense and exhausted. Abe sinks to the couch, is silent. Esther asks, "You're selling?" Abe replies with, "A little. Yeh, we're selling, we're selling." That is Grandpa's cue: "Ach, Abe, how many times didn't I tell it to you, you will only sell when you get enough stock." Abe, close to the breaking point, still not raising his voice, asks Esther to take him to the other room. Grandpa becomes excited. He feels he is being dismissed from family councils as though he were dumb, which he is not. He rebels, shakes off Esther's hand, and with rising voice and agitation begins a recall of all the occasions on which his advice was disregarded, all mistakes by Abe, on and on, becoming more excited by all efforts at restraint.

Abe rises to his feet and says, "Stop that, Isaac," as the grandfather, stepping closer in front of Abe and approaching hysteria, rushes on: "You will never make money! . . . . You never will be no good. I . . . ." Abe says, "Shut up, you damn fool!" and pushes the grandfather in the chest. Grandpa staggers back, coughing violently. Ben and Arnold ease him into a chair. Ben rushes off for water, Arnold unbuttons his collar and vest. Esther wipes his face, Abe stands haggard and exhausted. Then, softly, "Esther . . . . I . . . . I . . . . didn't hurt him, did I?" A slow curtain follows.

The structure of *No Villain* is linear. *They Too Arise* has a tripodal structure. It is not the death of the grandfather, which comes as in *No Villain* by telephone to the office the next day, but Abe's raising his hand against an old man that creates the crisis of the play, the turning point in Abe's consciousness that leads to his dominating place in the resolving scene. Three stresses come together to determine that crucial gesture. One is from the office, the struggle to save the business intensified by the Roth-Ben complication; the meeting provides the second stress; and for the third, in his home, the grandfather has been given precisely the traits that can precipitate all the stresses into one outrageous act.

The following day at the office, the frustrations of Ben's futile attempts at delivery recur. As in *No Villain,* the man comes from the bank for evidence of delivery and replies to Abe's declaration that he has thousands of orders with the comment that everyone has those same orders, and each will belong to whoever delivers first. There is a small addition over *No Villain*: "Unless these customers are regular with you." Abe is recharged. He asks the man to wait. He'll show him he has regular customers and friends, who will tell him the orders are still good. He makes two calls, receives the same reply: the order has been filled, one by Schaft, presumably with strikebreakers. Miss Lambert at Haynes Stores hangs up on Abe's extended protests. The man leaves, the telephone rings. Abe is sure it is Miss Lambert calling back. He tells Ben to answer and runs out to return with the man by the arm. As he begins, "What'd she say?" Ben hangs up and says, "Grandpa's dead, Dad." The man exits quietly. Abe, after a long pause, almost whispers, "Ach . . . . . . he . . . . *(breaking)* . . . . he was a good man." The scene ends. Another powerfully condensed summation has been given to Abe.

The final scene of *They Too Arise* takes place at home in the evening. Esther, Abe, and Arnold are present. Ben, Abe tells Esther, is out walking, will be back. The funeral appurtenances in *No Villain* are absent. The scene opens gently. Esther's crying has subsided; she will wait for Ben's return and then go to bed. They talk quietly. Roth and Helen enter and offer condolence. Roth tells Abe he has heard the

banks have closed in on him. He wants to tell him about the day Ben
called up. If he'd called any other day but that one, he would have
been able to help him out. He was opening two stores in San Francisco and Seattle, and—he begins to stumble a bit. Abe and Esther
each express understanding. Roth presents his proposal of Helen
and the business any time Ben will say the word. What do they think?
To Esther, of course, it's all right. Abe says, better wait for Ben.

When Ben arrives, Roth comes to the point. By some skillful
questioning, Ben leads Roth into answers that make it clear he was
the one who filled Abe's order, and with strikebreakers. Abe rises and
says, "Roth, that was my order!" and "We'd a been in business with
that order!" Past Roth's denials, Ben pursues: "Why didn't you loan
us the money?" Esther explains to Ben that Roth couldn't, to which
Ben replies, "The hell he couldn't. All we needed was his name." In
They Too Arise, it is Abe, who over Esther's cries of protest, orders,
"Get out Roth!" Roth and Helen leave.

The house of Esther's dreams has been pulled down. She is
desolate, sobbing: "So what's going to be with your sons? Two young
boys like that and no business to go into?" Abe doesn't know what
his sons are going to do, but they are not going to get rich by killing.
He is going to see they don't go through what he did to end up with
nothing, that they don't waste their lives trying to get rich. To
Esther's, "What then? What're they gonna do?" Abe replies "vig-
orously":

> I'll tell ya what they're gonna do, Esther . . . When I lifted that hand
> against the old man it was like some kind of . . . of a thing ya can't see
> was pushing me . . . it was something dirty . . . something rotten.
> Esther, I knew it . . . and when I see what a man like Roth's gotta do to
> stay where he is! . . . It's gotta be wiped out! I don't know how, I don't
> know where but I gotta do it!

This last speech marks the completion of an admirable structural
strategy. It puts in place the lens through which Abe now sees, as if
for the first time, the world in which he has lived. Esther is incon-
solable. She wants to go upstairs. Leaving, she says, "Ach, Abe, new
ideas you got in your head. I don't understand what's come over
you."

> *Arnold.* We can't let her go like that, Dad. She's got to understand.
> *Abe.* She'll understand, she'll understand. (*Taking them by the shoulders.*)
> You got a mother what always understands. Give her time, give her
> time. Meanwhile we got six good arms and three good heads. We

ought to be able to learn a lot . . . we can change a lot with such . . . with such equipment. A lotta changing we can do . . . a lotta changing.

They Too Arise might have been entitled *The Education of Abe Simon*. The events and experiences of the play, culminating in Abe's raising his hand against the grandfather, lead into an acute guilt consciousness in Abe that links *They Too Arise* to *All My Sons*, *Death of a Salesman*, *The Crucible*, *A View from the Bridge*, *After the Fall*, *Incident at Vichy*, and *The Creation of the World*. Whether a consciousness of guilt is constructive or destructive, however, depends on what is done with it. A guilt wave that swept France in the twelfth century built cathedrals. The renewed emphasis on guilt in our own time has been attributed to the disclosure of the Nazi Holocaust. A sense of common guilt spread through Europe and America that this horror had, somehow, been allowed to occur. In *No Villain*, Ben conveys his awareness to Arnold that every blow against the striking workers is evil. That is what in his curtain speech he says must be changed. *They Too Arise* goes much further. Guilt is vividly dramatized in the Liebowitz episode and the Manufacturers Association meeting, and brought to a stunning climax in Abe's one act of physical violence against Grandpa Stein. If there were no *They Too Arise*, it might be possible to attribute the thematic place of guilt in *All My Sons* (1947) and in Arthur's later writing to the post-Holocaust atmosphere of that time. In view of *They Too Arise*, we must conclude that the theme had its rise in his personal consciousness, although naturally he would be sensitive, as well, to the current of guilt feelings in society, having always held firmly and consistently to the position that serious theater is inescapably social.

In *Incident at Vichy*, when Von Berg becomes aware of the Nazi camps, a sense of communal guilt is one of the motives leading him to give his pass to Leduc, the Jewish doctor. In *After the Fall*, the fact of the Holocaust plays a prominent role in Quentin's restoration from his overwhelming sense of guilt, and with it his near loss of hope for humanity. Here the theme of guilt consciousness is explored with a complexity far beyond that in any other of Arthur's plays. Secondary characters and incidents embody variations on the theme. The principal plot line is Quentin's retracing in recall his descent from what seemed a peak of happiness and fortune to a long, agonizing struggle to preserve his suicidal wife's life while receiving from her spiritual blow on blow. A momentary impulse to do nothing leaves him bewildered by the discovery in himself of the capacity to kill, even though he had "loved that girl." Knowledge of the Holocaust and his own self-knowledge combine into a question: how can one keep hope for humanity and the future? Perhaps, courage . . . love . . . forgiveness, "again and again . . . forever?"

Although it is a far cry from Abe Simon's comparatively simple consciousness of guilt to Quentin's complexities, there is an essential truth in each—guilt recognized and fully faced can be a constructive experience; otherwise, it is merely wasteful and destructive. This conviction is the touchstone applied to every instance of guilt in the protagonists of Arthur Miller's plays. Guilt as a theme, however, is absent from the next three of his early plays. *Honors at Dawn* and *The Great Disobedience* are crusading plays, *The Grass Still Grows* is a comedy, and guilt is not found in any of the protagonists, only in the villains.

They Too Arise leads directly to *Death of a Salesman* through the principal characters and thematic content. A good deal of Abe Simon reappears in Willy Loman, including the mercurial moods, the emotionality, the unquenchable optimism, and the comradeship of a father with two sons. Abe's gesture of taking them both by the shoulders for his "we have six good arms and three good heads" speech recurs when Willy embraces his two boys in a memory scene. Out of frustration brought on by the strike, Abe unjustly berates Ben, just as Willy unjustly attacks Biff out of inner denial that his guilty affair with the woman in Boston is the cause of Biff's lost morale. Thus, guilt moves through both plays as a destructive force.

Both fathers are devoted to the well-being of their sons, but define it in their own limited terms. Abe's dream was to make a healthy, honest business to leave to his sons. All Willy had to give to his sons from a lifetime of selling was his own unfulfilled ambition, to get rich, as revealed in the memory scenes with Uncle Ben. The trouble with Abe's dream, as he himself recognizes, is that his sons don't want what he has to give. In both Abe Simon and Willie Loman, Arthur celebrated a passing class: in Simon, the owners of small manufacturing businesses at a time when production was becoming concentrated in big business; in Loman, the army of travelling salesmen, the men with "personality," who helped the spread of big business until they in turn were submerged by the mudslide of TV commercials.

In the spring of 1937, *They Too Arise* won a scholarship of $1,250 in the Bureau of New Plays national contest conducted by the Theatre Guild. It was produced in Ann Arbor, Michigan, by the B'nai B'rith Hillel Foundation with a highly talented teaching fellow in theater,

Fredrick Crandall, as director, and presented in the university theatre and in Detroit. I have a pleasant recollection of Arthur during the first rehearsal. The cast was reading at a long conference table in Hillel House. When one of the actors could not be present, Fred handed Arthur a script and asked him to read the part. The cue for the first speech of the part came round and there was dead silence. Arthur was sitting motionless, head turned toward the last speaker, on his face an expression familiar to me over the years—the wonder of hearing for the first time what one has written spoken by an actor.

Although two other plays were completed between *They Too Arise* and *The Grass Still Grows,* the latter's closest relationship, as one of *The Abe Simon Family Trilogy,* is with *They Too Arise.* The shift to comedy brought radical revision. The strike is omitted, and the strikebreakers are replaced by complications of romance. Abe is provided with a bookkeeper, Louise, capable and personable, with whom Ben is in love—a fresh obstruction to Roth's joint business and marital proposal. Helen Roth is reborn a proper comedy heroine. Arnold, hitchhiking home from Johns Hopkins, now a graduated M.D., is also a much enlivened personality. Dependable Ben is unchanged. Abe, maturer, is funnier. Better educated and more sophisticated than Abe, Esther is crisp of mind and speech. The grandfather (now Gramp) is equally endearing and enlivening, full of good will, advice, and activity.

The play gets quickly to the action. Esther is happy because Roth is coming about a loan Abe needs and is bringing Helen with him. Abe comes home, Ben soon after. Roth and Helen arrive. With Helen and Arnold off for a ride in the new Packard, Roth makes his proposal to Ben. Once Ben says the word, on the day of the wedding he will loan Abe the $3,000 with no interest. To Ben's query, Roth says not to feel rushed about the answer; he will stop in at the office next day to hear Ben's decision. Abe points out that the note is due in two days. Would Roth ask Dawson in the bank to give Abe a couple weeks more as a favor? Roth agrees and leaves. Abe is optimistic, but Gramp warns, "Be careful, Abe. Roth is a smart man."

The next day at the shop it comes out that Abe cannot compete while paying union wages with the big men who use scab labor and cut their prices. Ben advises that they liquidate while they still can. Abe rejects his advice. Creating the business to hand over to a son has been his whole life. Ben and Louise have a talk. If there is no other way than Roth's, he can't let his father lose his business. "I guess it's simply . . . that I love him . . . that's all." Louise replies with,

"I suppose I might even be able . . . to love you for that too . . . I'm that big a fool."

Max Schneeweiss, Abe's shop foreman, enters with a proposition. The men don't want Abe to lose his business, and they don't want to work somewhere else. They will put $4,300 in the business—their savings—if Abe will reincorporate as a cooperative with them, all sharing equally if there are profits, all on salary. Abe would be the manager, they'd make the coats. This way they'd be able to run the scab shops out of the industry, unless they went cooperative or unionized. Abe is moved, but cannot adjust at once to the idea of being a manager and not the boss. He tells Max he will think about it. At a few minutes after four they call the bank. Roth has not been in. Roth arrives and apologizes for not having seen Dawson; he couldn't get away. Roth asks Ben if he has decided. Ben says, all right, he accepts. Roth proposes a drink, calls out, "Girl, girl," to Louise, and gives her a number to order a bottle of port sent over and charged to him. Louise starts to dial, breaks into tears, and rushes out. Ben rushes out after her. Roth asks softly, "That's his girl, Abe?" To Abe's nod, after a pause, he says, softly, "Well, that's the way it goes. Love . . . is a terrible thing." He will be over Sunday; Esther can set the date. After a subdued good-bye, he adds, "I'll hold off Dawson for a week." (Gramp was right.) Roth's remark on love is one of those speeches that is both true to the speaker and true in a far deeper and more poignant sense than the speaker understands.

The following Sunday morning at seven o'clock, Helen Roth climbs through a front window of the Simons' home after several attempts at awaking Arnold, whose room is next to the stairs. She tells Arnold that she met Louise in Macy's and that Louise is a very unhappy girl. Helen has a solution: why don't she and Arnold drive to Connecticut and get married? She has the car and has left a note that she will meet her father that afternoon at the Simons. After some considering, they agree. As Arnold heads for the stairs to get dressed, Gramp appears at the top hugging a huge vase (he rearranges things). He is happy to find company and is told they are going for a walk. On learning that Ben is not with them, he shrewdly suspects the truth and gives the alarm. Helen grasps Arnold by the pajama collar and pulls him toward the door, Arnold protesting he needs clothes. She says they'll stop by and get a suit from her father's closet. Abe appears, Esther follows in close pursuit. Helen yanks Arnold to the door. Gramp says he thinks they are getting married. The roar of a motor is heard just as Ben appears. Abe tells him it looks as though

Arny and Helen went off together for a little wedding, and smiles. Ben says, smiling, "Ahh. What a guy."

The last scene of the play opens with Esther seated on the couch knitting "almost viciously." Abe is on the chair by the radio. It is nearly four o'clock; Roth may arrive at any moment. After an interval, Abe comes directly to the point: "What did I do? I need to know." Esther answers that he ruined both their sons' lives. He could have stopped Arnold and Helen, but did not; what was happening suited him fine. With Ben and Helen, there would have been money; with Louise, nothing. As for Arnold, he should not have married for four or five years until he was set up in his profession. Now Roth will not give Helen a cent. She doesn't understand what has come over Abe.

Abe says let him tell her something. He describes the scene in the office when Ben ran out after Louise, for love. And he was proud of him, because for "one of the few times in my kind of life I saw a man obey himself." Esther restates her position, as she sees it, with logic and clarity: ". . . all I know is, that in this world it is very few people who can be poor and happy. And I want them to be happy. And they're poor. I know what love is."

They discuss their own marriage, which was arranged, in which they have found love, but as Abe points out, neither was in love with anyone else. Esther is no longer angry. She is searching, trying to understand these new points of view. She asks Abe about the business: "Is it down the river?" "No," he says, "not down the river yet."

The doorbell rings. Instead of Roth, it is Abe's younger brother, Dave. He has stopped in to say goodbye and is going to Bermuda to take up an opportunity there. The opportunity is a seventeen-dollars-a-week job on a boat. He is ashamed to be working on a boat, he should have a business. Abe tells him working with his hands is honorable. Earlier, Abe had referred Dave to Roth, who reported he had put him on as a salesman. Dave now reveals he was a lousy scab in Roth's shop, where he was paid twenty-one dollars a week. His wife, Marian, has left him. Dave sees Roth approaching and leaves by the back door. If he were to meet Roth, he would knock him down.

As a new character, Dave is important, a catalyst. The men of the Abe Simon world have shielded their wives from the harshness of business. To Esther, Roth has been simply an old friend, rich, with a fine daughter, and presumably capable. Dave's visit provides a new view of Roth and what he represents, a lift toward her understanding and acceptance of new ideas by the end of the scene. Now she is prepared for Roth and his agitated inquiries. Abe is a romantic, bold, hopeful, responsive to basic emotions, love and anger. Dave provides him with his anger.

Abe confronts Roth directly with the lie about Dave and takes the initiative in renouncing his aid to save the business. An interruption comes when Helen bursts in, laughing, but almost ready to weep. She throws her arms around her father, who tries frantically to learn if she is married or not. Her narrative finally reaches the moment when she and Arnold were standing before the Justice of the Peace: "He looked at me, and he said, 'Helen, are you sure?' And then I looked at him, Daddy, and I said, 'I don't know.' And then he said, and he smiled—'You know, Helen, your father's a son of a bitch but I think we ought to ask him first.'" Roth, with an ecstatic smile, exclaims, "Arnold said that?" Helen, with equal ecstasy, cries, "Yes, Daddy!" Roth "embraces her hugely."

Helen then relates that Arnold put her in a cab, said he had to go for somebody, and drove off in the car. Just as Roth is getting angry about his new car, Arnold enters in a suit too large for him with safety pins holding up the pants. He turns to the door and says, "Come in, Max," and Abe's shop foreman enters. Arnold takes charge and cuts to the facts: Roth has no intention of loaning money to Abe, and Abe is broke. He calls on Max to present his proposition. Past Roth's outraged, "Since when do shop foremen make propositions?" Max repeats the cooperative plan, with the addition that the men will put in $5,000 instead of $4,300. To Roth's indignant protests that it will ruin the industry, Abe replies that Roth means it will ruin his scab shop, and that won't worry him or any other honest man. Abe accepts Max's proposal and makes an appointment for Monday morning eight o'clock at the shop, everyone present.

Abe wants Roth to understand he does not feel disgraced by becoming a working man. Roth calls on Helen to go home. She says, "No, Daddy," she and Arnold are going to be married soon. Until then, although going home to sleep, she will stay here. Roth moves for reconciliation and determines that Helen is sure. He turns to Arnold with, "Then . . . at least if you're going to be my son-in-law, don't go around looking like a bum. That suit, y'know, looks like something you picked out of a garbage pail." Arnold says softly, "Ah . . . this is your suit, Mr. Roth." Roth shakes his head slightly, turns up his palms with a "Well," and exits.

Then begins a delicately conceived and written family finale, in which Ben and Louise enter and announce they, too, would like to get married, all of which Esther meets with a gracefully humorous warmth while delivering a serious and beautiful prewedding address to her two daughters-in-law to be. As the young people go out for a walk, Esther and Abe watch them from a window. Esther asks, "Do you think they will be all right?" to which Abe says, "Why not? They got the main thing." Esther wonders, "I don't know . . . it should have been planned more. It should have taken more time." There follows a prose litany to time: time is for spending, not for saving. Gramp appears with decorations; Esther and Abe depart for a walk; Gramp is left happily decorating as a surprise for the young people's return. There are at least six possible curtain speeches following Esther's welcoming of Helen and Louise, and I would not readily give up a line of any of them. *The Grass Still Grows* is a happy blend of serious and hilarious, sentiment and philosophical reflection.

III

Honors at Dawn and *The Great Disobedience* come between *They Too Arise* and *The Grass Still Grows*. They are crusading or social protest plays, with the same basic theme, the power of big industrialists to exercise corrupting control within major social institutions; in *Honors at Dawn* a large university; in *The Great Disobedience* a big federal penitentiary. Although they contributed valuable experience, both plays were a digression, worthy in themselves but limited, a trial flight in the mode of the day in which they were written, and one that Arthur has not repeated. He has better things to do. He is a revealer, not a reformer, and almost from the beginning has been concerned more with the impact of society on people than with that of people on society. The inward moral orientation of *The Abe Simon Family Trilogy* is its most striking feature and casts its shadow ahead over all of the future plays.

Approaching the end of this reassociation with Arthur's first five plays, I lean back in my study chair and let my mind take its own way. What a superb storyteller he is, and was from the beginning. Each play caught me up and drew me along as it did some forty years ago. Sir Philip Sidney's praise of the poet—his word for any creator of fictional literature—played in and out of my mind in the rereading: "With a tale, forsooth, he cometh unto you, with a tale that holdeth children from play and old men from the chimney corner." And what a master of language he is, especially of speech creative and expressive of character, the language of which plays are made. I think he might agree with Joseph Conrad, another great storyteller, that the first responsibility of a writer of fiction is to make his narrative shipshape, but his end is to create living people through the tensions of the story and the revelations of the language. This Arthur has done also from the beginning. I love every member of the Abe Simon family and their daughters-in-law to be, and Max in *Honors at Dawn,* and, among others, some of the prison inmates in *The Great Disobedience.* Some day, years hence, if someone should ask, as of Charles Dickens, how he felt about his life, Arthur Miller might respond like Dickens with a wave of his hand toward the shelf of his works and say, "There are my people!"

For a period of years now it has been hard to decide whether one is more appalled or bored by the moral vacuousness of much of our theater. We are moral beings, and a theater without moral consciousness is a theater populated by characters of half-life. The best that can be given them is pity. Maxim Gorki through Sahtin in the last act of *The Lower Depths* speaks for Man: "Do not demean with pity. Give respect!"

I think of Arthur Miller as a dramatist of respect. Linda demands that attention must be paid even to such a man as Willy Loman. *Death of a Salesman* is that payment. After *A View from the Bridge* and a few years before *After the Fall,* I received a letter from Arthur referring to a conversation we had had in Ann Arbor. He was searching for a tragic protagonist who might be the modern equivalent in a democratic society of Hamlet, a man in a position of authority representing a high level of intellectual, educational, and moral development. He closed the letter with the sentence "I hope to say a good word for man." Each new play by Arthur Miller has always been a surprise relative to what had preceded. I feel one assurance, however, about his next play—that whatever it may be otherwise, it, too, will say a good word for man.

The Action and Its Significance: Arthur Miller's Struggle with Dramatic Form

by Orm Överland

"There are two questions I ask myself over and over when I'm working," Arthur Miller has remarked. "What do I mean? What am I trying to say?"[1] The questions do not cease when a play is completed but continue to trouble him. In the "Introduction" to his *Collected Plays* Miller is constantly asking of each play: "What did I mean? What was I trying to say?" These questions and the playwright's attempts to answer them are directly related to his account of how he planned and wrote his next play.

The process of playwriting is given a peculiar wavelike rhythm in Miller's own story of his efforts to realize his intentions from one play to the other. Troughs of dejection on being exposed to unexpected critical and audience responses to a newly completed play are followed by swells of creativity informed by the dramatist's determination to make himself more clearly understood in the next one.[2] This wavelike rhythm of challenge and response is the underlying structural principle of Miller's "Introduction" to his *Collected Plays*. Behind

"The Action and Its Significance: Arthur Miller's Struggle with Dramatic Form" by Orm Överland. From *Modern Drama,* 18 (March 1975), 1–14. Copyright © 1975 by the University of Toronto, Graduate Centre for Study of Drama. Reprinted by permission of the author and editor of *Modern Drama,* Jill Levenson.

[1] Quoted in Benjamin Nelson, *Arthur Miller: Portrait of a Playwright*, London, 1970, p. 320.

An early version of this essay was discussed in a seminar at the University of Bergen, Norway, and presented as a lecture at the Universities of Debrecen and Budapest, Hungary.

[2] For instance: "In the writing of *Death of a Salesman* I tried, of course, to achieve a maximum power of effect. But when I saw the devastating force with which it struck its audiences, something within me was shocked and put off . . . the emotionalism with which the play was received helped to generate an opposite impulse and an altered dramatic aim. This ultimately took shape in *The Crucible. . . .*" "Introduction," *Collected Plays*, New York, 1957, p. 38. Page references in parentheses are to this edition.

it one may suspect the workings of a radical distrust of his chosen medium. The present essay will consider some of the effects both of this distrust of the theater as a means of communication and of Miller's theories of dramatic form on his career as a dramatist.

Arthur Miller is not alone in asking what he is trying to say in his plays, nor in being concerned that they may evoke other responses than those the playwright thought he had aimed at. From the early reviews of *Death of a Salesman* critics have observed that a central problem in the evaluation of Miller's work is a conflict of themes, real or apparent, within each play.

The case for the prosecution has been well put by Eric Bentley:

> Mr. Miller says he is attempting a synthesis of the social and the psychological, and, though one may not see any synthesis, one certainly sees the thesis and the antithesis. In fact, one never knows what a Miller play is about: politics or sex. If *Death of a Salesman* is political, the key scene is the one with the tape recorder; if it's sexual, the key scene is the one in the Boston hotel. You may say of *The Crucible* that it isn't about McCarthy, it's about love in the seventeenth century. And you may say of *A View from the Bridge* that it isn't about informing, it's about incest and homosexuality.[3]

John Mander points to the same conflict in his analysis of *Death of a Salesman* in his *The Writer and Commitment:*

> If we take the "psychological" motivation as primary, the "social" documentation seems gratuitous, if we take the "social" documentation as primary, the "psychological" motivation seems gratuitous. And we have, I am convinced, to choose which kind of motivation must have the priority; we cannot have both at once.[4]

Mr. Mander's own image of this conflict of themes within Arthur Miller's play is the house divided and its two incompatible masters are Freud and Marx.

More sympathetic critics find that the plays successfully embody the author's intentions of dramatizing a synthesis of the two kinds of motivation. Edward Murray, for instance, has made the same observation as have Bentley and Mander, but in his view the difficulty of branding Miller either a "social" or a "psychological" dramatist points to a strength rather than to a flaw in his work: "At his best,

---

[3]*What is Theatre? Incorporating the Dramatic Event and Other Reviews 1944–1967*, New York, 1968, p. 261.
[4]London, 1961, p. 151.

Miller has avoided the extremes of clinical psychiatric case studies on the one hand and mere sociological reports on the other. . . . he has indicated . . . how the dramatist might maintain in delicate balance both personal and social motivation."[5]

Miller himself has often spoken of modern drama in general and his own in particular in terms of a split between the private and the social. In the 1956 essay, "The Family in Modern Drama," he claims that the various forms of modern drama "express human relationships of a particular kind, each of them suited to express either a primarily familial relation at one extreme, or a primarily social relation at the other."[6] At times he has pointed to his own affinity with one or the other of these two extreme points of view on human relationships, as when he talks of the forties and fifties as "an era of gauze," for which he finds Tennessee Williams mainly responsible: "One of my own feet stands in this stream. It is a cruel, romantic neuroticism, a translation of current life into the war within the self. The personal has triumphed. All conflict tends to be transformed into sexual conflict."[7] More often, as in "The Shadow of the Gods," Miller has seen himself primarily in the social tradition of the Thirties. It is in this essay that Miller makes one of his most explicit statements on the need for a synthesis of the two approaches:

> Society is inside of man and man is inside society, and you cannot even create a truthfully drawn psychological entity on the stage until you understand his social relations and their power to make him what he is and to prevent him from being what he is not. The fish is in the water and the water is in the fish.[8]

Such synthesis, however, is fraught with problems which are closely connected with Miller's medium, the theater.

Indeed, for Miller synthesis has largely been a question of dramatic form, and the problem for the playwright has been to create a viable form that could bridge "the deep split between the private life

---

[5]*Arthur Miller: Dramatist*, New York, 1967, p. 180. Compare Sheila Huftel, *Arthur Miller: The Burning Glass*, New York, 1965, p. 60: "the synthesis of social and psychological in *After the Fall* has always been with him, the cornerstone on which his plays are built."

[6]*The Atlantic Monthly* 197, April 1956, p. 35.

[7]Henry Brandon, "Sex, Theater, and the Intellectual: A Conversation with Marilyn Monroe and Arthur Miller," *As We Are,* New York, 1961, p. 125.

[8]"The Shadow of the Gods: a Critical View of the American Theatre," *Harper's Magazine* 217, August 1958, p. 39. A similar statement is made in the "Introduction" to the *Complete Plays*, p. 30.

of man and his social life." In addition to his frustration with audience responses and his desire to make himself more clearly understood, part of the momentum behind Miller's search for new and more satisfactory modes of expression after the realistic *All My Sons* has been the conviction that the realistic mode in drama was an expression of "the family relationship within the play" while "the social relationship within the play" evoked the un-realistic modes."[9]

In retrospect Miller found that the theme of *All My Sons* (1947) "is the question of actions and consequences" (p. 20), and the play dramatizes this theme in the story of Joe Keller, for whom there was nothing bigger than the family, and his son Chris, for whom "one new thing was made" out of the destruction of the war: "A kind of—responsibility. Man for man" (p. 85). When Miller is slightly dissatisfied with his first successful play, it is because he believes that he had allowed the impact of what he calls one kind of "morality" to "obscure" the other kind "in which the play is primarily interested" (p. 18). These two kinds of "morality" are closely related to the two kinds of "motivation"—psychological and social—that John Mander and other critics have pointed to. The problem may be seen more clearly by observing that the play has two centers of interest. The one, in which Miller claims "the play is primarily interested," is intellectual, the other emotional. The former is mainly expressed through the play's dialogue, the latter is more deeply embedded in the action itself.

Joe Keller gradually emerges as a criminal. He has sold defective cylinder heads to the air force during the war and was thus directly responsible for the deaths of twenty-one pilots. The horror of this deed is further brought home to the audience by the discovery that Keller's elder son was a pilot lost in action. This is what we may call the emotional center of interest, and most of the plot is concerned with this past crime and its consequences for Keller and his family. But it is this emotional center that for Miller obscures the real meaning of the play.

Miller wanted his play to be about "unrelatedness":

[9]"The Family in Modern Drama," pp. 40, 36. Miller often returns to this point, for instance in the essay "On Social Plays," published as an introduction to *A View from the Bridge*, London, 1957, where he refers to "prose realism" as "the one form that was made to express the private life," and writes of the "struggle taking place in the drama today—a struggle at one and the same time to write of private persons privately and yet lift up their means of expression to a poetic—that is, a social—level." (pp. 7–8)

Joe Keller's trouble, in a word, is not that he cannot tell right from wrong but that his cast of mind cannot admit that he, personally, has any viable connection with his world, his universe, or his society. . . . In this sense Joe Keller is a threat to society and in this sense the play is a social play. Its "socialness" does not reside in its having dealt with the crime of selling defective materials to a nation at war—the same crime could easily be the basis of a thriller which would have no place in social dramaturgy. It is that the crime is seen as having roots in a certain relationship of the individual to society, and to a certain indoctrination he embodies, which, if dominant, can mean a jungle existence for all of us no matter how high our buildings soar (p. 19).

This, then, is the intellectual center of the play. Any good drama needs to engage the intellect as well as the emotions of its audience. Miller's problem is that these two spheres in *All My Sons* are not concentric. When a play has two centers of interest at odds with each other, the emotional one will often, as here, have a more immediate impact on the audience because it is more intimately related to the action of the play.[10] Invariably action takes precedence over the sophistication of dialogue or symbols.

Death of a Salesman (1949) may serve as further illustration of the point made about the two centers of interest in *All My Sons*. Bentley wrote that the key scene of the play could be the one in Howard Wagner's office or the one in the hotel room depending on whether the play was "political" or "sexual." There is no doubt, however, as to which scene has the greater impact in the theater. The hotel room scene is carefully prepared for. The constant references to stockings and the growing tension around the repeated queries about what had happened to Biff after he had gone to ask his father's advice in Boston are some of the factors that serve to high-light this scene. A more immediate impression is made on the audience by the mysterious laughter and the glimpse of a strange woman quite early in the first act. The point is, however, that it is primarily on the stage that this scene makes such an overwhelming impact that it tends to over-shadow the other scenes that together make up the total image of Willy's plight. If the play is read, if one treats it as one would a novel,

---

[10]Raymond Williams has made a similar point in his *Drama from Ibsen to Brecht*, London, 1968, p. 270: "The words . . . expressing Keller's realization of a different kind of consciousness, have to stand on their own, because unlike the demonstration of ordinary social responsibility they have no action to support them, and moreover as words they are limited to the conversational resources so adequate elsewhere in the play, but wholly inadequate here to express so deep and substantial a personal discovery (and if it is not this it is little more than a maxim, a 'sentiment')."

balance is restored and a good case may be made for a successful synthesis of "psychological" and "social" motivation as argued, for instance, by Edward Murray.[11]

Miller seems to have become increasingly aware of the difficulty of making a harmonious whole of his vehicle and his theme. His story would have sexual infidelity (consider for instance the prominence this factor must have in any brief retelling of the plot of *Death of a Salesman* or *The Crucible*) or another personal moral failure at its center, while the significance the story held for the author had to do with man's relationship to society, to the outside world. The one kind of "morality" continued to obscure the other. When starting out to write *A View from the Bridge* (1955), Miller had almost despaired of making himself understood in the theater: no "reviews, favorable or not," had mentioned what he had considered the main theme of *The Crucible* (1953). Since he, apparently, could not successfully merge his plots and his intended themes, he arrived at a scheme that on the face of it seems preposterous: he would "separate, openly and without concealment, the action of the next play, *A View from the Bridge*, from its generalized significance" (p. 47).

With such an attitude to the relationship between story and theme or "action" and "significance" there is little wonder that Miller was prone to writing plays where critics felt there was a conflict of themes. For while Miller's imagination generates plots along psychoanalytic lines, his intellect leans towards socio-economic explanations.

The story was, according to his own account, his starting point for *A View from the Bridge:*

> I had heard its story years before, quite as it appears in the play, and quite as complete.... It was written experimentally not only as a form, but as an exercise in interpretation. I found in myself a passionate detachment toward its story as one does toward a spectacle in which one is not engaged but which holds a fascination deriving from its monolithic perfection. If this had happened, and if I could not forget it after so many years, *there must be some meaning in it for me, and I could write what had happened, why it had happened, and to one side, as it were, express as much as I knew of my sense of its meaning for me. Yet I wished to leave the action intact so that the onlooker could seize the right to interpret it entirely for*

[11]This is in fact the way in which Murray arrives at his evaluation. Discussing *The Crucible* he writes, "The crucial question, however, is: Does Miller succeed in fusing the 'personal' and the 'social'? A close reading of the play would suggest that he does." (p. 73)

himself and to accept or reject my reading of its significance (pp. 47–48, author's italics).

This decision, Miller explains, led to the creation of "the engaged narrator" (p. 47), the role played by Alfieri in *A View from the Bridge*.

The narrator is hardly an innovation in the history of dramatic literature, especially when seen in relation to the chorus in Greek drama. In our own time widely different playwrights like Thornton Wilder (*Our Town*) and Bertolt Brecht (*The Caucasion Chalk Circle*) have made successful use of the narrator. Such historical antecedents and the widespread use of narrators in modern drama should not be lost sight of when considering this aspect of Arthur Miller's plays. Miller's narrators, however, are closely connected with his reluctance to let his plays speak for themselves. They are born from his long and troubled struggle with dramatic form.

Arthur Miller had tried his hand at fiction as well as drama before he achieved success on Broadway with *All My Sons* in 1947. When he thought of his next play, his aim was to achieve "the density of the novel form in its interchange of viewpoints" (p. 30). Again and again he comments on *Death of a Salesman* in terms of a prose narrative, as when he contrasts its sense of time with that of *All My Sons*: "This time, if I could, I would have *told the whole story* and set forth all the characters in one unbroken speech or even one sentence or a single flash of light. As I look at the play now its form seems the form of a confession, for that is *how it is told* . . ." (p. 24).[12] Although this may merely be a manner of speaking, as suggested by his own critique of the movie version where "drama becomes narrative" (p. 26), it does point to an attitude that in certain respects runs counter to drama: the story as something to be *told* as opposed to something to be *shown* or dramatised.

In fact, however, *Death of a Salesman* succeeds precisely because Willy's story is shown on the stage, not told. The possible uncertainty as to motivation does not detract from the intense and unified impact of the drama in the theater. The characters reveal themselves through action and dialogue supported by what Miller has called the play's "structural images" (p. 30). All the more striking then, the need Miller evidently felt to have the characters stand forth and give their various interpretations of Willy's life after the drama proper has

---

[12]My italics. Compare phrases like "The way of telling the tale . . ." (p. 26) and "the form the story would take" (p. 31).

closed with Willy's death. The chorus-like effect of the "Requiem" is obviously related to Miller's conscious effort to write a tragedy of "the common man," a drama which places man in his full social context, which in his essay "On Social Plays" is so clearly associated in Miller's mind with Greek drama. From another point of view the "Requiem" may also be seen as the embryo of the narrator figure who becomes so conspicuous in *A View from the Bridge* and *After the Fall:* after the play is over the characters stand forth and tell the audience what the play is about.

Miller's reluctance to let a play speak for itself became even more evident in his two attempts to add extra material to the original text of *The Crucible* after its first production in 1953. The first of these additions, a second scene in Act Two, helps to explain Abigail's behavior in Act Three, but, as Laurence Olivier told the playwright, it is not necessary.[13] Although Abigail's psychotic character is brought out entirely in action and dialogue, in an encounter with John Proctor on the eve of the trial, and there is no suggestion of extra-dramatic exposition, the added scene is nevertheless evidence of Miller's sense of not having succeeded in making himself understood in the original version of the play.

More striking is the evidence provided by the series of non-dramatic interpolated passages in the first act, where the playwright takes on the roles of historian, novelist and literary critic, often all at once, speaking himself *ex cathedra* rather than through his characters *ex scena.* There is an obvious difference in intent as well as effect in writing an introductory essay to one's play and writing a series of comments that are incorporated in the text itself. The material used need not be different. For example, some of the comments on Danforth in the "Introduction" to the *Collected Plays* are quite similar to those on Parris or Hale incorporated in the play. In the one instance, however, he is looking at his play from the outside, as one of its many critics, in the other he has added new material to the play and has thus changed the text.

In effect the play has a narrator, not realized as a character but present as a voice commenting on the characters and the action and making clear some of the moral implications for the reader/audience. The director of the 1958 Off Broadway revival of *The Crucible* drew the

[13]See Arthur Miller, *The Crucible*, ed. by Gerald Weales, New York, 1971. Olivier's remark is quoted in "A Note on the Text," pp. 153–54. The extra scene is printed in an appendix. It was first published in the edition of the play that appeared in *Theatre Arts* 37, October 1953.

consequences of the revised text and introduced "a narrator, called The Reader, to set the scenes and give the historical background of the play."[14] Besides his function as one of the minor characters, this is what Alfieri does in *A View from the Bridge*. The introduction of a "narrator" element in *The Crucible* is closely related to Miller's attempts to have a separate voice present the author's view of the "generalized significance" of the "action" in the later play.

The interpolated expository passages of *The Crucible* serve two different purposes. Frequently the comments on a character merely repeat points made in that part of the drama which may be acted on the stage. Indeed, the opening words of the following paragraph on John Proctor are suggestive of the Victorian novelist guiding his readers through his story, making sure that no point, however obvious, may be missed:

> But as we shall see, the steady manner he displays does not spring from an untroubled soul. He is a sinner, a sinner not only against the moral fashion of the time, but against his own vision of decent conduct. These people have no ritual for the washing away of sins. It is another trait we inherited from them, and it has helped to discipline us as well as to breed hypocrisy among us. Proctor, respected and even feared in Salem, has come to regard himself as a kind of fraud. But no hint of this has yet appeared on the surface, and as he enters from the crowded parlor below it is a man in his prime we see, with a quiet confidence and an unexpressed, hidden force. Mary Warren, his servant, can barely speak for embarrassment and fear (p. 239).

Proctor's sense of guilt is central to any understanding of him as a dramatic character, but certainly this is made sufficiently clear by, for instance, the several explicit remarks made by Elizabeth as well as by his behavior on the stage.

While such passages are further instances of Miller's apparent distrust of his medium as a means of communication, other passages speak of an impatience with the limitations of the dramatic form. Miller had researched this play thoroughly, and it is as if on second thought he has regretted that he had not been able to bring as much of his research and his historical insights into the play as he would have liked. But when he in the interpolated passages takes on the roles of historian and biographer he tends to confuse the sharp line that must be drawn between the characters in a play called *The Crucible* and a group of late seventeenth-century individuals bearing

---

[14]*Ibid.,* p. 169n.

the same names as these characters. Thus, in the first of the two paragraphs that serve to introduce Proctor as he enters on the stage, Miller tells us:

> Proctor was a farmer in his middle thirties. He need not have been a partisan of any faction in the town, but there is evidence to suggest that he had a sharp and biting way with hypocrites. He was the kind of man—powerful of body, even-tempered, and not easily led—who cannot refuse support to partisans without drawing their deepest resentment. In Proctor's presence a fool felt his foolishness instantly— and a Proctor is always marked for calumny therefore (pp. 238–39).

The change in tense in the paragraph that follows (quoted above) suggests that Miller had a different Proctor in mind in each paragraph: the historical Proctor and the character in the play. This confusion runs through the various character sketches or brief essays on for instance Parris (pp. 225–29), Putnam (pp. 234–35) and Rebecca and Francis Nurse (pp. 242–43). It should further be noted that these interpolated expository passages are often concerned with motivation, and that both psychological, religious and socio-economic explanations of the trials are given. While the information is interesting in itself and throws light on the Salem trials, it cannot add to our understanding of the drama as acted on the stage. Whatever needs to be known about these characters and their motives by the audience must be expressed in action and dialogue. That is, if we do not accept the dichotomy of "action" and "significance," with the latter element presented by a representative of the author, a "Reader" or a narrator.

The assumption of such a dichotomy, according to Miller, lies at the heart of the structure of his next play, *A View from the Bridge.* Here, and in *A Memory of Two Mondays,* the one-act play originally presented on the same play bill, Miller thinks of himself as having followed "the impulse to present rather than to represent an interpretation of reality. Incident and character are set forth with the barest naiveté, and action is stopped abruptly while commentary takes its place" (p. 49). On the face of it, however, it is difficult to see why such commentary should be found necessary, unless the playwright had given up trying to make himself understood through "action" alone or, rather, to let his "action" carry the full weight of the "significance" he saw in it.

In his "Introduction" Miller claims at the outset that his "approach to playwriting and the drama itself is organic" (p. 3), and he insists that "the play must be dramatic rather than narrative in concept and execution" (p. 4). When towards the end of the "Introduction" he explains that "the organic impulse behind" his early plays was "split apart" in *A View from the Bridge,* it is as if he admits the failure of this approach. The organic structure of the early *All My Sons,* however, has already been questioned by Miller in his critique of its two centers of interest. As in this earlier play, the emotional center of *A View from the Bridge* is embedded in the action. But in the latter play Miller explains that he deliberately tried not to have the dialogue of the characters involved in the action carry any burden that goes beyond this action. The aspect of the play that dialogue attempted to express in *All My Sons* is now delegated to the narrator. The more explicit splitting apart of "the organic impulse" has been observed in *Death of a Salesman* with its concluding "Requiem." Moreover, Miller has also been seen to depart from the second of his two basic principles of playwriting in introducing narrative and expository passages into *The Crucible.* With *A View from the Bridge* he wrote a play that approaches illustrated narrative.

Alfieri, the lawyer-narrator, opens the play by telling a little about himself and his neighborhood and suggesting some of the themes of the play to follow. When Eddie appears on the stage, the verbal tense Alfieri makes use of is striking in its implications: "This one's name *was* Eddie Carbone" (p. 379, author's italics). Later in the play Alfieri consistently refers to Eddie in the past tense. The story is obviously Alfieri's story. What we see on the stage is Alfieri's memory of Eddie as he ponders on its significance: "This is the end of the story. Good night," he concludes the original one act version of the play.[15] The past tense is the mode of narrative; drama is enacted in the present.

The title *A Memory of Two Mondays* is in itself interesting in this connection as it suggests an implied narrator, someone whose memory is projected on the stage as is Alfieri's. This technique is developed to its furthest extreme in *After the Fall,* where *"the action takes place in the mind, thought, and memory of Quentin."*[16] The play has become illustrated narrative, and is essentially a two act monologue which the narrator and main character, Quentin, directs at the audience. Significantly, since the flow of narration is essential to the play and the many dramatizations of situations in the narrative are incidental, Quentin's audience is in Miller's stage directions defined

---

[15]Quoted from the periodical version, *Theatre Arts* 40, September 1956.
[16]New York, 1964, p. 1.

as a *"Listener, who, if he could be seen, would be sitting just beyond the edge of the stage itself."*[17]

The images presented on the stage are illustrations of Quentin's consciously controlled discourse or of the working of his sub-consciousness as he struggles for self-understanding and self-acceptance. In either case, the device of giving characters within *"the mind, thought, and memory of Quentin"* a semi-independent status on the stage and allowing them to speak for themselves, makes possible an objective view of the self-image projected by Quentin in his discourse. Essentially, however, Miller has placed a character on the stage and given him the opportunity of examining his life and motives and explaining himself to a Listener through a monologue that lasts the whole length of a two act play. From point of view of genre the result is a cross between expressionist drama, stream of consciousness novel and dramatic monologue. The result, however, is good theater: it works on the stage. The critical attacks on *After the Fall* have mainly been concerned with Miller's subject matter and theme, not his experiment with dramatic form.

Rather than add a clarifying "Requiem," as he did with *Death of a Salesman*; rather than interpolate expository passages in the published play to make himself more readily understood, as he did in *The Crucible*; and rather than introduce a narrator, somewhat to the side of the central plot, who could explain the author's "reading of its significance," Miller in *After the Fall* made the narrator's attempt to arrive at the significance of his own life and explain himself directly to the audience the center of the play. Ironically, Miller may never have felt himself so misunderstood by audiences and critics alike as after the first production of *After the Fall* in 1964, the play that may be seen as the culmination of a series of efforts to develop a form that would allow him to present his intentions unmistakably and clearly to his public.

Some years earlier, in his "Introduction" to the *Collected Plays*, Miller had observed that "the intention behind a work of art and its effects upon the public are not always the same" (p. 8). His answers to the question of how to avoid this communication gap could not, finally, have struck him as successful in practice. In his next play, at least, *Incident at Vichy*, written immediately after the critical disaster of *After the Fall*, he returned to the form of the straightforward, realistic play. By concentrating on one of the two poorly integrated themes of

[17]*Ibid.*, p. 2.

After the Fall, that represented by the concentration camp tower, the later play, moreover, avoids the conflict between two different kinds of "morality" or "motivation" many critics have found in his plays up to and including *After the Fall*. *Incident at Vichy* may be too much the drama of ideas (and not very new or original ones at that) to be successful in the theater, and Von Berg's development may not be quite convincing on the stage; but at least there is no need for any "Requiem," explanatory footnotes or narrator to express the play's dominantly public theme.

Four years later Miller returned to the material of *All My Sons, Death of a Salesman* and *After the Fall* in another family drama, *The Price*. The play is also a return to the realistic style and retrospective technique of *All My Sons*. But of course Miller had traveled a long distance since 1947. There is a greater economy of characters and incidents, a more subtle and dramatically integrated use of symbols, no more need for manipulative, mechanistic devices like surprise arrivals or unsuspected letters. Two hours in an attic with old furniture and four people—and the experience in the theater is of something organic, something that comes alive and evolves before us on the stage. The playwright appears relaxed, confident that the "action" expresses its "generalized significance": the characters speak for themselves and the play speaks for Arthur Miller.[18]

The critics who found, I think rightly so, a confusion of private-psychological and public-political themes in Miller's plays were addressing themselves to the very problem Miller has repeatedly pointed to as the central one for the dramatist in our day: how to create a form that can bridge "the deep split between the private life of man and his social life." Miller's belief, expressed in several essays in the mid-fifties, that it is the unrealistic modes of drama that are capable of expressing man's social relationships, as opposed to the realistic drama which is best suited to present the private life, is seen most clearly at work in *A View from the Bridge* from 1955. The "bridge," however, is rather crudely built: to the side of the realistic action

---

[18]The "Author's Production Note" to *The Price* may suggest, however, that Miller was not entirely confident that he had succeeded in making himself understood. He takes care to explain that "A fine balance of sympathy should be maintained in the playing of the roles of Victor and Walter," as if the text itself does not make clear that "both men" are presented "in all their humanity and from their own viewpoints." He even finds it necessary to give his view of the theme of the play: "As the world now operates, the qualities of both brothers are necessary to it; surely their respective psychologies and moral values conflict at the heart of the social dilemma." (London, 1968, p. [117])

stands the narrator, who in the first version of the play spoke in verse—poetry, according to Miller, being the style most closely related to public themes. In the light of such theories the author's misfired intentions with *After the Fall,* his most "unrealistic" play, may be more easily understood; and the irony of its reception as his most embarrassingly private play more readily appreciated. There is further irony in the successful synthesis of the public and the private spheres in *The Price.* For according to Miller's theory, the realism of this or any other play "could not, with ease and beauty, bridge the widening gap between the private life and the social life." But in his essay on "The Family in Modern Drama," Miller had also wondered: "Why does Realism always seem to be drawing us all back to its arms? We have not yet created in this country a succinct form to take its place."[19] This was written at a time when Miller was trying to break away from realism. This movement, however, had its temporary conclusion in *After the Fall*, the play that more than any other must have led Miller to despair of communicating his intentions to his audience.

The ironies of Arthur Miller's career as a dramatist were further compounded with the production of *The Creation of the World and Other Business* in 1973. In spite of the success, with audiences as well as with critics, of *The Price*, following the disastrous reception of his experiments in *After the Fall*, Miller seems unable to rest comfortably in the strong and protective arms of Realism. His latest play is his first attempt to express himself through comedy and pure fantasy, and in this his most radical departure from realism his earlier concern with the problems of integrating man's private and social life has given way to teleological speculation. Behind the fanciful cosmological draperies, however, one may discover the playwright's old story of the two sons and familial conflict. Indeed, the new play serves as a reminder that the Cain and Abel story is an archetypal pattern in *All My Sons*, *Death of a Saleman*, *After the Fall* and *The Price*.

In a different guise the old question of the two centers of interest is also raised by Miller's attempt at comedy. While God and Lucifer incessantly come together on the stage to discuss the Creator's design, Miller's alleged theme, the audience, who cannot but grow restless after two acts with God, his Angels and a boring couple named Adam and Eve, are finally given the two sons, the responsible and respected Cain and the irresponsible and loved Abel. The rather

[19]"The Family in Modern Drama," pp. 40, 36.

simplistic psychological presentation of the conflict between them is the kind of dramatic material Miller has successfuly handled before, and both because it is welcome relief from the overall tediousness of the rest of the play and because it has dramatic potential, it will easily lay claim to the attention and the interest of the audience at the expense of the play's concern with the human dilemma. Miller's latest Broadway venture thus is not only thematically related to his first one but shows that the playwright has still not been able to solve the problem of dramatic form he then felt had served to obscure his main theme.

The story of Arthur Miller's struggle with dramatic form had its beginning in his realization of the two centers of interest in *All My Sons*. His subsequent theories of social drama and its relationship to the realistic and unrealistic modes of drama should be regarded primarily as rationalizations of his own attempts to express himself clearly, to bridge the gap not so much between the social and the private as between his conscious intentions and the audience and critical responses. This was fully demonstrated in his attempts deliberately to separate the action of a play from its significance. His distrust of the realistic drama as a usable medium was thus properly a distrust of the theater itself as a medium, as evidenced in his use of intermediary commentary and narrators and in his tendency towards illustrated narrative. Realism nevertheless has proved to have a strong hold on Miller, and it is the mode with which, the evidence of his plays suggests, he is most at home. *The Creation of the World and Other Business* marks a break with the tone and style of all his previous plays, but it is impossible at this point to guess whether it will turn out to be a new departure in his career or a dead end. Although Miller, like the devil in Ibsen's *Peer Gynt*, has not always been able to reckon with this audience, he has demonstrated that he has been extremely sensitive to their responses. He may therefore accept the common verdict of critics and audiences and return to the kind of work that has placed him in the front rank of contemporary dramatists.

Work as Alienation in the
Plays of Arthur Miller

by Paul Blumberg

If, as sociologist, one wanted to play the devil's advocate for a moment, one might argue that of the two forms of the study of social man in contemporary society, sociology on the one hand, and the social novel or the social play on the other hand, it is truly the social novel or play which offers the more incisive social analysis.

The sociologist, the argument would go, merely provides us at most with a series of generalizations which represents the culmination of research involving concepts, hypotheses, empirical regularities and so on. By providing the generalizations at various levels of abstraction, or perhaps in linking these together in some more or less systematic fashion, the sociologist regards his task as essentially *completed*.

But the social novelist or the social playwright, on the other hand, cannot be content to stop at the level of generalization; indeed, he must make the sociological generalization *his point of departure*. At the level of generalization, the social novelist or playwright is just beginning, because he must now take that generalization and proceed to illustrate it, to dramatize it, to particularize it imaginatively in the form of a scene, an act, an episode, a chapter, a story or an entire novel or play. The generalization which for the sociologist is a finished product is for the fiction writer, with sociological inclinations, merely the barest raw material. In this sense—without forgetting the dissimilarity of their tasks, purposes, objectives or methods—the social novelist or dramatist is truly the sociologist par

From Paul Blumberg, "Work as Alienation in the Plays of Arthur Miller" (editor's title), *American Quarterly*, 21, No. 2, Pt. 2 (Summer 1969), 291–310. Originally published as "Sociology and Social Literature: Work Alienation in the Plays of Arthur Miller." Copyright © 1969, Trustees of the University of Pennsylvania. Pages 291–303 and 306–10 are reprinted here by permission of the author and publisher.

excellence, because he must carry the sociological generalization to a further and more sophisticated point. . . .

Of all our modern playwrights, Arthur Miller is certainly the one who has the most to say to contemporary sociologists. He is an avid, militant, eager and articulate defender of the "social play." He has written long and often in its defense, declaring that, contrary to critical opinion, the social play need not be synonymous with social *criticism*, although the two are often seen as identical. To summarize Miller's views, a social play, in contrast to a nonsocial or a psychological play, demonstrates the impact of social forces—the class structure, the economy, the system of norms and values, family patterns, etc.—on the raw psychology and lives of the characters; exposes the basic similarity of men, not their uniqueness; and, finally, addresses itself to the question, as did classical Greek drama which Miller regards as the forerunner of all social plays, "how are we to live?" in a social and humanistic sense.[1]

Miller expressed his basic attitude toward the role of social forces in drama in an address he delivered some years ago in which he said:

> I hope I have made one thing clear . . . —and it is that society is inside of man and man is inside society, and you cannot even create a truthfully drawn psychological entity on the stage until you understand his social relations and their power to make him what he is and to prevent him from being what he is not. The fish is in the water and the water is in the fish.[2]

Moreover, Miller has constantly reiterated his belief in the futility of a playwright's attempting to explore the psychological side of man in vacuo, without recourse to his social milieu. Thus, he has written: "I can no longer take with ultimate seriousness a drama of individual psychology written for its own sake, however full it may be of insight and precise observation."[3]

One of the overriding themes in Miller's plays, from his first successful Broadway production, *All My Sons*, to his most recent, *The Price*, is what might be called the quest for community. How in the modern world is it possible to recapture the "primary group" values

[1] "On Social Plays," in *Two One-Act Plays* by Arthur Miller (New York, 1955).

[2] "The Shadow of the Gods: A Critical View of the American Theater," *Harper's*, CCXVII (Aug. 1958), 39.

[3] "On Social Plays," p. 8.

of affection, compassion, solidarity and responsibility? It is the tragedy of the industrial world, according to Miller, that the idea of community has withered, atrophied, and the humanistic links connecting man to man have been severely damaged. A great respecter of the engaged, the committed, the connected, the "political" man, Miller is correspondingly impatient with the complete privatization of life, both by ordinary men themselves in the course of their daily existence, and by playwrights who write psychological drama of unconnected, unrelated, atomistic men. He sees this theme as really the concern of all great plays: this struggle between what he calls "family relations" and "social relations" and what those in sociology would call a struggle between *Gemeinschaft* (community) and *Gesellschaft* (society) values. Miller writes:

> all plays we call great, let alone those we call serious, are ultimately involved with some aspect of a single problem. It is this: How may a man make of the outside world a home? How and in what ways must he struggle, what must he strive to change and overcome within himself and outside himself if he is to find the safety, the surroundings of love, the ease of soul, the sense of identity and honor which, evidently, all men have connected in their memories with the idea of family?[4]

Miller's great reverence for the family is reflected in many of his plays, including *All My Sons, Salesman, A View from the Bridge, The Price* and others.

The theme of work alienation, the central subject of this essay, is actually a sub-theme in Miller's overall treatment of the alienation of contemporary man from a sense of community or relatedness to others. Although his plays, in themselves, illustrate well the concept of work alienation, he has spelled it out for us, in general terms, in an essay. This will be our point of departure for an examination of some of Miller's plays in which this theme is most apparent. Miller writes:

> The deep moral uneasiness among us, the vast sense of being only tenuously joined to the rest of our fellows, is caused, in my view, by the fact that the person has value as he fits into the pattern of efficiency, and for that alone. The reason *Death of a Salesman*, for instance, left such a strong impression was that it set forth unremittingly the picture of a man who was not even especially "good" but whose situation made clear that at bottom we are alone, valueless, without even the elements of a human person, when once we fail to fit

---

[4]"The Family in Modern Drama," *Atlantic Monthly*, CXCVII (Apr. 1956), 36–37.

the patterns of efficiency.... In short, the absolute value of the individual human being is believed in only as a secondary value; it stands well below the needs of efficient production. We have finally come to serve the machine. The machine must not be stopped, marred, left dirty, or outmoded. Only men can be left marred, stopped, dirty, and alone.

Nor may the exponents of socialism take heart from this. There is no such thing as a capitalist assembly line or drygoods counter. The disciplines required by machines are the same everywhere and will not be truly mitigated by old-age pensions and social security payments. So long as modern man conceives of himself as valuable only because he fits into some niche in the machine-tending pattern, he will never know anything more than a pathetic doom.[5]

A persistent thread running through Miller's writing is his concern with the world of work and his effort to illustrate the alienating character of labor in the modern world. Miller's plays are unusual in the sense that the characters in many of them spend much of their time at work, in work-related activities, talking about work or in reaping the (usually negative) consequences of their labor. This is true, for instance, in *All My Sons, Salesman, The Misfits, A Memory of Two Mondays, The Price* and, to a lesser extent, in *A View from the Bridge.* Miller's concern with work as basic to men's lives dates really from his youth. As an adolescent during the depression in Brooklyn, he became painfully aware of the importance of work and the devastating consequences of its absence; he was bewildered at society's mysterious magic as it transformed successful businessmen into paupers. "Suddenly," Miller wrote of this period in his life, "overnight, in fact, the postman became an envied character because he could not lose his job and even had a paid vacation.... The star football player [in high school] became a shipping clerk, and was glad to have the job...."[6]

The depression affected Miller personally. His father, who had been a prosperous ladies' coat manufacturer, apparently suffered grave losses during the depression, and after Miller's high school graduation, he "couldn't even afford the fare" to go to college, and had to take a job. Miller's own manual work experience has been broad and varied for an artist-intellectual, and accounts for the familiarity he demonstrates in his plays with the artifacts and processes of work in industrial society. As a boy, Miller delivered rolls

[5]"On Social Plays," p. 10.
[6]"A Boy Grew in Brooklyn," *Holiday*, XVII (Mar. 1955), 122.

and bread for a bakery. Later, he worked in a warehouse, from which experience he was ultimately to write his *Memory of Two Mondays*. He drove a truck, worked as a waiter, as a crewman on a tanker and so on. John Chapman, writing in 1949, claimed that Miller "spends a few weeks each year working in a factory so he will remember what it feels like to stand on one's feet in one place eight hours a day."[7]

It comes as no surprise, then, that in his writings, Miller has often stressed the importance of work in shaping the lives and personalities of his characters. In probably the most explicit statement of his belief in the imporatnce of work to men, Miller has written:

> I read books after I was seventeen, but already, for good or ill, I was not patient with every kind of literature. I did not believe, even then, that you could tell about a man without telling about the world he was living in, what he did for a living, what he was like not only at home or in bed but on the job. I remember now reading novels and wondering, What do these people do for a living? When do they work? I remember asking the same questions about the few plays I saw.[8]

It is not surprising, then, that when Miller himself began to write, the arena of work, of job, of career, became so often a central focus for him, and that within this arena, Miller attempted to dramatize the malaise and alienation of contemporary man. Let us follow this thread through a few of Miller's dramatic works.

Joe Keller, manufacturer, and central figure in *All My Sons*, has a moral perspective no larger than the fence that surrounds his factory or the grass growing evenly around his own house. Joe Keller is not a selfish, disagreeable or greedy industrialist; he is, really, an ignorant, good-natured and kindly fool, whose love for his wife and family is genuine and unselfish. Yet, in a very thoroughgoing sense, he is deeply antisocial, alienated both from his work and from the larger society around him. Keller's alienation, however, stems not from personal inadequacy or from a unique flaw in his character, but from the larger influence upon him of a society built around the values of rugged individualism and a total absence of any sense of social or community responsibility. The social milieu which created a Joe Keller is the same milieu, Miller might tell us, that created the fallout shelter fad some fifteen years later, where men stocked their family shelters with guns in orders to shoot a hapless neighbor who might desperately, though presumptuously, attempt to enter; or a milieu

---

[7]Quoted in Dennis Welland, *Arthur Miller* (New York, 1961), p. 5.
[8]*Harper's*, CCXVII, 36.

which creates a climate where persons on a city street indifferently observe a fellow citizen being assaulted or murdered.

Keller's especial sin in *All My Sons* involves the fact that during the just-completed Second World War, he was a manufacturer of engines for fighter aircraft. Keller's factory was responsible for turning out more than one hundred defective cylinder heads which led to the tragic deaths of more than twenty American pilots who flew the P40s with the faulty engines. We discover, through the action of the play, that although Keller denies any complicity or responsibility for shipping out the damaged parts, and has succeeded in having the entire episode blamed on his partner who lands in jail, that Keller was, in fact, a knowing party to the scandal. The play is, in fact, built around the growing awareness of Joe Keller's guilt, on the part of Keller himself and of his family.

In a sense, Joe Keller is the dramatic antithesis to the character of Roslyn in *The Misfits*. In Roslyn we have someone whose nerve endings are, so to speak, linked in with every other living thing, whose sense of relatedness to the world is jarred and upset when the most insignificant living thing has to be injured. Joe Keller, on the other hand, though not a hard or a ruthless character—Miller's compassion prevents him from portraying almost any character as exclusively and unforgivingly evil—is, nevertheless, a man whose sense of human responsibility has been thrust aside by the every-man-for-himself individualism rampant in American society.

Joe Keller's wife has been vaguely aware of his guilt all along, but she is totally preoccupied with the hope and faith that the Keller's older son, a pilot who has been missing in action for years, is still alive somewhere. Keller's younger son, Chris, is a character akin to Roslyn in *The Misfits*, a man whose sense of relatedness and responsibility to others makes his father's guilt totally abhorrent and vile. Chris is his father's perfect opposite. While Joe cannot see beyond his family's dining-room table, Chris feels a sense of unity with the world. Describing his own wartime experiences to the girl he hopes to marry, he speaks of the courageous men in his company:

> They didn't die: they killed themselves for each other. I mean that exactly; a little more selfish and they'd've been here today. And I got an idea—watching them go down. Everything was being destroyed, see, but it seemed to me that one new thing was made. A kind of—responsibility. Man for man. You understand me?[9]

[9]*Collected Plays* (New York, 1957), p. 85.

In a confrontation between the two men, when Joe's guilt and complicity is finally apparent, Chris and his father argue at each other, but they do not connect. For Joe's sense of alienation from anything beyond his home prevents him from comprehending Chris' feelings of a broader responsibility. Joe struggles with the arguments of a trapped man: that he had no other choice but to ship out the cracked cylinder heads, that his forty-year-old business would have been ruined in a day had he interfered, that he intended to notify the authorities in due time to prevent the use of the faulty parts, that he did it all only for his family, for his wife and to save the business for Chris.

Chris can only respond in terms of a wider responsibility: that there is something larger than the family, a human commitment that goes further.

Chris, barely in control, shouts:

> For me! Where do you live, where have you come from? For me!—I was dying every day and you were killing my boys and you did it for me? What the hell do you think I was thinking of, of the Goddam business? Is that as far as your mind can see, the business? What is that, the world—the business? What the hell do you mean, you did it for me? Don't you have a country? Don't you live in the world?[10]

The play reaches its climax when it is discovered that Keller was himself responsible for his elder son's death: that Larry killed himself when he discovered his father's incredible responsibility in the defective engine scandal. Chris, trying to explain the significance of it all to his mother, exclaims: "Once and for all you can know there's a universe of people outside and you're responsible to it, and unless you know that, you threw away your son because that's why he died."[11]

Keller's alienation, once again, his sense of estrangement from everyone outside his immediate family was traceable in part to his relationship to his work, which encouraged an unrestrained and boundless individualism, a social indifference and a measuring of value in terms of personal profit and loss, rather than in terms of any wider or more general social values.

Miller summarized the condition of Joe Keller's alienation:

> Joe Keller's trouble, in a word, is not that he cannot tell right from wrong but that his cast of mind cannot admit that he, personally, has

[10]*Ibid.*, pp. 115–16.
[11]*Ibid.*, pp. 126–27.

any viable connection with his world, his universe, or his society. He is not a partner in society, but an incorporated member, so to speak, and you cannot sue personally the officers of a corporation. I hasten to make clear here that I am not merely speaking of a literal corporation but the concept of a man's becoming a function of production or distribution to the point where his personality becomes divorced from the actions it propels.[12]

Miller adds that what makes this a social (or a sociologically relevant) play is not the fact that a man sold defective parts to the armed forces during wartime. That incident, in itself, could form the plot of the most common detective or crime story. Rather, what is important and sociologically pertinent with respect to the theme of social alienation, estrangement, unrelatedness or "loneliness" in Miller's plays is that "the crime is seen as having roots in a certain relationship of the individual to society, and to a certain indoctrination he embodies, which, if dominant, can mean a jungle existence for all of us no matter how high our buildings soar."[13]

Before William Whyte wrote of the organization man and the social ethic, before David Riesman had sketched the characteristics of the modern other-directed man, before C. Wright Mills had given us a bitingly critical portrait of the contemporary personality market in the white collar world, and before Erich Fromm's concept of the marketing personality as a characterological type had gained currency—before all of these, Arthur Miller gave us his powerful—nay, definitive—portrait of the prototype of the alienated white collar man in the character of Willy Loman.

In Willy Loman, Marx's concept of work alienation is extended. For Marx, the modern wage worker's labor was alienated in the sense that his work was repetitive, routine, fragmented and dull, that the worker was merely "an appendage to the machine"; that work was for someone else and under someone else's jurisdiction, not one's own; that in his work the worker was separated or alienated from ownership of the factory, the tools with which he works, the product of his labor and so on. But at least the modern wage worker retained spiritual autonomy from the system, retained the means of hating it and withholding commitment to it. But in Willy Loman, as prototype of the alienated white collar worker, both body and soul are thrown

[12]*Ibid.*, p. 19.
[13]*Ibid.*

into the industrial cauldron, and both are consumed. Willy, a poor victim of a singleminded allegiance to false and hollow values of material success, allows what is most uniquely his, his personality, to be molded, transformed and vulgarized in accordance with what he believes others expect of him. Worse yet, the self-hatred eating at his soul because of his failure to achieve these goals leads him to destroy his precious and once warm relationship with his sons, and finally leads to his own self-destruction. Long before Willy's physical suicide, his self-hatred has brought him to spiritual suicide, and he is only temporarily sustained in his growing madness by his transparent self-deception and dreams of successes past and false illusions of successes future. Willy Loman is, in short, the tragic personification of the other-directed, success-seeking new middle-class man of mid-20th century corporate America. The incredible impact of this play on American audiences, its reception and acclaim are apt testimony to the fact that Miller captured the emerging social character of the American new middle class.[14]

In a sociological framework, we see that Miller made a fundamental distinction between the social character of the *old* entrepreneurial middle class and the social character of the *new*, salaried middle class. The contrast between Willy Loman and brother Ben is crucial. In sociological terms, Ben is a classic representative of the old, 19th-century middle class, while Willy represents the new, dependent, salaried, pathetically other-directed middle class. Ben's character is clearly inner-directed; he has all the 19th-century middle-class virtues: he is hard, unscrupulous, firm, self-reliant, full of the self-confident energy of the 19th-century captain of industry or robber baron. While Willy stresses the importance of personality, of being "well liked" and acceptable to the world, of pleasing others, while insisting on proper form, dress, manner and style, Ben ignores all of this. Ben is presented as a satiric caricature of the old, independent entrepreneur. Setting out to make his fortune in Alaska, he instead found himself in Africa because of his "poor sense of direction." But, never mind. Africa: gold, diamonds, riches of all kinds! And he walked into the jungle at seventeen, walked out at twenty-one, and, by God, he was rich! Willy pleads for "the answer," begs Ben for the "secret to success," hanging on his every word. But, just as in the popular American success literature of our day,[15] we get

[14]See Miller's *Collected Plays*, pp. 27 ff. for a brief personal account of the impact of the play.

[15]See Ely Chinoy, *Automobile Workers*, for a description of the elusiveness of the advice in American success literature.

nothing but vague generalities, imprecise slogans and stirring calls to action. Ben's entrepreneurial advice, "Never fight fair with a stranger, boy," sets the competitive old middle-class mood, but it leaves Willy as baffled and helpless as ever.

Compared to Ben, Willy represents another age, another stage in the development of the American economic system. Ben's world is one in which there are still frontiers to cross, new empires to build, before every corner of the economy was organized and incorporated and covered. As an independent agent, self-employed and self-reliant, Ben has no need to rely on the other-directed values of sociability. The key to success for the old middle-class entrepreneur was less his smile than his fist. His independence meant, in essence, that he didn't have to please anyone or be particularly "well liked." As Willy's neighbor, Charley, says to him at one point after another one of Willy's sermons on popularity-as-a-means-to-salvation: "Why must everybody like you? Who liked J. P. Morgan? Was he impressive?"[16]

Willy's world is different, however. For the new middle-class salaried employee, especially the salesman, success and promotion up the organizational hierarchy *does* depend upon pleasing others: pleasing one's superiors, one's peers, one's customers, one's buyers and a whole host of others. In this respect, Willy was correct: in the world of the salaried new middle class, it is important, crucial, in fact, to be well liked, to sell your personality as well as your "labor power."

As Willy says to Ben, during one of his recurring hallucinations:

> Without a penny to his [Biff's] name, three great universities are begging for him, and from there the sky's the limit, because it's not what you do, Ben. It's who you know and the smile on your face! It's contacts, Ben, contacts! The whole wealth of Alaska passes over the lunch table at the Commodore Hotel, and that's the wonder, the wonder of this country, that a man can end with diamonds here on the basis of being well liked![17]

And yet, Willy is unsure of his own values, for he seems wedged in transition somewhere between the ideology of an old-fashioned and a contemporary business world. And it is a measure of Willy's insecurity that in this speech he is asking Ben as well as telling him. But this is not Ben's way. He ignores Willy's remarks and only sounds

[16]*Collected Plays*, p. 192.
[17]*Ibid.*, p. 184.

the call to action once more: "There's a new continent at your doorstep, William. You could walk out rich."[18]

Earlier we said that one of the persistently recurring themes in Miller's plays is the struggle to realize primary group or *Gemeinschaft* values in a world increasingly dominated by the impersonality of secondary or *Gesellschaft* values, with the ensuing isolation and privatization of life, and the alienation of the individual from his fellows. This clash between "family relations" and "social relations," as Miller calls them, probably finds its most powerful dramatic illustration in *Salesman* when Willy confronts his young boss, Howard.

Willy, sixty-three years of age, is exhausted by his decades of service to the company. He is gradually going mad because of this exhaustion and his self-evident failure to realize the values of material success which he holds so dear, made infinitely worse by the knowledge that his sons, upon whom he has transferred his desperate quest for success, are also both "failures." Willy goes to Howard now to say that he is too ill to travel any more, that Howard must find a place for him in the office. The conversation between Willy and Howard represents the struggle of *Gemeinschaft* with *Gesellschaft* values and the ultimate triumph of the latter. This is not party-line writing, as a few critics once asserted. Howard is not portrayed as the greedy, selfish, heartless capitalist, but merely an understandable victim of the ideology of "business is business," an ideology which has clearly estranged him from any deeper human values. Howard bears Willy no malice, but simply has no place for him in the office; it's simply a matter of dollars and cents: "Kid, I can't take blood from a stone, I—." Not only doesn't Howard have a job for Willy in the office, but, later in the scene, is forced to tell Willy that he has been reluctantly putting off telling him that he can no longer represent the firm at all.

Willy's appeal—so strange and incongruous for a hard-headed salesman—is an appeal to "family relations," to "particularism" in the framework of sociologist Talcott Parsons.

> *Willy.* God knows, Howard, I never asked a favor of any man. But I was with the firm when your father used to carry you in here in his arms.
> *Howard.* I know that, Willy, but—
> *Willy.* Your father came to me the day you were born and asked me what I thought of the name of Howard, may he rest in peace.[19]

But all of this is simply irrelevant now. Howard is a stranger and Willy

[18]*Ibid.*
[19]*Ibid.*, p. 179.

is alone, and the only pertinent point is that Willy is unable to sell any more. Later, as the argument heightens:

> *Willy.* I'm talking about your father! There were promises made across this desk! You mustn't tell me you've got people to see—I put thirty-four years into this firm, Howard, and now I can't pay my insurance! You can't eat the orange and throw the peel away—a man is not a piece of fruit![20]

And so Willy hammers away helplessly at the invincible doctrine of economic efficiency.

Later, Willy tells Charley that he's been fired: "That snotnose. Imagine that? I named him. I named him Howard." But Charley only chides him for his naiveté:

> Willy, when're you gonna realize that them things don't mean anything? You named him Howard, but you can't sell that. The only thing you got in this world is what you can sell. And the funny thing is that you're a salesman, and you don't know that.[21]

Willy wasn't really cut out for selling; he was far more talented and gained much more satisfaction working with his hands. As Biff said at the funeral, the memorable days were on Sundays, seeing his father "making the stoop; finishing the cellar; putting on the new porch; when he built the extra bathroom; and put up the garage." Biff adds: "You know something, Charley, there's more of him in that front stoop than in all the sales he ever made." But as happy as he was with this as an avocation, Willy could never have accepted the life of a worker for, as Biff said, "He had all the wrong dreams. All, all wrong." Willy swallowed whole the success ideology of the new middle class; and it eventually poisoned and killed him. Biff, Willy's favorite son, on the other hand, knew the white collar world for what it was—and despised it. He hated the routine of getting on the subway on hot summer mornings, of devoting his whole life to "keeping stock, or making phone calls, or selling or buying. To suffer fifty weeks of the year for the sake of a two-week vacation, when all you really desire is to be outdoors, with your shirt off. And always to have to get ahead of the next fella."[22]

Biff decided to quit this life in spite of his father's desperate urgings, and he went West, into the outdoors, to work on farms, ranches, away

[20]*Ibid.*, p. 181.
[21]*Ibid.*, p. 192.
[22]*Ibid.*, p. 138.

from the city, away from a regimented white collar existence. But being Willy's son, he could never quite emancipate himself from the nagging thought that, however free he was in the outdoors, he wasn't getting anywhere; he wasn't "building a future." Willy's suicide finally frees Biff of the last longings he ever had for a middle-class career; he sees finally and powerfully what it did to his father. And, as the play closes, he has firmly decided to go West again, and stay there, and he urges his brother to join him.

But his brother, Happy, draws another lesson from his father's tragedy. He is resolved to succeed where his father has failed, to accept his father's values of material success in an urban, industrial, new middle-class milieu. Where Biff seeks to escape the corroding sense of work alienation that destroyed his father, Happy resolves to win the game his father has lost. He says resolutely to Biff at his father's grave: "I'm gonna show you and everybody else that Willy Loman did not die in vain. He had a good dream. It's the only dream you can have—to come out number-one man. He fought it out here, and this is where I'm gonna win it for him. . . ."[23]

A Memory of Two Mondays is a simple one-act play, and although it has been called one of Miller's lesser works, he himself has said that "nothing in this book [of collected plays] was written with greater love, and for myself I love nothing printed here better than this play."[24] It can be considered a lesser work only in terms of its length.

The play is set entirely in a dingy auto parts warehouse in New York in the early 1930s and concerns the lives of a miscellaneous group of workers employed there. Set there, it is one of the few modern American plays which takes place in an actual industrial work situation and is, thus, naturally of central importance in Miller's dramatic treatment of the world of work. As Miller described the play and its setting: "It is a kind of letter to that sub-culture where the sinews of the economy are rooted, the darkest Africa of our society from whose interior only the sketchiest messages ever reach our literature or our stage."[25] *A Memory of Two Mondays* is certainly Miller's clearest dramatic statement about the alienation of the manual worker in an industrial milieu. In one act, Miller magnificently conveys the routine, the stultification, the deadening effect of year after year of repetitive and uncreative industrial labor. "There's a good deal of

[23]*Ibid.*, p. 222.
[24]*Collected Plays*, p. 49.
[25]*Ibid.*

monotony connected with the life, isn't it?" says Kenneth, the new, young, articulate Irish worker. "You ain't kiddin'," replies Larry, nearly forty years of age, with years and years on the job, but struggling financially and desperately in need of a $5 raise. Kenneth continues, exploring Miller's theme of alienation: "Oh, there must be a terrible lot of Monday mornings in sixteen years. And no philosophical ideas at all, y'know, to pass the time?"[26]

With pathos, insight and humor, Miller captures the working-class conversations about cars, women, drink, the fear of being fired—a recurrent theme in Miller's plays—money, sports and the painful boredom of the job. He captures also the attempts by the workers to transcend the daily tedium: the endless horseplay and joking, the countless treks to the toilet as a refuge and momentary escape from the monotony of their tasks.

In the midst of the men and women destined to spend their entire working lives in this dusty, shabby warehouse is Bert—an obviously autobiographical character—an 18-year-old boy who is working there to save enough money to go to college. Bert, just beginning to find himself intellectually, comes to work every day with *The New York Times* and a copy of *War and Peace* which he has been reading for an interminable duration. Bert here is a kind of observer of this industrial scene, in it but not really of it, a stranger in their midst, a momentary passerby. He is there as an almost invisible witness, a marginal man and thus a fairly keen observer. Miller's sensitive portrayal of Bert makes him the magnificent prototype for all those young boys, bound for college and eventually for the white collar or professional world, who take a temporary manual labor job and encounter an unfamiliar world. These college-bound youths meet people whom they will never again contact from the inside, with whom they have little in common except perhaps for an elemental sympathy and compassion, and with whom communication is strained, artificial and reduced to elementary essentials. For most of the warehouse workers there is an awkward, defensive misunderstanding of the world of books and university life which Bert will soon enter. Raymond, the manager, looking at Bert's copy of *War and Peace*, says, "What do you get out of a book like that?" Bert answers, "Well, it's—it's literature." Raymond, mystified, changes the subject.

On one level, the play is about Bert's contact with the other

[26]*Ibid.,* p. 347.

workers: they all inhabit the same world of the warehouse, but, with a couple of exceptions, they pass Bert by with a bare bit of communication and understanding. As a play about a college-bound boy who briefly encounters the blue collar world, it is a brilliant illustrative teaching instrument which college students, most of whom have had such experiences, are able to recognize immediately.

The play on another level abounds in dramatic illustrations of the theme of the alienation of wage labor. Kenneth is, perhaps, affected most strongly by the situation. A recent Irish immigrant, the young man is, at first, full of poetry, idealism, hope and optimism. He hates the dirt and the ugliness of the warehouse, but somehow, in the beginning, manages to rise above it. Searching always after a little beauty in life and nature, Kenneth suggests that Bert help him wash the big windows that have been so covered with dust for years that they are completely opaque. Kenneth says: "I've often thought if we could see a bit of the sky now and again it would help matters now and again. . . . With all this glass we might observe the clouds and the various signs of approaching storms. And there might even be a bird now and again."[27]

Trying to bring a little beauty and a little of God's nature into this industrial scene, however, proves hopeless. Kenneth finally convinces Bert to help him wash the big windows, but, significantly, the view from the workshop floor serves only to reveal a little more of the sordid human condition; a brothel opens up next door, and the newly washed windows reveal all—to the delight of the other workers but to the very proper Kenneth's disgust. The boss's only answer to it: "Shouldn't have washed the windows, I guess," Toward the end, the warehouse has drained all the poetry out of Kenneth's heart and as the play closes he is drifting dangerously toward alcoholism.

On his last day on the job, Bert reflects and wonders why it is he who is able to leave forever this industrial jail, while the others seem trapped forever. And he expresses his awe and respect for the men and women he'll leave behind, respect for their capacity to endure the endlessness of this warehouse life.

> I don't understand;
> I don't know anything:
> How is it me that gets out?
> I don't know half the poems Kenneth does,
> Or a quarter of what Larry knows about an engine.

[27] *Ibid.,* pp. 347–48.

> I don't understand how they come every morning,
> Every morning and every morning,
> And no end in sight.
> That's the thing—there's no end!
> Oh, there ought to be a statue in the park—
> "To All The Ones That Stay."
> One to Larry, to Agnes, Tom Kelly, Gus. . . .[28]

A Memory of Two Mondays is Arthur Miller's own monument to these workers.

Reluctant as I am to categorize Arthur Miller's art—it seems almost irreverent to do so, especially with someone whose art one respects—it is perhaps justifiable in terms of the rich sociological material contained in these plays and the great illustrative sociological relevance which his plays possess. By way of summary then, Miller's plays seem often to treat, directly or indirectly, the theme of work alienation. Sociologically conceived, the alienation of labor has many dimensions and has been dramatically treated by Miller in the following ways:

1. Alienation as a perversion or misuse of the products of one's own labor *(All My Sons, The Misfits);*

2. Alienation as the estrangement from community or *Gemeinschaft* values; it is the retreat in one's work into a super-privatized world where one feels no responsibility to anyone except one's immediate family or circle of friends regardless of the possible destructive social consequences of one's work. This type of alienation, dramatically presented in *All My Sons*, represents an antisocial closing-off of responsibility, an emphatic rejection of *Gemeinschaft* relationships, of community, of relatedness or feelings of solidarity with others in society;

3. Alienation as the transformation of oneself into an other-directed organization man; one who sells his integrity, the genuine and unique core of one's personality in order to please others and to achieve success in the new middle-class salaried world of the large organization *(Death of a Salesman* and, to a lesser extent, his novel, *Focus);*

4. Alienation as the destruction of social relationships and of one's self-respect arising out of the self-hatred caused by the knowledge of failure to achieve material success *(Death of a Salesman);*

5. The classic form of work alienation described by Marx, the

---

[28]*Ibid.,* pp. 370-71.

alienation of the manual worker: the necessity to thrust oneself constantly into a form of toil which is dull, routine, repetitive, uncreative and stultifying *(A Memory of Two Mondays)*.

It should be noted, finally, that Miller has carried into his latest play the same themes of the quest for community and the alienation of labor that have pervaded so many of his earlier works. In its simplest form, *The Price* concerns the conflict of two middle-aged brothers, one of whom, Victor Franz, took the alienating dead-end job of an ordinary patrolman walking a beat and sacrificed school, career and success to care for his helpless father during the depression, while his brother abandoned the burdens and responsibilities of kin and went on to become a wealthy and successful physician. The brothers embody the struggle in American society between the private and the social instincts, between the contending ideologies of personal ambition and social responsibility. Victor Franz found that the price of compassion was a lifetime of alienated labor, and of frustration and bitterness.

The Articulate Victims of Arthur Miller

by Ruby Cohn

Philip Rahv has contrasted the American Paleface and Redskin traditions in literature, and the contrast holds for the stage as well. Wishing to write modern tragedy, Arthur Miller has created loquacious characters in both traditions. His Palefaces tend to preach morality through generalizations and abstractions; more memorable are his urbanized Redskins, who face disaster with concrete images and vigorous rhythms.

Conceived and partially written during World War II, Miller's *All My Sons* thrives on well-worn subjects: two war-hero brothers are in love with the same woman; two businessmen are involved in the same crime; a hidden letter leads to a dénouement; virtue triumphs when a guilty father commits suicide; pure young lovers are finally united. *All My Sons* is an old-fashioned problem play about a timely problem—war profits. But Miller's war profiteer, Joe Keller, inspires pity rather than hisses because he looks, thinks, and talks like a member of the Broadway audience. Just before his suicide, he refers to Miller's title with its biblical flavor: "Sure, [Larry] was my son. But I think to him they were all my sons. And I guess they were. I guess they were." A classical recognition.

Although Miller's play is based on an event in the Midwest, the drama is heightened by Joe's New York Jewish rhythms and vivid homely images: "You look at a page like this you realize how ignorant you are." "You can talk yourself blue in the face, but there's no body and there's no grave, so where are you?" "It's a tragedy: you stand on the street today and spit, you're gonna hit a college man." "A little man makes a mistake and they hang him by the thumbs; the big ones become ambassadors." "I'm his father and he's my son, and

"The Articulate Victims of Arthur Miller." From Ruby Cohn, *Dialogue in American Drama* (Bloomington, Ind.: Indiana University Press, 1971). Copyright © 1971 by Indiana University Press. Reprinted by permission of author and publisher. Pages 68–96 have been revised by the author for this volume.

if there's something bigger than that I'll put a bullet in my head!" In these sentences, rhythm underlines sentiment—respect for learning, cynicism about civic duty, adherence to family feeling. Father and son, Joe and Chris Keller are moral antagonists, and Miller gives them contrasting idioms. In moments of stress Chris pontificates in abstractions, whereas Joe cries out in pained expletives. It is the guilty father whom we remember.

Both *All My Sons* and Miller's best-known play, *Death of a Salesman*, presumably dramatize Wasp families, since Miller does not specify racial or religious origins. Various critics have attacked Miller for concealing the Jewishness of the Loman family, but Miller has countered that "Jewishing" the families would undercut their symbolic Americanism; the drive toward success is an all-American phenomenon.[1] In *Death of a Salesman* Miller uses informal grammar and casual repetitions to cement this basic Americanism, but he distinguishes the speech patterns of his main characters. Willy Loman speaks in clichés larded with repetitions of "man," "boy," "kid." His flat language contrasts with Charley's cynical urban wisdom, Uncle Ben's frontier aphorisms, Linda's sentimental outbursts, Happy's wise-guy banter, and Biff's lyricism about nature.

The original title of *Death of a Salesman* was *The Inside of His Head*, and Miller's achievement has been the skillful dramatization of Willy's last hours to reveal what goes on inside his head. In Act One, four extended memory scenes are climaxed by Biff's discovery of the woman in his father's hotel room. Near the end of Act Two, Willy has a fantasy of asking his dead brother Ben for advice about his own suicide. Through blocking, lighting, and music, Miller sets off these excursions into Willy's memory and fantasy, so that we never confuse them with the dreary present, in which he speaks the same colloquial idiom.

Miller has acknowledged his debt to Ibsen rather than Strindberg, and yet *The Dream Play* is an ancestor of *Death of a Salesman*, where dream is theme, refrain, and technique. Rather than a tragedy of failure, as the play is often described, *Death of a Salesman* dramatizes the failure of a *dream.* The intrusion of Willy's past and fantasy into his present resembles a dream, and the word *dream* recurs, from the early scenic direction: "*An air of the dream clings to the place, a dream rising out of reality*" through the introduction of Willy's two sons: "[Biff's]

---

[1]Robert A. Martin, "The Creative Experience of Arthur Miller: An Interview," *Educational Theatre Journal* (October 1969), p. 315.

dreams are stronger and less acceptable than Happy's" to the triple evocation in the Requiem:

Biff. He had the wrong dreams.
Happy. He had a good dream.
Charley. A salesman is got to dream, boy. It comes with the territory.

Miller's play is as much about a salesman's dream as about his death, but death lies immanent in Willy's dream.

Willy has enough faith in his success dream to reject Charley's advice and money, and yet he carries on a lifelong debate with his successful brother Ben. Charley and Ben—small businessman and robber baron—are foils for Willy, and their idioms contrast with his pat phrases about success through popularity. Charley speaks salty proverbs, and Ben speaks active epigrams. But repetitively and almost monosyllabically, Willy preaches the popularity he can only occasionally achieve. Willy sometimes claims to be well liked, but he confides to Linda that people laugh at him instead of liking him. Even his infidelity is the result of making a woman laugh. Unintentionally, he makes us laugh, often by the juxtaposition of his ephemeral dream against the irritating concreteness of his Chevvy, Studebaker, and Hastings refrigerator. We may not know what Willy sells, but we know what he buys: "The refrigerator consumes belts like a goddam maniac."

Willy's linguistic poverty reflects the poverty of his dream, as well as of a real world "full of aspirin, arch supports, saccharine (all the wrong cures for what ails Willy), Studebakers, Chevrolets, shaving lotion, refrigerators, silk stockings, washing machines."[2] But the first three items are remedies, and most of the others are flawed. Willy's life teeters between these petty concrete objects and his grandiose verbal projections. In past, present, and fantasy, Willy expresses himself through clichés and repetitions in a formulaic chant. However, he achieves neither popularity nor success as a salesman, and he fails as gardener, mechanic, husband, father.

This "low man" accounts for the play's wide appeal, in spite of flaws in two key scenes. A phoney dream of success should be exploded by a scene about the phoniness of success, and not about illicit sex. Nevertheless, Biff's discovery leads to a fine scenic image of Willy's self-contradiction—begging on his knees as he threatens Biff with a beating.

---

[2]Henry Popkin, "Arthur Miller: The Strange Encounter," in *American Drama and Its Critics*, ed. Alan Downer (Chicago: University of Chicago Press, 1965), p. 234.

As the climax violates the thematic drive of the play, so the Requiem violates its form. *Death of a Salesman* is not rigidly contained within Willy's mind, but the Requiem is jarringly outside it. More importantly, the epilogue does not provide new insight. We have already heard the divergence of Willy's sons in their judgment of their father; Happy remains prey to Willy's dream while Biff attains self-recognition in Oliver's office; it need not be spelled out again. Charley, on the other hand, changes unconvincingly; having repeatedly urged Willy to give up his phoney dream, Charley suddenly becomes sentimental about that dream of a salesman.

Linda, however, is least convincing in the Requiem. We have followed her devotion to her husband, and we pity her in her grief. When Linda found the rubber pipe near the gas jet, she worried, but she did not wonder *why* Willy wanted to kill himself, discouraged and exhausted as he was. Desperate and deluded by the end of the play, Willy does carry out his threat. Linda's astonishment arises less from her character than from Miller's bid for audience sympathy.

Near the beginning of the play, Willy grumbles: "Figure it out. Work a lifetime to pay off a house. You finally own it, and there's nobody to live in it." Miller skillfully has Linda echo him at the play's end: "I made the last payment on the house today. Today, dear. And there'll be nobody home." What neither of them learns—but what we learn—is that a house is not a home when it is built on clichés. Nevertheless, much of the play's strength lies in the carefully rhythmed poverty of Willy's words. His mass-produced phrases belie his claim to special attention. His sentimental fantasies are punctured by malevolent objects. Rather than risk independent thought, he risks and loses his life. And we sympathize with him, as with few characters in modern drama.

After *Death of a Salesman* Miller created several protagonist-victims who he sought to elevate to tragic stature. In *The Crucible* the hero-victim preserves integrity by sacrificing his life. In Miller's first three published plays, then, he moves from villain-victim (Joe Keller) to protagonist-victim (Willy Loman) to hero-victim (John Proctor), all highly verbal while conveying an impression of inarticulacy.

Since *The Crucible* is set in colonial New England, Miller invents a language that vaguely suggests colonial English; it relies mainly on *be* as a main verb and *do* as an auxiliary verb. Uncolloquial, Miller's dialogue permits poetic flights. Willy Loman expressed his love of nature: "The trees are so thick, and the sun is warm." John Proctor is more mannered: "Lilacs have a purple smell. Lilac is the smell of nightfall, I think. Massachusetts is a beauty in the spring!"

Many of the *Crucible* scenes are histrionic, but the moral choices turn upon the simple word *name*. Abigail brazenly assures her uncle: "There be no blush about my name," and she accuses Elizabeth Proctor of blackening her name. The importance of a good name is insidiously shifted by the witch-hunters into the naming of names. Giles Corey, foreshadowing John Proctor's heroism, preserves his good name by refusing to name names. As John Proctor's peril grows, he indulges in abstractions, which Miller anchors in repetition and the word *name*. John tarnishes his name by confessing his adultery, so as to stain Abigail's name. When Elizabeth lies about John's adultery, he cries out: "She only thought to save my name." Ready to sacrifice his name in exchange for his freedom, John is not willing to testify that his fellow-victims spoke to the Devil: "They think to go like saints. I like not to spoil their names."

After John signs his confession, he refuses to relinquish the document: "God has seen my name on this! It is enough!" Guilty in the sight of God, Proctor is not willing to have his neighbors know his guilt, and he pleads: "I have given you my soul; leave me my name!" Only slowly does he come to realize that his soul and his name are virtually synonymous. With stock gestures of melodrama, he utters sanctimonious last words: "You have made your magic now, for now I do think I see some shred of goodness to John Proctor. Not enough to weave a banner with, but white enough to keep it from such dogs. *Elizabeth, in a burst of terror, rushes to him and weeps against his hand.* Give them no tear! Tears pleasure them! Show honor now, show a stony heart and sink them with it!" The shift from "name" to "honor" weakens these heroics.

Turning away from heroics and histrionics, Miller next wrote his own favorite play, *A Memory of Two Mondays*. In the form of nostalgic memory, the play contains very loose blank verse. But the New York City speech sounds like prose, flavored by the dialects of Slavic Gus and Irish Kenneth. Midway through the play, college-bound Bert and lyrical Kenneth wash the warehouse windows, and they burst into verse at the sight of summer outside. However, the verse barely scans and is almost barren of imagery.

A View from the Bridge, originally performed on the same program as *A Memory of Two Mondays*, also blends verse into prose—in the original one-act version. The colorful colloquialisms of Eddie Carbone, the longshoreman protagonist, contrast with the rhetoric of Mr. Alfieri, the commentator-lawyer, who speaks in free verse. Leonard Moss describes the contrasting speech patterns: "[Alfieri's] sonorous periodic sentences (with repeated connectives, in the biblical tradition), his dignified diction, elegant imagery, and legendary allusions are obviously far removed from the protagonist's lower-class Brooklynese."[3] The play's title may even be a pun; Alfieri, an American attorney of Sicilian origin, is the bridge between two civilizations, the one founded on written law and the other on tribal loyalty.

Eddie Carbone, frustrated by his unacknowledged lust for his niece, seeks legal recourse against her marriage, but he thereby betrays the tribal code. A man who thinks with his fists, Eddie is nevertheless endearing because of his salty speech. "Most people," he instructs his niece, "ain't people." Or, warning her against the blonde Rodolpho, he claims: "That's a hit-and-run guy, baby; he's got bright lights in his head, Broadway." Or, "Just remember, kid, you can quicker get back a million dollars that was stole than a word that you gave away." To his wife he complains: "It's a shootin' gallery in here and I'm the pigeon." Such vivid images contrast not only with Alfieri's rhetoric but with the formal phrases of the "submarines." As in *The Crucible*, a play of very different language, Miller invests the repeated word *name* with thematic importance. Challenging Marco to fight, Eddie is as irascible as Hotspur: "Wipin' the neighborhood with my name like a dirty rag! I want my name, Marco!"

After Eddie's death in the duel, Alfieri delivers a confusing eulogy: ". . . not purely good, but himself purely, for he allowed himself to be wholly known." But Eddie did not know himself, and since we know him through Alfieri's "view from the bridge," *is* he wholly known? Alfieri's final sentence provides no answer: "And so I mourn him—I admit it—with a certain . . . alarm." As usual when Miller resorts to abstraction—alarm—his meaning is fuzzy. In the original one-act version of the play, Alfieri's verse provides a bridge between instinctual man and codified law. In the revised two-act version, Miller added dialogue that blunts the play's drive and the protagonist's passion, mainly through spelling out sexual detail. Miller feels that the additions result in "a clearer statement,"[4] but the clarity makes Eddie a victim of specific circumstance, to whose fate Alfieri's choral commentary seems irrelevant.

[3]Leonard Moss, "Arthur Miller and the Common Man's Language," *Modern Drama* (May 1964), pp. 52–59.
[4]Arthur Miller, "Introduction" to Bantam edition of *A View from the Bridge*, p. x.

As the narrator Alfieri is intended to broaden the meaning of *A View from the Bridge*, an unnamed Listener ("God or analyst") is intended to broaden the meaning of *After the Fall*. Although the opening scenic direction claims: "*The action takes place in the mind, thought, and memory of Quentin*," the play is less "mental" than *Death of A Salesman* because Quentin addresses himself *consciously* to the Listener, whereas Willy is at the mercy of random association. Willy dreams of success as a result of being well liked, and Quentin looks for innocence as though the Fall had not taken place. Each play's dialogue underlines the illusion of its protagonist—*well liked* and *innocent*.

Miller's Quentin undertakes a quest in self-exploration, during the course of which he asks a good many rhetorical questions, but his specific question—whether to marry for the third time—is petty against the concentration camp background, and yet Miller does not seem aware of its pettiness. Quentin himself is supposed to learn through the drama. We witness some dozen incidents of Quentin's life, as opposed to the four main events of Willy's past and fantasy. We don't know what Willy sells, but we don't know Quentin's family name or background. Although his parents and friends are Jewish, Quentin's speech is free of Jewish inflection, and it is burdened with abstractions.

After the Fall begins with Quentin's extended address to the Listener, which runs through a catalogue of abstractions—decision, success, feeling, despair, way of life, hope. Quentin often generalizes with such words as *one, whoever*, editorial *we*. Leonard Moss counts one hundred repetitions of the word *love* and about fifty each of *death* and *truth* in the first published version of the play[5]. Although some of these were subsequently deleted, many remain, along with some dozen repetitions of *power* and *innocence*. Arguing with his first wife Louise, Quentin charges: "We are killing one another with abstractions." Louise seems to learn abstraction from Quentin, but he alone is capable of the sententiousness of: "We conspired to violate the past, and the past is holy and its horrors are holiest of all!"

Although it may not have been Miller's intention, Quentin's images and repetitions serve, like his abstractions, to reveal his self-obsession and the shallowness of his understanding. Willy's clichés are exploded by the thematic drive of *Death of a Salesman*, but Quentin's limitations become the limitations of *After the Fall*. Examining himself, he says that self-knowledge is futile; attractive to

[5]Moss, "Arthur Miller."

women, he is a misogynist; confessing his guilt, he covertly implies his innocence; dulled by abstraction, he seeks significance in the boyhood joy with which he wakens each morning; steeped in personal particulars, he strains for universal significance.

After the Fall, written after an eight-year silence, must have exacted a personal price from Miller, but perhaps that very price hindered his main dramatic skill—to evoke pity through poignant scenes centering on a protagonist who expresses himself in rhythmed colloquialisms. Miller himself declared: "Look, *After the Fall* would have been altogether different if by some means the hero was killed or shot himself. Then we would have been in business."[6] In his next play, *Incident at Vichy*, Miller was "in business."

The title *Incident at Vichy* points to an un-American setting, and the drama is meant to be a morality play that could take place anywhere. Threatened by Nazis, a group of French Jews guess at their fate. The first words of the non-Jew Von Berg pose the problem: "Have you all been arrested for being Jewish?" When there is no answer, he adds: "I'm terribly sorry. I had no idea." A little later he steadies an old Jew and asks him: "Are you all right, sir?" The question recalls bitter Jewish jokes about minor aches and pains during the holocaust. In Miller's play, however, only the painter Lebeau speaks with bitter Jewish wit. Although the play's Jews are anxious about their fate, they discuss it with the impersonal pronoun, *one*, and they speak in abstractions. The psychiatrist Leduc enunciates what seems to be the play's message, in a passage that recalls Sartre's *Anti-Semite and Jew*: "Until you know it is true of you you will destroy whatever truth can come of this atrocity. Part of knowing who we are is knowing we are someone else. And Jew is only the name we give to the stranger, that agony we cannot feel, that death we look at like a cold abstraction. Each man has his Jew; it is the other. And the Jews have their Jews. And now, now above all, you must see that you have yours—the man whose death leaves you relieved that you are not him, despite your decency. And that is why there is nothing and will be nothing—until you face your own complicity with this . . . your own humanity." Leduc scarcely seems concerned about his own fate, so that Miller has to reintroduce an offstage but specific Nazi relative of Von Berg, to motivate the nobleman's sacrifice of his own life for Leduc's.

In the play's final scene, Von Berg confronts the cultivated

---

[6]"Arthur Miller" in *Writers at Work: The Paris Review Interviews*, Third Series (New York: Viking Press, 1967), pp. 223–24.

German major. Although both are contemptuous of the "racial anthropologist," only the nobleman has courage as well as culture. In a new departure for Miller, he renders Von Berg's moral triumph silently. After Leduc's exit with Von Berg's pass, "*Von Berg turns and faces* [the Major].... *The moment lengthens, and lengthens yet . . . They stand there, forever incomprehensible to one another, looking into each other's eyes.*" The two men stand in silent opposition after the many long discussions in the body of the play. Like the homespun heroics of *The Crucible*, the many arguments of *Incident at Vichy* seek to explore moral depths. Proctor's "You are pulling Heaven down and raising up a whore!" is nevertheless more graphic than Leduc's "It's not your guilt I want, it's your responsibility." The context fails to dramatize the final prolonged silence.

After such heroics—noble suicides articulating abstractions of nobility—Miller wrote his least ambitious play of a protagonist-victim, *The Price.* The play's seed appears to be a character who figures minimally in the plot—Gregory Solomon, eighty-nine-year-old dealer in second-hand furniture.[7] In *The Price*, Victor Franz, policeman, has concealed from himself the motives that led him to interrupt his scientific education so as to support his father who was ruined by the 1929 stock market crash. His adult life is the price he paid for that self-concealment. His surgeon brother has paid the price of personal relationships to succeed professionally. The play's concern with moral price is reflected in the price for a house full of furniture, crammed into a single stage room.

Divided brothers is an old romantic theme, and Miller has dramatized it in earlier plays—*All My Sons, Death of a Salesman* (twice), *A View from the Bridge, After the Fall.* For the first time, however, divided brotherhood is his central theme, and yet one cannot distinguish these brothers by their speech—both loquacious while implying that they are not, both educated but careless of grammar, both ready to draw generalizations from their separate lives. Although Walter succumbs to success and Victor to family loyalty, each is temporarily seduced by the other's motive. Walter notes: "It's almost as though we're like two halves of the same guy."

The Price is an unpretentious exploration into a family relationship, enlivened by the experiential wisdom of the appropriately named furniture-dealer, Gregory Solomon. His salty Jewish expressions provide both comic relief and a feeling of tragic endurance in a world

7Ibid., p. 198.

of uncertain values: "The price of used furniture is nothing but a viewpoint." At the play's end, when ironically named Victor realizes that nothing has come of his talk with his brother, Solomon comments on the incalculable price of human pain: "I had a daughter, should rest in peace, she took her own life. . . . But if it was a miracle and she came to life, what would I say to her?" None of Miller's articulate victims attempts an answer.

In spite of personal idealism and public optimism of their author, Miller's plays are remarkably full of suicide. Larry Keller crashed his airplane, and Joe Keller shot himself. Willy Loman crashed his car and did not die his dream death of a salesman. John Proctor (as well as lesser characters) of *The Crucible* went to death to assert his smirched integrity. Lou and Maggie killed themselves in despair in *After the Fall*. Prince Von Berg sacrificed his life to prove his faith in individual life, and Gregory Solomon lost his daughter by a suicide that contributed to his wisdom. For all of them Miller seeks our pity, through tightly structured plays, tense scenes, and—at his best— crisp dialogue. Miller is sometimes said to create inarticulate characters, but they all speak freely. Incisive idiom etches Miller's low men in our minds; Joe Keller, Willy Loman, Eddie Carbone, Gregory Solomon are vigorous with concrete images, Jewish inflections, and rhythmic repetitions of everyday words. However, Miller sometimes tries to convert his low man into Everyman, or—worse—into the Tragic Hero, and that betrays him into sonorous abstraction. It is in the seemingly trivial that Miller achieves his truest drama.

The Mills of the Gods:
Economics and Law
in the Plays of Arthur Miller

by Thomas E. Porter

I

Two recurrent themes mark the plays of Arthur Miller: business and law. The Great Depression was a central experience of the playwright's youth, and his concern with the American economic system testifies to its abiding effect on him.[1] The investigations of the so-called McCarthy Committee in the 1950s, in which Miller was called as a "witness," made a profound impact on his adult life and raised questions for him about the administration of justice under law. His major works may be divided into two "trilogies" on this basis: three plays about business and three about the judicial process. His treatment of these themes, of economics and law in the American experience, strikes a nerve in all Americans.

When the playwright speaks about his preoccupation with these systems, he uses expressions more characteristic of earlier cultures. He unabashedly talks of "big gods" and "hidden laws of fate":

> The hidden laws of fate lurked not only in the characters of people but equally if more imperiously in the world beyond the family parlor. Out there were the big gods, the ones whose disfavor could turn a proud and prosperous and dignified man into a frightened shell of a

"The Mills of the Gods: Economics and Law in the Plays of Arthur Miller," by Thomas E. Porter, appears in print for the first time in this volume, with the author's permission.

[1]In his latest play, *The American Clock*, Miller returns again to the subject of the Depression. Like *After the Fall*, the play draws on personal experience and treats the stock market crash from a familial as well as a national perspective.

man whatever he thought of himself, and whatever he decided or didn't decide to do.[2]

These expressions have associations with antiquity, with Greek *moira* and *ananke*, with the whimsical determinations of the Olympians. Miller quickly withdraws to a safe distance by qualifying his statement: "I too had a religion, however unwilling I was to be so backward. A religion with no gods but with godlike powers. The powers of economic and political imperatives which had twisted, torn, eroded, and marked everything and everyone I laid eyes on."[3] These "powers," economic and political, operate in society and have a daimonic effect on the destinies of individuals, for good or evil. If the gods are gone, an aura of the divine surrounds, at least for the playwright, the economic system and the judicial process.

Miller's metaphors of "the hidden fates" and the "big gods" correspond to a sense of the necessary and the inevitable in the dramatic action. In Greek tragedy, for example, the gods always represent a specific force working in the culture, a basic attitude or institution that articulates a vision and/or maintains order in society. The oracle of Apollo in *Oedipus Tyrannos* insists on the fallibility of all men and, when the legendary hero faces the possibility that he is not in total control of his (and the City's) destiny, the dramatic conflict of the play is generated. With the recognition of a more humane order in the cosmos, Oedipus's fabled response to the Sphinx, wise by the standards of the legendary past, turns out to be incorrect. It is no longer Man who goes by different stages of locomotion, but Oedipus himself. The oracle cancels the prerogatives of the demigod hero and puts government in the hands of the fallible human individual. The inevitability of the tragedy depends on the recognition that every man learns only by suffering and that no man is exempt from this law. The oracle represents a necessity that the culture has discovered. In the same way the "godlike powers" that Miller describes create in the plays a sense of inevitability, an uncomfortable awareness of the laws of fate. In the movement of the action, the mills of the gods can be heard, grinding exceedingly small.

For purposes of analysis, we will divide the major plays into the categories noted above: the business plays—*All My Sons, Death of a Salesman, The Price*—and the judicial plays—*The Crucible, A View from the Bridge, After the Fall*—in order to describe these systems and to consider their function in the context of the dramatic action.

[2]Arthur Miller, "Shadow of the Gods," *Harper's Magazine*, 217 (1958), 36.
[3]Ibid.

II

The mills of the gods that work in the business plays have some affinity to Blake's "dark Satanic mills." The actions of *All My Sons, Death of a Salesman,* and *The Price* are grounded in what Miller calls the "iron necessities of economics."[4] In these plays the iron necessities affect the action in a manner analogous to the impact of the oracle on *Oedipus.*

Miller observes about *Salesman* that "it refused admission to its author's opinions and himself, opened itself to a revelation . . . social laws of action no less powerful in their effects upon individuals than any tribal law administered by gods with names."[5] It is perhaps the author's privilege to see these laws as "facts" rather than as part of his invention. Certainly the economic system, as defined in the plays, operates with the force of a divine decree.

Miller is helpful, too, in describing the matrix and nature of this system; he intends, in *Salesman,* to "speak commonsensically of social facts which every businessman knows and talks about, but which are too prosaic to mention or are usually fancied up on the stage as philosophical problems. When a man gets old you fire him, you have to, he can't do the work."[6] He is drawing on common sense, what the man-in-the-street knows about business, that is, the conventional wisdom that is a combination of naive theory and practice. The system here is rule-of-thumb American capitalism, not far removed from the classical principles of political economy enunciated by Adam Smith, David Ricardo, and Alfred Marshall.

The basic underlying concept of modern economic theory that emerges from these nineteenth-century analysts and passes into conventional wisdom is the market system. Polyani describes the emergence of this system:

> (Adam Smith), living in the . . . monetarized economy of England, was able to include wages and rent in the group of "prices" and thus, for the first time, glimpse a vision of the wealth of nations as an integration of the various manifestations of an underlying system of markets. Adam Smith became the founder of political economy because he recognized, however dimly, the tendency toward interdependence of these different kinds of prices insofar as they resulted in competitive markets.[7]

---

[4] Arthur Miller, *Collected Plays* (New York: Viking Press, 1957), p. 54.

[5] Ibid., p. 32.

[6] Ibid., pp. 30–31.

[7] Karl Polyani, *The Livelihood of Man,* ed. Harry W. Person (New York: Academic Books, 1977), pp. 7–8.

The supply-demand-price triad, operating to constitute the market, became the unchanging assumption behind all capitalist theory. Polyani points out that the market system "grew swiftly into one of the most powerful forces ever to enter the human scene."[8] Although Smith's successors refined and modified the founder's insights, they "assumed as a matter of course that the agency by which all ordinary business activities are organized and interrelated is 'the market.' "[9] The plays assume the validity of economic principles, with supply-and-demand regulating price in the marketplace.

In *All My Sons,* the first play in the business trilogy, the crisis turns on the revelation that the protagonist, Joe Keller, deliberately shipped an order of defective airplane parts from his factory and allowed his partner to take the blame. When Joe justifies this decision to his son, Chris, he appeals to supply-and-demand, the competitive nature of business:

> I'm in business, a man is in business; a hundred and twenty cracked, you're out of business; you got a process, the process don't work you're out of business; you don't know how to operate, your stuff is no good; they close you up, they tear up your contract, what the hell's it to them?[10]

Joe knows the rules; "they" are entitled to tear up the contract, to destroy the company, if Joe cannot compete. Chris, the son who speaks for a different set of principles—the larger community, self-sacrifice, and comradeship—admits the force of the economic imperative under which Joe was operating: "This is the land of the big dogs, you don't love a man here, you eat him! That's the principle; the only one we live by—it just happened to kill a few people this time, that's all" (*All My Sons*, p. 124). Joe responds with a reference to the market: "Who worked for nothin' in that war? When they work for nothin', I'll work for nothin' " (*All My Sons*, p. 125). In the system everybody gets his price, *quid pro quo*. And Chris, the idealist, has no practical alternative to propose. He will leave and find a job elsewhere; he knows "a couple of firms" where he can get a place. He must continue to live in "the land of the big dogs." (It requires only a simple transposition to read "dogs" as "gods.") In an

---

[8]Ibid., p. 9.

[9]C. E. Ayres, *The Theory of Economic Progress* (New York: Schocken Books, 1962), p. xii.

[10]*All My Sons* in Miller, *Collected Plays*, p. 115. Quotations from the play are from this version, cited in the text as *All My Sons.*

economic frame of reference, Chris has no adequate response to Joe Keller's argument. When Joe puts a bullet in his head, it is in response to a humanitarian, not an economic, judgment.

All My Sons presents a protagonist who understands the rigor of the marketplace and loses his family because he follows its dictates. *Death of a Salesman* offers a failure who suffers because, among other considerations, he does not comprehend the practicalities of the system. The aura that American optimism sheds around the "iron necessities" of the system draws Willy like a magnet. He rides out into the marketplace with the blessings of Horatio Alger, of Roger Babson, and Dale Carnegie. He regards the demigods of success—the robber barons, Edison, and Red Grange—and resolves to emulate them. The success mythology in America grew up around the economic system; opportunities to compete in the marketplace along with plentiful resources and the vertical mobility of an egalitarian society provided fertile soil for the entrepreneur. The inventor of a better mousetrap did not lack for householders with mice. The self-help literature cited appropriate examples of "rags-to-riches," and many a "poor boy" made good.[11]

Whether built on the doctrine of hard work or on the cult of personality, the success legends do not contravene the principles of the market system. Willy has reached the end of the road; he can no longer sell. Howard, Willy's "heartless" boss, makes the inevitable decision; he fires Willy because the aging salesman can no longer do the job. Willy protests: "You can't eat the orange and throw the peel away—a man is not a piece of fruit!"[12] (*Salesman*, p. 181). Willy may not be a piece of fruit, but by economic standards his labor is a commodity, subject to the law of supply-and-demand. Charley, Willy's friend and a modest success, spells this out in no uncertain terms:

> Willy, when're you gonna realize that them things don't mean anything? You named him Howard, but you can't sell that. The only thing you got in the world is what you can sell. And the funny thing is that you're a salesman, and you don't know that (*Salesman*, p. 192).

When the Loman brothers decide to go into the sporting goods business, only a Willy would view their scheme with approval and enthusiasm. They, too, have nothing to sell; Biff meets an altogether

---

[11]See Thomas E. Porter, *Myth and Modern American Drama* (Detroit: Wayne State Univ. Press, 1969), pp. 128–31.

[12]*Death of a Salesman* in Miller, *Collected Plays*, p. 181.

predictable rebuff. In the end, when all Willy's resources fail him and he tries to convert his life to cash, he implicitly acknowledges the "iron law"; he is a commodity worth only the face value on his insurance policy. Although from his own perspective, he is searching for diamonds in brother Ben's mythical jungle, from the perspective of the system, he is literally cashing in the only chip he has left, himself. Unwittingly, Willy obeys the principle of the system: when a man ceases to be productive in the business world, he self-destructs. For the man who "succeeds," the big gods appear to be allies; for the disillusioned, they are the "big dogs."

The third drama that deals with business announces the relevance of economics in its title: *The Price*. Unlike Joe Keller or Willy Loman, Victor Franz decided not to compete in the marketplace. His decision to look after his father, ruined in the crash of 1929, precluded his attending college, so he joined the police force and spent twenty years at a routine job—one clearly beneath his capabilities. Now nearly fifty, he faces retirement; still relatively young with his health and ambitions intact, he has nothing to sell and nowhere to go. Standing dissatisfied midway in his life, he questions the price that filial loyalty exacted of him.

At this point, the action of the play veers away from this issue into an investigation of the causes for Victor's decision and the responsibility that Walter, his successful doctor-brother, shares for it. Walter would like to make it up to Victor and seal the breach between them, but time will not turn back and doors once open are now closed. When Walter offers him a job as a laboratory assistant, Victor acknowledges the rigors of the system: "Walter, I haven't got the education, what are you talking about? You can't walk in with one splash and wash out twenty-eight years. There's a price people pay. I've paid it, it's all gone, I haven't got it any more."[13] At this juncture, a job from Walter would be charity, and Victor can no more accept it than Willy Loman could. Not to participate in the competition amounts to failure in the long run. Esther, Victor's not-so-long-suffering wife, puts it flatly to her husband: "We can never keep our minds on money! We worry about it, but we can't seem to *want* it. I do, but you don't. I really do, Vic" (*Price*, p. 19). Thus, she and Walter do not trust Victor to strike a good bargain in selling the furniture in the flat. He has not entered the marketplace; he lacks the credentials. The economic wheel of fortune does not yield to *contemptus mundi* in

---

[13]Arthur Miller, *The Price* (New York: Bantam Books, 1969), p. 99.

this society. By not competing, Victor paid his price to the system, to the "big gods" that made his father tremble at the prospect of the poor house.

The final revelation that the elder Franz was not destitute, that Victor could have borrowed college money from his father, is anticlimactic, a piece of ancient history that does not touch Victor's present. Walter justifies his own departure from the family circle by pointing to the operative values of the household: "[T]here was no love in this house. There was no loyalty. There was nothing here but a straight financial arrangement. That's what was unbearable" (*Price*, p. 111). The family itself turned out to be a marketplace where those rules obtained. If indeed the elder Franz had four thousand dollars "under his ass," then by these rules Victor was a fool. He cannot simply blame Walter for his own failure to recognize the operation of the business code in the bosom of his family. Familial virtue reaps no reward in the land of the big dogs.

The Price explicitly focuses on two social categories that are excepted from the operation of the economic mills: the educated and the outsider. Victor cannot take advantage of Walter's offer because he does not have the education. The professional class—doctors and lawyers principally—are not subject to economic laws in the same way the uncredentialed businessman is. In *All My Sons* and *Salesman*, the same exemption obtains. When Charley delivers his apologia for Willy, he makes this point: "He don't put a bolt to a nut, he don't tell you the law or give you medicine." The man who works with his hands, because he cannot rise, will not fall; the professional, the lawyer or doctor, will always be in demand. Bernard, Biff's boyhood friend and adulator, has his law degree; he goes off to try a case before the Supreme Court, tennis racket in hand. Willy asks him, the erstwhile pitiable grind, for the secret of success. Joe Keller, like Victor, has no education on which to fall back. A self-made man, he worked his way up the ladder and "college men" intimidate him: "I don't know, everybody's getting so Goddam educated in this country there'll be nobody to take away the garbage. . . . It's a tragedy: you stand on the street today and spit, you're gonna hit a college man" (*All My Sons*, p. 96). When George, the son of his partner, "gets his degree" and becomes a lawyer, Joe worries that the case of the cracked cylinder heads will be reopened. The educated pose a threat to self-made men like Keller who, although he is boss, is afraid to ask college graduates to sweep the floor. To Willy, they represent secure accomplishment and an embodiment of the success mystique. To

Victor, they are a reminder of lost opportunity. This attitude is typical of the first sociological generation of immigrants who saw education as a ladder to a higher socioeconomic bracket and acceptance into the American mainstream. In any event, professional credentials, in these dramas, provide financial security of a kind that preclude dilemmas like those vexing the protagonists.

Miller also includes in the business plays personae who have managed modest success outside the professions. In *Salesman*, Charley is the notable instance. He knows the rules; as remarked above, he tutors Willy in economics. His "secret" is the lack of a driving ambition. He does not identify himself with his career—in fact, his occupation is never specified. Neither does he, like Willy, drive his son toward achievement. Along with his humane concern for his neighbor, his generosity, and common sense, "not taking an interest in anything" is his virtue (*Salesman*, p. 191). Charley does not tempt the gods with his aspiration. In *The Price*, the octogenarian furniture buyer thrives on a similar philosophy. A Russian-Jew, he has seen too much and lived too long to worry about success. It is not part of his cultural equipment. He will not cheat Victor: "I left Russia sixty-five years ago, I was twenty-four years old. And I smoked all my life. I drinked, and I loved every woman who would let me. So what do I need to steal from you?" (*Price*, p. 35). He comes from a tradition in which doing business is a ritual of communication. He wants to know his customer, to engage the person in the transaction. Walter's proposals for a tax deduction make good financial sense, but they efface Solomon's contribution, reducing his role to assayer. His arguments to the "boys," in the face of Walter's practicality, are grounded in his concern for Victor and his need to carry on his trade. In the old man these two motivations intertwine. Walter sees only the sharp dealer—"rob them blind, you old mutt"—who is picking Victor's naive bones. Victor sees a friend: he takes Solomon's word on the appraisal of the goods and his advice on dealing with Walter. When Victor closes the deal with a handshake, he participates in a tradition in which friends can do business. For Victor, it is a small triumph over the financially successful doctor, and it hinges on the complicity of a man from an alien tradition. Charley and Solomon, both wise in the ways of the marketplace, are, for different reasons, not trapped by the compulsions it generates.

Those personae in the plays who escape the stresses of the system only serve to heighten the dilemma of the protagonists. For Joe Keller, Willy Loman, and Victor Franz, the economic system works like fate—inexorably, impersonally—and it determines their identities, their status, and their destiny. It is tempting, then, to conclude that they are victims, pathetic creatures in the grip of forces they cannot control, flies to the gods who kill them for sport. In fact, the protagonists are not let off so easily. Joe Keller callously permits his partner to go to jail, Willy smiles indulgently at his son's thefts and cheats on his wife, Victor refuses to acknowledge his father's deception. In each case another member of the family accuses and condemns the protagonist for his "crime." Chris rejects his father for not taking responsibility; Biff, on discovering Willy's philandering, calls him a "phoney, little fake"; Walter points out that Victor deliberately closed his eyes to their father's duplicity. In short, the "iron necessities" of economic law do not exculpate the perpetrators. The impersonality of the system is experienced as a daimonic force because the consequences of its operation are intensely personal.

The impersonal machinery of the economic system—stock market fluctuations, supply-and-demand in the labor pool, cost of living—assume the aspect of "big gods" when the protagonists internalize the values of the system. When Willy loses his position, he does not react as a statistic. The seemingly whimsical economic forces become, for the individual who suffers because of them, intensely personal in their effects. Miller, at the conclusion of his introduction to the *Collected Plays*, contrasts determinism and free will, the "godlike power" and the responsibility of the individual:

> The history of man is a ceaseless process of overthrowing one determinism to make way for another more faithful to life's changing relationships. And it is a process inconceivable without the existence of the will of man. His will is as much a fact as his defeat. Any determinism, even the most scientific, is only that stasis, that seemingly endless pause, before the application of man's will administering a new insight into causation.[14]

The romantic implications of this declaration, to strive and not to yield, do not speak to the tension in the plays whose protagonists strive sufficiently, but are doomed from the start. The Puritan would be more comfortable with the destiny of the protagonists than the Romantic might. Miller's personae are more predestined than determined; that is, the impersonal system defeats them in a very personal way; they are, at the same time, responsible for their own destiny.

---

[14]Miller, *Collected Plays*, p. 54.

Any form of determinism—physiological, socioeconomic, or psychological—effectively relieves the individual of responsibility for his or
her actions. The common Reformation teaching on predestination
does not excuse the reprobate from responsibility. The mystery of
election, in Reformation doctrine, raises the sinner to a new life of
radical innocence by an unmerited divine decree.[15] The nonelect
remained mired in a depraved or, at best, deprived state of nature
inherited from Adam. Various "convenant" theologies, in the wake
of this stern doctrine, concentrated on the search for "signs of
election," some palpable evidence of God's favor. It is not surprising
that, in the midst of subtle theological dispute about the relationship
between grace and nature and the popular concern for certitude, a
moral life and material prosperity should become indices of divine
predilection.

The secular mythology of success in America has a strong strain
that draws on this doctrine; even when all traces of the theology that
originated it have disappeared, the aura of "election" clings to the
successful.[16] Miller has seized on a dimension that the public would
rather ignore: the plight of the "reprobate" on whom the big gods do
not smile. The energy of the preacher, whether in the pulpit or in the
executive suite, tends to be focused on salvation, on the hope of
election, on the dream of success. Galbraith quotes one of the
exemplars of the business elect:

> As John D. Rockefeller explained to a fortunate Sunday school class:
> "The growth of a large business is merely the survival of the fittest. . . .
> The American Beauty rose can be produced in the splendor and
> fragrance which bring cheer to its beholder only by sacrificing the
> early buds which grow up around it." As with the rose, so with the
> Standard Oil Company. "This is not an evil tendency in business. It is
> merely the working-out of a law of nature and a Law of God." This
> aligned God and the American Beauty rose with railroad debates,
> exclusive control of pipelines, systematic price discrimination, and
> some other remarkably aggressive business practices.[17]

There is no need to mourn the losers, either on secular or religious
grounds. Nature and nature's God have rejected them, so they are

[15]For a treatment of the common concern with depravity and justification and of
variant theological approaches by the Puritans, see Norman Pettit, *The Heart Prepared*
(New Haven: Yale Univ. Press, 1966), pp. 2–9.

[16]See Porter, *Myth and Modern American Drama*, pp. 34–35.

[17]John Kenneth Galbraith, *The Affluent Society* (Boston: Houghton Mifflin, 1958),
p. 60.

snipped off like the early buds. When Willy's long-suffering wife cries for attention to the salesman and his plight, she is a voice in the wilderness. The anomalies are patent and irresolvable: the impact of an impersonal set of economic laws devalues the individual; although the economic system is theoretically under the control of the experts, it operates whimsically and autonomously to crush the unlucky (read: nonelect).

The final movement of the action in the business plays is bound to include these anomalies, not resolve them. For those who lack professional credentials, who believe blindly in the beneficence of the system, who drop out of the competition—in short, the losers— disaster is predictable. One can only make peace with the dangling sword and try to maintain integrity and a place in society in spite of it. Biff, Chris, and—ultimately—Victor know the truth, but it does not set them free. Presumably Biff accepts the fact that he is "a dime a dozen." Chris hopes that he can escape the blight of competition by leaving town. Victor accepts Solomon's philosophy, dons his uniform, and goes to the movies. The system with its potential for destruction remains firmly in place; the economic mills grind on.

III

In the remainder of the Miller canon—*The Crucible, A View from the Bridge,* and *After the Fall*—the action focuses on the law, the judicial system that is presumably the bulwark of justice and order in society. The protagonists in this set of plays are economically secure and, although economic motivations are at work, they do not figure principally in the action. For Miller the legal establishment is the agent of justice, the arbiter of guilt and innocence in society. The plays explore the limits of this system on its own terms—rules of evidence, indictment, due process, judgment. The personae, exempted by their status and/or their circumstances from the operation of economic necessities, still have to confront the issue of "election" on internal grounds, their individual and social innocence or guilt.

Of the three plays, only the action of *The Crucible* contains an explicit courtroom sequence: the witchcraft proceedings that take place in a public forum with all the legal panoply. The limitations of the legal system appear clearly. A narrow-minded, fanatical judiciary applies an outmoded law in a hysterical atmosphere. The startling

and unsettling feature of this judicial process is the careful application of rules of evidence, due process, and seeming impartiality.[18]
John Proctor, a sturdy farmer and a "good" man, along with other
"good" citizens of Salem, is found guilty of witchcraft by the court.
This miscarriage of justice is palpable; the verdict exonerates Proctor
because it represents the malice of the community—jealousy and
greed among the citizenry and lust for power among the magistrates.
If *The Crucible* were a traditional courtroom drama, this outcome
would suffice to establish the protagonist's innocence. But the playwright is not satisfied with a legal vindication; he adds a final act in
which Proctor is tested further. The legal verdict excludes Proctor
from the society of the corrupt and the malicious without necessarily
incorporating him into the company of the saintly Rebecca Nurse
and the indomitable old prophet, Giles Corey. Unlike them, he did
contribute to the evil perpetrated by the court. His adultery with
Abigail put knowledge into her heart and, for fear of losing his
reputation in the community, he waited too long to denounce her in
public. Although both faults seem minor and understandable, for
Proctor, they blight his sacrifice and cast doubt on his personal
goodness.

When Proctor appears, before his execution, to converse with his
wife, he is shaken by doubts about his worthiness. He considers
confessing to traffic with the devil because of his past sins:

> I cannot mount the gibbet like a saint. It is a fraud. I am not that
> man . . . My honesty is broke, Elizabeth; I am no good man. Nothing's
> spoiled by giving them this lie that were not rotten long before.
>
> Let them that never lied die now to keep their souls. It is pretense for
> me, a vanity that will not blind God nor keep my children out of the
> wind.[19]

Proctor speaks here like a dyed-in-the-wool Calvinist. Once soiled,
the garb of innocence cannot be cleansed. To this point in the play,
Proctor's religious beliefs have had a liberal, even a contemporary
cast; he did not attend church, for instance, because of the minister's
fire-and-brimstone theology. Now, searching his soul, he finds no
evidence of the signs of election. He is "no good man" and unworthy
of inclusion in the company of the saints.

His view contrasts sharply with that of Reverend Hale, whose

[18]Porter, *Myth and Modern American Drama*, pp. 191–92.
[19]*The Crucible* in Miller, *Collected Plays*, pp. 322–23.

confident assessment of witchcraft in Salem has been shaken by the condemnations. Distraught by the turn the trials have taken, Hale's admonition to the imprisoned Elizabeth is radically different from his earlier position:

> Life, woman, life is God's most precious gift; no principle, however glorious, may justify the taking of it. I beg you, prevail on your husband to confess. Let him give his lie. Quail not before God's judgment in this, for it may well be God damns a liar less than he that throws his life away for pride (*Crucible*, p. 320).

Proctor does not accept this argument; when he does give his lie in confessing to Danforth, he ascertains from Elizabeth and Rebecca that it is an evil action that they would not take for all the world. If God's law has gone dark and mysterious for Hale, it remains clear to Proctor: he knows his confession is false.

Elizabeth, in her interview, testifies to her own part in John's fault. She points out her complicity: "It needs a cold wife to prompt lechery" (*Crucible*, p. 323). She insists that he is taking her sins on himself and asks his forgiveness. John will not accept this mitigation of his fault. When she tells him that she never knew such goodness before, he cannot accept that judgment, either. His own awareness of his guilt drowns out any testimony to the contrary.

The confessional interview with Danforth in which Proctor effectively admits his unworthiness resembles the first stage of the Puritan conversion experience.[20] He only speaks to his own guilt and he considers that a private act. "I have confessed myself! Is there no good penitence but it be public? God does not need my name nailed upon the church! God sees my name; God knows how black my sins are! It is enough!" (*Crucible*, p. 327). God knows his unworthiness and, to that extent, his confession is no lie. He has passed through the first phase of conversion by recognizing his sinfulness.

The apotheosis of this sequence comes when Proctor "sees" his

---

[20]In many seventeenth-century New England churches, admission to full communion required a "scrutiny" before the elders and open confession before the congregation. William Haller gives this description of a Puritan's conversion experience: On looking into his heart, "what he saw there, of course, was sin, the innate propensity of all flesh to evil, the original corruption of man's nature. . . . Suddenly his sins came before him and would not be put out of mind. He was in the hands of a greater power than himself or any man, a power, however, which revealed to him thus suddenly the hell within in order as suddenly to save him from it. God 'saith of and to my Soul, yea live, yea live I say.' " *The Rise of Puritanism* (New York: Columbia Univ. Press, 1938), p. 77.

own goodness. He will not betray the saints and lend his name to the injustices of the court. He calls it a marvel and magic that he can go forth to hang with Rebecca and Martha Corey. The imagery is traditional, the white banner of resurrection: "I do think I see some shred of goodness in John Proctor. Not enough to weave a banner with, but white enough to keep it from such dogs" (*Crucible*, p. 328). This falls just slightly short of the "amazing grace" that crowns the conversion experience of the reformed churches—a lightening-flash vision of "goodness" that covers guilt. Rebecca adds the appropriate Amen to Proctor's witness, telling him to fear nothing, for another judgment awaits. Elizabeth delivers the benediction: "He have his goodness now. God forbid I take it from him!" (*Crucible*, p. 329). John Proctor passes through the fire; he is purified like gold in the crucible.

This "conversion," and, indeed, the whole fourth-act sequence, has an air of anticlimax about it. The paroxysm of guilt that shakes John Proctor in prison is explicable only in terms of the sufferings of his imprisonment. He has shown no signs heretofore of an engrossing concern about his own goodness. In coming forward to testify in court, he acted for the community; there he confesses his adultery and his self-interest in failing to speak out earlier. Moreover, to this point, his religious convictions seem quite commonsensical; he does not approve of Mr. Parris's hellfire-and-brimstone sermons, and he stays away from meeting if there is plowing to be done. This sudden apperception of his sinfulness is quite out of character. It adds a new dimension to the final sequence—Proctor's relationship with "God."

While the period of the play may account for the theological rhetoric, it does not account for Proctor's self-denigration. His sense of unworthiness can be interpreted in the light of the doctrine of total depravity, but Proctor has no such theological awareness elsewhere in the play. Hale's doctrine that "life is God's most precious gift" and the desire to keep his children "out of the wind" provide sufficient rationale for his recantation; he need not grovel in unworthiness. Thus, it is striking that his progress in this sequence should embody a seventeenth-century Puritan conversion experience: admission of sinfulness, testimony to the workings of grace, acceptance by the community of the elect. This "amazing grace" is the more amazing because its source—divine action—is uncredited. In the end a mysterious personal vision of "goodness" admits Proctor to the circle of the "saints."

In *A View from the Bridge*, the protagonist moves (or is moved) in a direction diametrically opposed to John Proctor's. Although Eddie Carbone is manifestly guilty, he maintains his essential innocence to the end. He is blinded by his passion for Catherine, his seventeen-year-old niece/ward, and so betrays his countrymen by reporting them to the Office of Immigration, convinced to his death that he is justified. No apocalyptic vision like John Proctor's shows Eddie the error of his ways, and he goes determinedly to a death that the narrator-observer, Alfieri, describes as "useless." All that can be said for him is that his ignorance is as invincible as his will is indomitable. This strange combination makes his doom inescapable.

Unlike Miller's other protagonists, thoroughly assimilated Americans, Eddie belongs to the second sociological generation of immigrants. He is a man between cultures—American in his aspirations and bound to Sicilian traditions, subject to two different allegiances. This cultural bind is illuminated for the audience from the outset by Alfieri, who has himself emerged from the immigrant status. He ticks off the conflict of cultures: the Sicilian code of honor, omerta and revenge, versus the American legal system. Although these codes work to Eddie's destruction, it is significant that the motivation that insures it derives from a law of nature: his passion for his niece.

The subterranean impulses at work sparking his desire to keep Catherine are familiar to every amateur psychologist. When, however, Alfieri explains the problem to Eddie, he assigns a nonpsychological explanation:

> You know, God sometimes mixes up the people. We all love somebody, the wife, the kids—everyman's got somebody he loves, heh? But sometimes . . . there's too much . . . You know? There's too much, and it goes where it mustn't.[21]

Alfieri suggests that Eddie examine his motives. But the longshoreman cannot or will not admit his passion. God has mixed him up and presumably God will have to sort him out.

This "God," ostensibly operating in human nature, has no official representation in Eddie's intercultural situation. In *The Crucible*, there are, if anything, too many spokesmen for the divine; John Proctor has to sort them out. Eddie, however, except for the prayers of Alfieri's "old woman," has none of the strategies of the old country at his disposal: the wisdom of the elders or of the Church. Like a good citizen, he goes to the lawyer. Surely the law will recognize his rights and protect his interest in Catherine. Again like an American, he has

---

[21]*A View from the Bridge* in Miller, *Collected Plays*, p. 409.

encouraged her to better herself; the education he provided was designed to make her independent. When she exercises her liberty by choosing a man, he (officially, anyway) feels that his prerogatives have been ignored and seeks redress with the law. Alfieri disillusions him about his recourse. "The law is not interested in this"; there is no direct legal action that will prevent Catherine's marriage to the "submarine" Rodolpho. Alfieri cannot recommend a psychiatrist, given his perspective; this middle-class remedy would mean nothing to Eddie. So, with no authority figure to set him straight, Eddie is left with his guilty passion. He deals with it as best he can.

At first he tries, in various ways, to alienate Catherine and Rodolpho. He casts aspersions on Rodolpho's mannerisms and manhood, he appeals to Catherine's sense of obligation, he invokes patriarchal privilege of the tribal code. When none of these strategies work, he uses the letter of the law and reports Rodolpho and Marco to the Immigration authorities. Since the law cannot help him directly, he invokes it in an attempt to solve his problem indirectly. In so doing, he violates the injunction of both cultural codes against informing.

The legal system—a light that failed in *The Crucible*—abets injustice again in *Bridge*. The law's disinterest in Eddie's problem and its proscription of illegal aliens conspire with Eddie's obsession to destroy the harmony of Red Hook society. His only justification, which everyone—including his wife—condemns, is his unalterable conviction that he is saving Catherine, a conviction motivated by his unacknowledged passion. Having broken the code and so forfeited his reputation, Eddie appeals to an older law by which he hopes to vindicate his honor—a duel of honor, a trial by combat. Eddie will, inevitably, lose, for the outcome of a fight with Marco has been foreshadowed by an earlier test of strength. The efficacy of trial by combat is guaranteed by the invocation that traditionally precedes it: God defend the right. Alfieri makes this point obliquely when he warns Marco: "Only God makes justice" (*Bridge*, p. 435). Eddie refuses to accept Rodolpho's apology, spurns the offer to "go to church together" and insists on the duel. He dies on his own knife.

The direct line of the action to the protagonist's death and the ironic foreshadowing of it has, as Epstein remarks, overtones of Greek tragedy. "Eddie Carbone's fate is in the hands of the gods. How like Greek tragedy!"[22] And, one is tempted to add, "how

---

[22]Arthur Epstein, *"A Look at A View from the Bridge"* in *Critical Essays on Arthur Miller*, ed. James Martine (Boston: Hall, 1979), p. 113.

unlike." The God who "mixes Eddie up" sends him blind to his "just" punishment. A thumbnail comparison with the standard Greek tragedy, *Oedipus Tyrannos*, illuminates the differences between Sophocles' play and Miller's. Oedipus's fault is fixed in an irreversible past action; his search for the criminal responsible for the plague is dictated by his kingly responsibility. He has—with the sanction of tradition—exempted himself from the common fallibility of mankind; he is the demi-divine tyrant whose legendary defeat of the Sphinx saved the city. The oracle of the god, on the other hand, insists that he is fallible, a man like other men, and that he does not have absolute control over his own destiny. The oracle leads Oedipus to the truth about his parentage, his actions, and his nature. Conversely, Eddie's fault is a present passion—palpably human and reversible. The only oracle he has available, the lawyer, cannot, in this matter, speak with authority. What Oedipus discovers is his continuity with the human race; this is precisely what Eddie is prevented from seeing.

In *The Crucible*, John Proctor, vindicated by the verdict of a corrupt court, mysteriously sees his "goodness" and joins the saints in martyrdom. Eddie Carbone is condemned by an equally mysterious decree to a useless death at Marco's hands. These two protagonists share, however, a determination to protect their "names." Proctor's unwillingness to lend his signature to the perfidy of the court prepares his heart for conversion. Eddie determinedly confronts family and neighbors in blind self-justification. Alfieri's final tribute, the "something perversely pure" that calls to him from Eddie's memory, salutes an unwillingness to relinquish his place in the community. Neither Proctor nor Eddie run from their involvement; contrary judgments fall on them as they make a stand on their home ground.

After the Fall, perhaps because it includes elements of autobiography, combines the concerns of the business trilogy with those of *Crucible* and *Bridge*. Miller remarks that *After the Fall* is a memory play and that it deals with the inside of the protagonist's head. The principal episodes of the structure—anti-Communist investigations, divorce and remarriage to the show-girl, her suicide and a third marriage to a survivor of the concentration camps—clearly parallel Miller's life experience.[23] It is no accident that the protagonist is a

[23]The autobiographical element in the play drew considerable critical fire. John Simon remarks sharply that Miller has discovered "a new form of contrition called *tua culpa*"; Robert Brustein calls it an autobiographical "strip-tease while the band plays 'mea culpa.'" Simon, *Hudson Review*, 17 (1964), 235; Brustein, *New Republic*, 150 (February 8, 1964), 26.

lawyer, concerned with his livelihood, with his reputation, and with his personal guilt or innocence. The narrator-protagonist, Quentin, conducts a trial in which his actions and motivations are scrutinized by an unseen Listener—and the audience.[24] The most telling lines with regard to the judicial nature of the investigation are Quentin's:

> I looked at life like a case at law, a series of proofs . . . But underlying it all, I see now, there was a presumption. That I was moving on an upward path toward some elevation, where—God knows what—I would be justified or even condemned—a verdict anyway. I think now that my disaster really began when I looked up one day—and the bench was empty. No judge in sight.[25]

The conventional image of the divine tribunal—God as Judge—comes to mind, and when Quentin addresses the Listener, he often initiates his remarks with the expletive "God" (*Fall*, pp. 2, 7, 85). Although the bench "up there" is empty, Quentin presents his case to the powers "out there"—the Listener, the audience—and to himself.

As the Last Judgment image indicates, the innocence with which Quentin (and Miller) is concerned, like John Proctor's, goes beyond simple legal imputation. He seeks a verdict on a transcendent innocence that can be radically attributed to the individual. In the encounter with Felice, the girl whose life he changed in a casual conversation, Quentin's unselfish giving culminates in a blessing. This benediction sticks in his mind as evidence that he may be "good." But, by and large, as he declares when reflecting on his relationship with Holga, he feels "unblessed" (*Fall*, p. 31). He associates this feeling with betrayal and separateness, the seed and fruit of guilt. Significantly, throughout the play the accusations of betrayal either pivot on economic considerations or are couched in economic terms. The principal motive for turning from spouse or friend is self-preservation in the socio-economic order. When Quentin's colleagues, Mickey and Lou, confront the loyalty hearings, Lou accuses Mickey of "selling me for your own prosperity" (*Fall*, p. 50). Quentin does not really want to espouse Lou's case; he is afraid of losing his position in the firm as well as his reputation. His first reaction to Lou's suicide is relief, followed by a sense of guilt. When the relationship with Maggie breaks down, economic issues provide the club with which they hit one another. Quentin raises the hard

---

[24]Critics have noted the trial structure in *After the Fall*, e.g., Benjamin Nelson, *Arthur Miller: Portrait of a Playwright* (New York: McKay, 1970), p. 250.

[25]Arthur Miller, *After the Fall* (New York: Bantam Books, 1965), pp. 4–5.

economic facts: they have fallen behind in their tax payments; Quentin has been neglecting his practice, logging forty percent of his time in dealing with Maggie's affairs (*Fall*, pp. 129, 136). She accuses him of using her for gain: "All you care about is money!" (*Fall*, pp. 139). These women are not Kate Keller or Linda Loman, totally dedicated to family. The voices from Quentin's childhood, interwoven with the incidents of adulthood, also illustrate the operation of economic imperatives. His mother threatens a divorce when she discovers that her husband sank his last dollar in a failing business. Quentin leaves his failed father behind to get a job "with pay" (*Fall*, p. 95). Those characteristics that make Quentin a successful lawyer and businessman alienate him from family and friends. The *suave qui peut* dictates of the economic system result in betrayal and alienation when viewed from a conscience perspective.

These episodes from the past are framed by a present choice that Quentin must make—he has met a woman. In the light of his past failures in marriage, he struggles with the problem of yet another commitment.

> I'm not sure, you see, if I want to lose her, and yet it's outrageous to think of committing myself again. . . . Well, yes. But look at my life. A life, after all, is evidence and I have two divorces locked in my safety deposit box (*Fall*, p. 4).

He finds himself hoping again—for love and new life; his exploration of the evidence is geared to "cornering that hope" and discovering if it is authentic or delusive. The "evidence" of the past indicates that he is both betrayer and betrayed and that alienation is the outcome when relationships are tested. But the promise held out by a commitment to Holga is different. It takes shape within an alien cultural context.

Holga represents another order; she has passed through the experience of Nazi Germany, the loss of family and country. Quentin sees her as mature—aware of the potential for evil. The tower of the concentration camp that looms over the stage is associated with Holga and her experience. With her, Quentin can confess the nature of his search for "some final saving grace" (*Fall*, p. 22). When he finally renders his verdict on his life, she provides him with the inspiration he needs. Looking up at the tower, he concludes that he is guilty, but that indeed all men are guilty.[26] "My brothers died here—

---

[26]"The guilt that Quentin assumes is something very like original sin—an acceptance that he, and all men, are evil or have evil in them, the capacity to kill." Gerald Weales. *The Jumping Off Place* (New York: Macmillan, 1969), p. 18.

He looks from the tower down at the fallen Maggie—but my brothers built this place; our hearts have cut these stones!" (*Fall,* p. 162). The coda to this outcry is his vision of Holga: "The woman hopes!" Because of her spirit, Quentin can determine to love again—without the illusion of innocence. He will live "unblessed" in the human condition that obtains after the Fall.

Quentin shares something with the other two protagonists in the judicial trilogy. His apperception of universal guilt owes a debt to the sense of man's total depravity that initiates Proctor's conversion. He is aware, as Eddie Carbone is not, of man's "killer" instinct, the moral manifestation of that depravity. But, unlike either Proctor or Carbone, Quentin does not confront the problem at home, in his own neighborhood. The "grace" that allows him to take up his life again emanates from a European woman's example of enduring hope and pervasive tyranny. Holga's survival has little in common with Quentin's experience. In contemplating marriage to her, he becomes the outsider drawing on a strength not his own. Holga's spiritual resources are not dramatized; they must remain a mystery to Quentin and to the audience.

The rhetoric of "innocence and guilt," "truth and love," finally focus on the symbol of the tower—for Quentin, a vicarious experience at best. By assimilating to another culture—its failures and its triumphs—he escapes the vexing problems of his own. The socio-economic system and the dubious values of the judicial process remain untouched by his decision. In short, Quentin opts for a fresh start in a new situation, a psychological version of the American myth that a spatial remove confers a new identity. "Salvation" is escape—to the West, to the Islands, to a new job, and a new wife. Quentin's quest for a favorable verdict from the Listener (and the audience) turns into a case of special pleading when he evades the "evidences" of his own past and takes refuge in a universal guilt and an alien culture.

IV

Lincoln once described Americans as an "almost chosen people."[27] This phrase catches, with a nicety, both the sense of superiority and

[27]Quoted in William C. McLoughlin and Robert N. Bellah, eds., *Religion in America* (Boston: Houghton Mifflin, 1968), p. 21.

the insecurity of the culture. As the nation has been chosen and blessed, so the ideal of community and innocence shines; the "almost" demands self-searching. The mystery of salvation frets all Miller's protagonists; the plays put the question "If I am confident and dedicated, why am I not prosperous?" and, more pathetically, "If I am prosperous, why am I guilty and unhappy?" When the gods were in place, there were theological answers (however unsatisfactory) to these questions. When the bench is empty, only the machinery remains; the mills grind on without plan or purpose.

In his dramas Miller presents, without cavil, the quasi-sacral systems that presumably guarantee prosperity and justice. His "commonsense" approach precludes a call to revolution. For better or for worse, society runs on capitalist practicalities and judicial principles. Man must succeed in the marketplace and be justified by the evidence. When the systems fail to effect prosperity or justice, the individual has to assume responsibility for his own destiny. Joe Keller, Willy Loman, and Victor Franz are subject to the "iron necessities" of economics; they also have no one to blame but themselves. When the limits of the law appear and fail to address substantive issues of innocence and guilt, the individual is obliged to adjudicate his own case. It is noteworthy that, in the judicial plays, the protagonist draws on resources outside the system. John Proctor undergoes a conversion appropriate to seventeenth-century Puritanism; Eddie Carbone reverts to a "duel of honor," a trial by combat reminiscent of his Sicilian origins; Quentin seeks strength and support from a woman of a different heritage. The final plays in each of the trilogies—*After the Fall* and *The Price*—both desert native ground in coming to closure. As Quentin makes a fresh start with Holga, Victor Franz takes inspiration from the old Russian-Jew who finds satisfaction in the humane pursuit of his occupation. If it should come, salvation from within or outside the individual arrives by virtue of influences alien to the American systems at work in the plays.

This conflict between the ideal and the actual constitutes the center of Miller's dramatic efforts. He balances the inevitability and limitations of the system against a striving for integrity and innocence. Because he does not devise utopias (even when he suggests the possibility, for example, Biff's naive agrarianism in *Salesman*) and because he does not mitigate responsibility, the plays retain dramatic impact. At the same time, the final movement inevitably disappoints. Because the economic system is impersonal and the judicial sharply limited, that is, neither one achieves the desired end, the resolution inevitably seems evasive. Escape to other cultural values or into values borrowed from the past is no adequate substitute.

While Miller's insistence on individual responsibility may seem, in the light of the inexorability of the systems he presents, fuzzily romantic, the ideal of prosperity and integrity is not unreasonable. Periodically, there is a call to the nation for renewal, a "war on poverty," revision of the civil rights laws. If the gods are gone, then people must be responsible for the machinery. After all, the economic and judicial systems were created by man for man; why then can they not be made responsive to human needs? This cry underlies the ideal of comradeship espoused by Chris Keller, Biff's anguished impeachment of his father's "wrong dream," Proctor's need for justification. With all the resources at hand, a more humane and cohesive society should be possible; Miller, like Quentin, refuses to abandon this hope.

Because his plays struggle with this dilemma, Miller is a quintessential American playwright. Consciously or not, he accepts the straits to which the experience of the "almost chosen people" has led. A culture built on the market system and the rule of law cannot escape the values they inculcate. The mills of the gods are created by the chilling recognition that many Americans are not in control of their own destiny and that they have no one to blame but themselves. The action in Miller's plays articulate this fear and this responsibility: the hidden fates are finally rooted in the American past.

Arthur Miller in the 1960s

by Gerald Weales

In 1964, after an absence of eight years, Arthur Miller returned to the New York stage. Within a year, he and the Repertory Theater of Lincoln Center offered two new plays—*After the Fall* and *Incident at Vichy*. The first of these is an excessively long self-analysis by a character whose biography so much resembles the playwright's that most critics take it as Miller's *Long Day's Journey into Night*. The second is a kind of roundtable discussion over a grave, during which one man finds the power to act. Although they are very different in superficial ways, the plays are alike in theme and tone. If they are inferior to the early plays—and I think they are—their shortcomings can best be seen in recognizing that there is not a complete break between early and later Miller. As a playwright concerned with both psychological man and social man (as his definition of social drama says that he should be), Miller is inevitably forced to deal with the problem of identity. This is what he has always written about, and it is as clearly the subject of *Incident at Vichy* as it is of *All My Sons*.

The basic premise of all his early work is that society is an image-making machine, a purveyor of myths and prejudices which provide the false faces and false values that modern man wears. The implication is that the individual has little choice—that he can conform and be destroyed, as Joe Keller (in *All My Sons*) and Willy Loman (in *Death of a Salesman*) are, or that he can refuse to conform and be destroyed, as John Proctor (in *The Crucible*) and Eddie Carbone (in *A View from the Bridge*) are. Despite the blackness of this description, the plays are not pessimistic, because inherent in them is a kind of vague faith in man, a suspicion that the individual may finally be able to retain his integrity. This possibility appears, most conventionally, in the platitudes of Chris, the avenging idealist of *All My Sons*, and in the romantic death of John Proctor. In *A View from the Bridge* it lies outside the action of the play, in Miller's attempt, speaking through the narrator Alfieri, to engraft a ritual purity on Eddie: "not purely good, but himself purely." In *Death of a Salesman*, it does not lie in the "right choice" implied by Biff's "He had the wrong dreams." It certainly does not lie in Biff himself, in all those references to working with the hands, nor in the alternative suggested by Charley and Bernard. It is in Willy's vitality, in his perverse commitment to a pointless dream, in his inability simply to walk away. Willy Loman is a character so complex, so contradictory, so vulnerable, so insensitive, so trusting, so distrustful, so blind, so aware—in short, so human—that he forces man on us by being one.

Although *After the Fall* and *Incident at Vichy* end in positive acts, the new plays are a great deal more somber than the early ones. Quentin in *Fall* goes to meet Holga, ready to commit himself once again to a personal relationship, which we are to take as a commitment to life. The Prince in *Vichy* gives up the pass that would free him to save the life of Leduc. Despite these acts, the new plays embody a philosophic idea which belies the positive conclusions and which separates *Fall* and *Vichy* from the earlier plays. The difference lies in the way Miller uses the problem of identity. I do not mean that he has ceased to accept that men have images forced upon them. One of the lines of action in *Incident at Vichy*—although it might be called a line of inaction—has to do with the failure of the waiting men to resist what is being done to them. A great deal of the discussion concerns the way one should act in the face of his destroyers, what role he should play in an attempt to save himself. The implication is that the victims' failure to agree to attack the guard is their way of consenting to their own destruction. Lebeau, the painter, admits that he feels guilty although he knows he has done nothing wrong and is not ashamed of being a Jew. He can say, "Maybe it's that they keep saying such terrible things about us, and you can't answer." It is Leduc, the psychiatrist, who states the proposition formally: "So that one way or the other, with illusions or without them, exhausted or fresh—we have been trained to die." There is a relationship between this kind of thinking and the conception of Willy Loman as a man attempting to be the success his society admires, but there is a great difference too. Willy, as a consenting victim, is a product of Miller's observation; the consenting victims of *Incident at Vichy* are products turned out on the Bruno Bettelheim-Hannah Arendt line—explanations of totalitarian success which almost become apologies for it.

There is, then, a qualitative difference between the conceptions of society in *Death of a Salesman* and in *Incident at Vichy*. That difference, however, is not apparent if we look at *After the Fall* alongside *Salesman*. The pressures that beset Quentin and his friends and relatives are not necessarily the same ones that push Willy around, but they are the same kind. It is clear in *After the Fall* that much of Maggie's behavior is the result of her doing what is expected of her, and that Louise sees herself and Quentin in the roles that her psychoanalysis forces them to play. In the political subplot, Mickey testifies and names names partly because his new affluence requires that he should, and Lou, who makes a John Proctor refusal, admits that in the past he has compromised his sense of his own honesty and tailored himself to fit party requirements.

Yet *After the Fall* and *Incident at Vichy* are thematically two of a kind. The real split between these two plays and the earlier ones can be found in what the heroes are looking for—or, at least, in what they find. Like John Proctor and Eddie Carbone, both Quentin and Von Berg are concerned about their names. When Leduc seems surprised that Von Berg should take his title seriously, the Prince answers, "It is not a 'title'; it is my name, my family." Since he goes on to use words like *dishonor*, one might assume that *name* has the same value here as it does in *A View from the Bridge* or *The Crucible*. At this point in the play, it may have such value, at least for Von Berg, but the lesson that the play is going to teach him is to understand *name* as Quentin uses it when he keeps asking over and over in whose name one turns one's back. In the early Miller plays the quest for identity, for name, was a search for integrity. In *After the Fall* and *Incident at Vichy* that quest has become an attempt to find a workable definition.

In *After the Fall*, Quentin is faced with the problem of coming to some conclusion about himself which will make it possible for him to operate in the world. He is attracted to Holga, but he hesitates to commit himself to her, because so many of the commitments of his past—personal, political, and professional—have collapsed, leaving him nothing. The play is Quentin's look at that past, his attempt to find meaning in it. Early in the work, he says sadly, "I feel . . . unblessed." He is bothered throughout the play by a girl named Felice, whom he cannot get out of his mind. Once, casually, he did something that changed the course of her life, and he continually sees her, her hand lifted in benediction, saying, "I'll always bless you." At the end of the play, when he faces the figures from his past, like the director in Federico Fellini's *8½*, he stops Felice from lifting her hand. He accepts that he is unblessed. What he learns in the course of the play is that he has spent his life trying, one way or another, to establish his innocence. The guilt that he feels about the way he has treated his family, about his two failed marriages, about his reluctance to defend his old friend has always been transferred to the other person in the relationship. At the end, he accepts that it is after the fall, that there is no innocence, that the guilt is his own. Earlier, Holga tells him her recurrent dream. In it, she has an idiot child, which she knows represents her life; she wants to run away from it, but she stays and finally brings herself to kiss it. In case Quentin or the audience has missed the point of the dream, she adds the moral: "I think one must finally take one's life in one's arms, Quentin."

Accepting one's life—at least in the context of *After the Fall*—is more complicated than simply recognizing that any relationship implies responsibilities on both sides. The guilt that Quentin assumes is something very like original sin—an acceptance that he, and all men, are evil or have evil in them, the capacity to kill. This idea is presented several ways in the play. Verbally, in Quentin's statements about his failure to grieve for his dead—for Lou, for his mother, for Maggie. Visually, in the scene in which he begins to strangle Maggie and finds himself strangling his mother. Metaphorically, in the concentration camp tower that broods over the whole play. This is the element of the play that is most difficult to take, but it is a necessary part of the idea Miller has imposed on his work. Near the end, Quentin turns toward the tower and says, "My brothers died here . . ." and then, looking down at Maggie lying at his feet, adds, "but my brothers built this place." What is finally being said in *After the Fall* is not that Quentin's life shows him capable of cruelty, of murder even, but that he must accept his complicity in all the evil in the world. Holga, who carries the messages for Miller, says, ". . . no one they didn't kill can be innocent again."

Incident at Vichy comes to the same conclusion. In this case, it is not self-examination that brings self-knowledge to Von Berg; it is a lesson forced on him from outside by Leduc, who from the beginning of the play has accepted that man is inherently evil. When he says he believes the rumor that there are furnaces waiting to destroy them all, it is not because the destroyers are Germans or Nazis, but "It's exactly because they are people that I speak this way." Von Berg, on the other hand, believes that there are "certain people," not identifiable by race or class, through whom all that is best in civilization will finally survive. He imagines that his sympathy for the suffering of the Jews separates him from their tormentors. He is so horrified by what has happened in his native Austria that he has, as he says, "put a pistol to my head!" But he has not pulled the trigger, and, as Holga points out in *After the Fall*, by being alive he fails to be innocent. Leduc reminds him that the cousin he mentions early in the play, a man for whom Von Berg obviously feels affection, is a Nazi. "It's not your guilt I want," says Leduc; "it's your responsibility."

That line, however, is false—if not for Leduc, certainly for Miller. What he wants in this play is for Von Berg to recognize his guilt, as Quentin accepts his in *After the Fall*. In an article in *The New York Times Magazine* (January 3, 1965) called "Our Guilt for the World's Evil," Miller set out to correct some misconceptions that he felt had grown up around *Incident at Vichy*. He makes quite clear that, to him, the story is relatively unimportant and that Von Berg's heroic act at the end is gratuitous. "The first problem is not what to do about it," he says, "but to discover our own relationship to evil, its reflection of ourselves." If Quentin is a usable analogy for Miller himself, it would seem that the events of the eight years prior to 1964 made him find in himself qualities that he can accept only with difficulty. The accepting becomes possible, however, by extending the *mea culpa* to take in all men. He chooses to do this by embracing the commonplaces of contemporary psychology, but—since he is still a social dramatist—he uses the complicity gambit to turn personal guilt into public guilt. What this means to Miller as a playwright is that he no longer deals with man's struggle against the images being forced on him; instead, he becomes an image-forcer himself. After all the identity searching, the name that Quentin and Von Berg end up with is Everyman as Executioner. Both plays suggest—insist, really—that once this label is accepted, once the illusion of innocence is pushed aside, a man is free to act, even to act as a lover (like Quentin) or a martyr (like Von Berg). These positive acts, however, are simply the residue left by the burning away of the naive belief in man implicit in the early plays. In *After the Fall* and *Incident at Vichy*, the heroes are not in a struggle; they are in analysis. The analysis is successful when they accept that they fit the love-hate stereotype of the psychological man.

Although what Miller has to say in the new plays is philosophically suspect, it is not his theme but his commitment to it that has crippled his work. His new truth is not an impetus to creativity, but a doctrine that must be illustrated. In the past, he has occasionally been criticized for his didacticism, but in none of the early plays—not even in *All My Sons* and *The Crucible*—has he sacrificed action to argument. There are defects enough in those plays—the hidden-letter trick in *All My Sons*, Elizabeth's loving lie in *The Crucible*—defects that grow out of a need to let the action make a social point. Even so, his main characters—even John Proctor—are more than one-dimensional vehicles. All of the early plays are attempts to understand man and his society by confronting a particular man with a particular situation. The generalizations to be made from that particularity lie outside the play—with the audience, with the critic, with the playwright in his theoretical writings. In the new plays, the situations and the characters are only demonstration models. The playwright has moved from the creation of character to the making of statements, from the concrete to the abstract. This can best be seen if we look at *After the Fall* alongside *Death of a Salesman*, the early play that it most resembles.

The first title for *Salesman* was *The Inside of His Head*, which would suit *After the Fall* just as well. According to the first stage direction of *Fall*, "The action takes place in the mind, thought, and memory of Quentin." Although the version of *Salesman* that finally reached the stage has objective scenes as well as subjective ones, both *Salesman* and *After the Fall* make use of the ideas and the devices of expressionistic theater. The barriers of time and space disappear. The skeletal set of *Salesman* and the free-form set of *After the Fall* were conceived to let Miller's heroes step freely from the present to the past or, particularly in the case of Quentin, from one moment in the past to another. Both plays are designed, then, to let the playwright (and his characters) escape the restrictions of conventional realism.

The difference between the two plays lies in the way the playwright uses his freedom. In *Salesman*, we follow Willy through the last desperate day of his existence, watching him clutch at impossible and mostly imaginary straws until, through Biff, he is able to find the release that will let him die. The jumble of memories that nag at him are not simply explanatory flashbacks, although there is exposition in them. Since they are as real to Willy as the immediate events, they contribute to his disintegration. In *Salesman*, then, all the scenes are part of the play's action. In *After the Fall*, this is hardly the case. In that play Quentin decides to go meet Holga at the airport; the action, presumably, is his process of reaching that decision. When we see him at the beginning of the play, he is somewhat worried by the fact that hope keeps sneaking up on him even though he knows how awful everything is. The play uses his life to explain to him that he is the psychological stereotype discussed above. Then, perversely hopeful in a terrible world full of potential killers like himself, he goes off to meet the girl. Although there are lines to suggest that Quentin is undergoing some kind of torment, the pain of his self-analysis is belied by the discursive, man-to-man stance which he takes during the narrative sections of the play.[1] The remembered scenes, then, do not have the look of experiences being undergone, but of illustrations to prove a point. Even if we were to believe that Quentin is actually coming to conclusions as we watch him, those conclusions—his acceptance of himself—do not lead logically or dramatically to Holga. It is as though he stepped to the front of the stage and said, "I have a few hours to kill before I meet a plane. Let me spend them describing the human condition."

"Let me give you a piece advice," says Gregory Solomon, the aged furniture dealer in *The Price* (1968); "it's not that you can't believe nothing, that's not so hard—it's that you still got to believe it. *That's* hard." As this speech makes clear, Miller's most recent play is set in the same thematic country as *After the Fall* and *Incident at Vichy*. Here again are the rival brothers and, in the expositional past, the father whose business failed and the mother whose marriage did, elements already familiar from *After the Fall*. In *The Price*, Miller brings the two brothers—one a policeman, the other a successful surgeon—to the top floor of a brownstone house, the family home before 1929, where, surrounded by the furniture of the past, they try to face the mutual accusation that has dogged them for years, the last sixteen of which they have not seen or talked to one another. Their encounter is a long, quarreling discussion, a kind of mutual analysis, which would be impossible (the characters are always saying that they want to get things clear, as though they were panel participants) if it were not that Miller so carefully builds the scene that the audience gets caught up in the self-justifying attacks, shifting allegiance from one brother to the other as new revelations, new modifications, new admissions are uncovered.

---

[1] Robert Anderson's most recent play, apparently an attempt to lay his own ghosts (as *Fall* must have been for Miller), suffers from the same problem. The narrator-protagonist of *I Never Sang for My Father* (1968), who feels guilty that he could never love his father, manages to reduce a human problem to a bromidic discussion, all the more unsatisfying because the old man is an admirable, unlikable, self-pitying bully, a character too idiosyncratic to fit the stereotyped pattern to which the play keeps reverting.

Victor, the policeman, blames Walter for not having lent him enough money to finish college and for having left him to care for the father, presumably broke and broken because of the crash. Walter accuses Victor of knowing that the father was not that helpless, at least financially, and of choosing his policeman's lot to keep Walter guilty. Although Miller says, in a "Production Note" to the published play, that a "balance of sympathy" in the playing of the brothers is a thematic and theatrical necessity, it is Victor, the conventional good son (whatever his motivation, he did look after the father) and the voice for the play's few social criticisms, who retains the sympathy of the audience. He is, after all, the protagonist. In an emotional paralysis as the play opens, he is unable to make a decision about his retirement from the force, an event toward which he and his wife once looked as a new beginning. Suspecting that his past has been meaningless and that his future can be no better, he hesitates to act, an indecision that is destroying his marriage. The play's action is to take him—as *After the Fall* takes Quentin—beyond all attempts to shift the blame for his life to his brother, his father, anyone outside himself. He learns to pay his own price for the choice he made, even though he recognizes that the choice was partly an accident of psychology and social situation. There is no grand revelatory moment as a result of his self-discovery. His wife does tell him not to bother to change out of his uniform as they go out to dinner and a movie, an acceptance on her part of what he is. No longer immobilized by the past, he is able not only to sell the furniture, but to take his fencing mask and foil as souvenirs.

If this were all there were to *The Price,* it would not be that welcome a change from *Fall* and *Vichy*. Its strength lies in the character of Gregory Solomon, who dominates the play when he is on stage and, through well-timed intrusions during the brothers' discussion, continues to be a formidable presence even when he has moved to the periphery of the central action. A man almost ninety years old, a retired appraiser, who finds in the furniture an opportunity to begin again, he is an embodiment of the idea that life is the product of belief beyond disbelief. More important he is Arthur Miller's first real comic character, a creation that realizes some of the possibilities implicit in Willy Loman's happier scenes. Solomon is a Russian-Jewish stereotype who escapes caricature and turns into a shrewd, garrulous, idiomatic, lovable old man. At the end of the play, he is left alone with the furniture. He turns on the Victrola and begins to play a laughing record from the 1920s that the audience has already heard. As the laughter begins, it has a sardonic quality about it, as though it were a comment on everything that the play has presented, but Solomon begins to chuckle, then to laugh with the record. The man swallows the machine, life pervades the stage, and *The Price* escapes being simply another demonstration about the nature of man.[2]

[2] I wrote this description of the end of the play after having seen the pre-Broadway tryout in Philadelphia, in which David Burns gave a remarkable performance as Solomon. When the play reached New York, the ending had been changed so that Solomon laughed alone. Whether it was a temporary change having to do with the replacement for Burns, who had become ill, or whether Miller imagined that he had improved his curtain, the new version was much less effective than the earlier one. The published play, which had been prepared for the press before the final changes were made (for instance, its two acts became one in New York), contains the original ending. Miller's description of the laughter, "howling helplessly to the air," suggests the double response I felt in Philadelphia. In that form, it is a superb miniature restatement of the play's theme.

Colloquial Language in *All My Sons*

by Leonard Moss

All My Sons, Miller's first success on Broadway, represents a considerable advance in the author's ability to manipulate language. To a casual observer the dialogue may appear to be simply a phonographic imitation of contemporary American idiom, replete with clichés and slang. In the opening scene, comfortable gossip circulated by the Kellers and their friends connotes the sense of security conventionally associated with everyday family and neighborhood life. The talk—ingenuous, friendly, relaxed—duplicates the good-natured banter one might expect to hear in any Midwestern suburban backyard on a pleasant Sunday morning.

This deliberate banality, however, encompasses more than mere linguistic verisimilitude: the common man's slangy syntax has been used for theatrical purposes. "The play begins in an atmosphere of undisturbed normality," Miller wrote. "Its first act was later called slow, but it was designed to be slow. It was made so that even boredom might threaten, so that when the first intimation of the crime is dropped a genuine horror might begin to move into the heart of the audience, a horror born of the contrast between the placidity of the civilization on view and the threat to it that a rage of conscience could create" (*C.P.*, 18).[1] Intruding upon the tensionless domestic world, with its chatter about want-ads, parsley, and Don Ameche, a terrible challenge to tranquillity becomes increasingly insistent, finally bursting apart the innocent verbal façade. The peaceful mood deceptively evoked by trite speech prepares the stage for desperate war.

A series of allusions that gradually reveal a hidden sin brings about the transition from tranquillity to fear—an Ibsenesque technique

---

"Colloquial Language in *All My Sons*" (editor's title). From Leonard Moss, *Arthur Miller* (New York: Twayne Publishers, 1967), pp. 37–43. Copyright © 1967 by Twayne Publishers, Inc., a Division of G. K. Hall & Co., Boston. Reprinted by permission of the author and publisher.

[1]*Arthur Miller's Collected Plays* (New York, 1957)—hereafter cited as *C.P.*

that Miller was to employ in later plays. The Kellers' elder son, Larry, was reported missing in action after a wartime flight; when a neighbor refers to Larry's memorial tree, which was "toppled" by a storm the night before, he sounds the first jarring note. As yet such references do not significantly affect the prevailing conversational tenor, pitched as it is to humorous trivia. Even Joe Keller's teasing a youngster about "jail" contributes to the conviviality. But Joe and Chris, his other son, begin to worry about the impact that the tree's destruction will have on Mother, who still hopes for Larry's return. By the time she enters, then, the initial calm has already been somewhat disrupted. Her outburst of grief for the missing flier further disturbs that calm. "Because if he's not coming back," Kate cries, "then I'll kill myself! Laugh. . . . [She points to tree.] Laugh, but there are meanings in such things" (italics are omitted in quoting stage directions here and elsewhere).

Now another complication emerges: Kate refuses to allow Chris to marry his brother's fiancée because that would acknowledge Larry's death. The problem seems to involve mother and son, primarily, with Joe Keller standing by as a concerned spectator: "well, that's only your business, Chris," he comments. Yet the facts rapidly coming to light in the dozen or more oblique and direct allusions to an old scandal begin to place him in a more central position; they introduce a contradiction between his apparent neutrality and his actual involvement. His former partner in the machine shop, the spectator soon learns, has been serving a prison term for shipping defective cylinder-heads that caused the death of twenty-one American pilots. "The story was," Keller recalls, "I pulled a fast one getting myself exonerated." And a friend comments, "everybody knows Joe pulled a fast one to get out of jail. . . . There's not a person on the block who doesn't know the truth."

A more dynamic style mirrors the rising apprehension felt by Keller and his wife as their secret rises from the past. Their questions, idly curious before, now become urgently incisive, demanding immediate solution: "now what's going to happen to Mother? Do you know?" "Why, Joe? What has Steve suddenly got to tell him that he takes an airplane to see him?" "She don't hold nothin' against me, does she? I mean if she was sent here to find out something?" (This last question is answered with another query: "Why? What is there to find out?") The need to "know"—the verb occurs almost two hundred times—assumes first importance. Within a family supposedly united by strong affection there is surprising uncertainty and, therefore, constant inquiry in respect to each other's motives: "I don't understand you, do I?" Keller asks Chris, a comment later echoed by Mother.[2]

The verbal contrast brings out a psychological contrast, as Keller's defensive questions reveal qualities not previously manifested by the industrialist: harshness starts to displace his simple folksiness, fearfulness displaces the comfortable self-assurance. The grave interrogation alternates with continued small talk. Keller dissembles his growing "nervousness" by performing as a homespun humorist: "I don't know, everybody's gettin so Goddam educated in this country there'll be nobody to take away the garbage. . . . No kiddin'. It's a tragedy: you stand on the street today and spit, you're gonna hit a college man." But in the second act such pleasantries only bring his terror into sharper relief.

The Kellers attempt to seduce George, the jailed man's son, from his threatening demand for truth with the girl friends, grape juice, and homely clichés that remind him of his carefree existence as a boy in their town. Joe Keller almost succeeds in this verbal enterprise; he woos George with nostalgic reminiscences while discrediting his father with a show of gruff honesty. Then Kate ruins her husband's plan through an incriminating slip of the tongue—a venerable theatrical convention. As excitement builds to a climax, the hectic dialogue mixes the antithetical accents of normalcy and urgency. Keller stubbornly conceals the truth; Kate frantically evades it; and George persistently drives to uncover it ("what happened that day, Joe?"). At the same time, Chris and the neighbors, unaware of the impending crisis, cheerfully pursue avocations ranging from love to astrology.

When Chris discovers that his father had allowed the defective engine parts to be shipped, ordinary speech is unable to carry the intense stress and must be supplemented with exclamation and with violent action. Kate "smashes [Keller] across the face," and Chris in "overwhelming fury . . . pounds down upon his father's shoulder" (author's directions). In a confrontation that climaxes the movement toward revelation at the end of the second act, the son takes up the role of interrogator with a vengeance:

> How could you do that? How? . . . What did you do? Explain it to me or I'll tear you to pieces! . . . God in heaven, what kind of a man are

---

[2]At one point in *All My Sons*, thirteen of twenty sentences spoken by Joe Keller are questions.

you? . . . Where do you live, where have you come from? . . . What the
hell do you think I was thinking of, the Goddam business? Is that as
far as your mind can see, the business? What is that, the world—the
business? What the hell do you mean, you did it for me? Don't you
have a country? Don't you live in the world? What the hell are you?
You're not even an animal, no animal kills his own, what are you?
What must I do to you? I ought to tear the tongue out of your mouth,
what must I do? . . . What must I do, Jesus God, what must I do?

Theme development, of course, proceeds simultaneously with the
skillful development of tension and character: an ethical disparity
causes the conflict between father and son. Joe Keller cares little for
public approval, everything for his son's admiration. To him, "the
world had a forty-foot front, it ended at the building line." "Nothin'
is bigger" than the family, in whose name even homicide can be
justified: "my only accomplishment is my son. . . . There's nothin' he
could do that I wouldn't forgive." "Joe Keller's trouble, in a word,"
Miller has stated, "is not that he cannot tell right from wrong but that
his cast of mind cannot admit that he, personally, has any viable
connection with his world, his universe, or his society" (*C.P.*, 19).

If the father is monomaniacal in his loyalty, the son qualifies his
familial devotion. Chris cares for his family—"you're the only one I
know who loves his parents," a friend remarks—but combat has
taught him a higher principle. The men in his command "killed
themselves for each other. . . . Everything was being destroyed, see,
but it seemed to me that one new thing was made. A kind of—
responsibility. Man for man." His belief recalls Lawrence Newman's
final wish for a society founded upon common welfare rather than
upon self-interest and mutual exclusion.[3]

---

[3] A similarity between the father-son oppositions in *All My Sons* and in *The Wild
Duck* suggests a possible debt to Ibsen. In both plays the owner of a factory has been
implicated in a business scandal and then exonerated, his partner disgraced and sent
to prison—the matter is alluded to fragmentarily in the early part of the two dramas.
Each of the former partners has a son: one young man was shamed by his parent's
imprisonment; the other, now heir to the business, counters his wealthy father's
materialism with idealistic notions. The two sons, having been out of contact for
years despite their common interest in a young lady, stage a reunion at the home of
the plant-owner during which they try to cultivate good humor with inconsequential
chatter. The reunion, however, is disturbed by intrusive reminders of the unpleasant
past. Finally, antagonism generated by the earlier situation ends in a suicide that is
announced by the sound of a pistol.

Correspondences exist also at the verbal level, so far as one can judge from a
translation of Ibsen (*Three Plays by Ibsen* [New York, 1959]). For instance, Werle, the

After bringing the conflict to its brilliant culmination, Miller mishandles the resolution. Joe Keller's inexplicable decision to commit suicide is the most obvious sign of this mishandling. At first, Keller holds firmly to his position; his obstinacy impels Chris to curse himself and his father, then determine to give up his home, career, and fiancée ("now I'm practical, and I spit on myself").[4] Instead of sacrificing his own life, however, Chris brings about his father's death by reading to Joe the letter in which Larry also had denounced his father and condemned himself. In this way, Chris damns Keller for Larry's suicide. More than that, the letter apparently demonstrates the validity of Chris's philosophy on universal brotherhood; for Keller hints at moral surrender in his cryptic statement before shooting himself: "sure, [Larry] was my son. But I think to him they were all my sons. And I guess they were, I guess they were."

If this vaguely worded last speech is supposed to indicate a sudden ethical conversion, it hardly suggests the process whereby Keller capitulates to an alien theory he had savagely resisted until that moment. More likely, and more appropriately after the gradual increase of tension during the first two acts, his suicide may be an emotional reaction to the rejection by both sons (he had warned that, should the bond with his surviving son be severed, "I'll put a bullet in my head"). But the speech does not express a feeling of deprivation strong enough to overcome Keller's staunch self-defense. The realization that he has driven one son to his death and alienated the other

entrepreneur in *The Wild Duck*, proposes that his boy join the firm, since "we are father and son after all"; Keller makes the same request, insisting "I'm his father and he's my son." Werle's son rejected the offer because, as another character says, "he is suffering from an acute attack of integrity"; in *All My Sons*, a minor character complains that Chris (who also spurns his father's business) "makes people want to be better than it's possible to be."

There are, of course, radical differences between the two plays. Moreover, Miller claims to have gotten the idea for his work while listening to "a pious lady from the Middle West [who] told of a family in her neighborhood which had been destroyed when the daughter turned the father in to the authorities on discovering that he had been selling faulty machinery to the Army" (*C.P.*, 17). Still, it may be that Ibsen's influence, which Miller admits was substantial enough in other respects, extended to the theme of father-son conflict. (In response to my inquiry, Miller stated that he could not remember whether Ibsen had influenced him in this connection.)

[4] Arvin R. Wells, *"All My Sons," Insight I* (Frankfurt, 1962), p. 169, remarks that "because [Chris] is closely identified with his father, his necessary sense of personal dignity and worthiness depends upon his belief in the ideal image of his father; consequently, he can only accept the father's exposure as a personal defeat."

might well be unbearable to a character who has predicated his existence upon pride as a father. But the disintegration of such pride seems gratuitous when manifested so casually.[5]

The lameness of the ending is compounded by the melodramatic plot devices: one familiar stage convention, an incriminating letter, leads to another, a suicide. Still others occur earlier in the play. There is coincidence: George's crucial interview with his long-imprisoned father takes place at the same time that Chris decides to marry Ann, George's sister. There is a prophetic symbol: the ruined tree portends the death of hope. And there is Kate's fatal slip of the tongue.[6] When such conventions operate in concert with expository methods of some subtlety, as in the first two acts, they remain unobtrusive. When they become the chief narrative means, as in the finale, their awkwardness reaches distressing proportions.

The narrative crudeness and verbal obscurity at the conclusion of *All My Sons* may be symptomatic of a shift in interest from the indignant father to the outraged son; after the last question spoken by Chris in the second act—"what must I do?"—Keller's defense no longer commands central attention. Miller seems to have become captivated by a figure recurrent in his work—a maturing individual (a New-man) who proclaims, in abstract terms, the interdependence of all men. The third act betrays a drift toward the rhetorical style Miller has called upon so freely elsewhere: sententious declarations delivered by Chris and by three colleagues in disenchantment differ radically in style both from the simple-minded banter prominent in the first act and from the intense exclamation and interrogation prominent in the second.

Keller's attempt to justify his crime remains relatively concrete even when the appeal is made on hypothetical grounds: "did they ship a gun or a truck outa Detroit before they got their price? Is that clean? It's dollars and cents, nickels and dimes; war and peace, it's nickels and dimes, what's clean?" His questions, now self-answered, continue to expose his apprehension and his toughness; their specificity suits well the narrowness and the urgency of his commitment. On the other hand, Chris, though his diction is plain, argues his case for mutual responsibility with hazy generalities: "once and for all you can know there's a universe of people outside

[5]The abruptness of Keller's conversion has disturbed other critics; for example, see Arthur Ganz, "The Silence of Arthur Miller," *Drama Survey*, III (1963), 232.

[6]Norm Fruchter also mentions these conventions, in "On the Frontier," *Encore*, IX (Jan., 1962), 19.

and you're responsible to it, and unless you know that, you threw away your son because that's why he died." Chris's wider concept is necessarily difficult to explain, but simplification of this kind does not clarify the idea.

No less than three other disillusioned, somewhat pretentious young men express disgust at the selfishness they encounter in the world; in so doing they reinforce the standpoint taken by Chris. Larry posthumously speaks his shame on learning of his father's indictment: "every day three or four men never come back and he sits back there doing business" (Act III). George has suffered from *his* father's disgrace: "when I was studying in the hospital it seemed sensible, but outside there doesn't seem to be much of a law" (Act II). And Jim gave up the dream of becoming a researcher: "these private little revolutions always die. The compromise is always made. . . . Every man does have a star. The star of one's honesty. And you spend your life groping for it, but once it's out it never lights again." (Act III).

These moralistic speeches place a disproportionate emphasis on the antagonist's position, a change in focus that may account for the inconclusiveness of Keller's pre-suicide statement, with its token acquiescence in Chris's theory. Besides disrupting the development of the main character, moreover, such judgments dissipate tension. They produce an effect opposite to that achieved early in the play by the judicious alternation of serious and comic moods. After the cleanly decisive second-act clash between father and son, Chris's cynical wisdom comes as a wordy letdown: "we used to shoot a man who acted like a dog, but honor was real there, you were protecting something. But here? This is the land of the great big dogs, you don't love a man here, you eat him! That's the principle; the only one we live by—it just happened to kill a few people this time, that's all. The world's that way, how can I take it out on him? What sense does that make? This is a zoo, a zoo!" (Act III). (Similarly, Sue's long, misleading, and irrelevant criticism of Chris unduly slows the pace after the suspenseful conclusion of the first act.)

The playwright probably directed attention away from the father's loss to the son's in order to show the consequences of a thoroughgoing tribal outlook; "the fortress which *All My Sons* lays siege to," Miller stated, "is the fortress of unrelatedness" (*C.P.*, 19). But in taking that course he undercut the source of emotional power he had cultivated during most of the play. *All My Sons*, for two acts an extremely well constructed work, reveals clearly what is evident in almost every play Miller has written—the habit of following a carefully prepared movement to crisis with an anticlimactic denouement. His desire to formulate "social" truths has restricted his talent for capturing inward urgencies in colloquial language.

Miller's Realism and *Death of a Salesman*

by Enoch Brater

It is always surprising to discover that Arthur Miller, whose best work for the theater makes its pact so soundly with conventional realism, began his playwriting career exploring the possibilities of some very different dramatic forms. Incorporating the techniques of expressionism, symbolism,and even verse drama, Miller's early unproduced plays bear little resemblance to the kind of realistic narration we associate with the concise arrangement of his mature style. "I wrote a verse, or near verse, tragedy of Montezuma and Cortez," he remembered, "which had no relation whatsoever to any Ibsenesque theatre. I wrote a rather expressionist play about two brothers in the University when I was a student" and "I wrote two or three attempts at purely symbolistic drama. . . . What bothered me was that I didn't believe in any of these plays that I had written."[1] Miller's youthful experimentation with the dramatic styles available to him was an earnest search for compatibility between the contingencies of his medium and his developing social consciousness. The spade-work proved crucial: it meant that on the road to realism Miller would take a variety of detours his work would never completely abandon.

Before *All My Sons* I had written 13 plays, none of which is realistic and none of which got me anywhere. So I decided at the age of 29 that I wasn't going to waste my life in this thing. I already had one child, and I couldn't see myself going on writing play after play and getting absolutely nowhere. I sat down and decided to write a play about which nobody could say to me, as they had with all the other plays, "What does this mean?" or "I don't understand that" or some such thing. And I spent two years writing that play just to see if I could do it that way. Because I was working in a realistic theater, which didn't

"Miller's Realism and *Death of a Salesman*" by Enoch Brater appears in print for the first time in this volume, with the author's permission.

[1]Robert A. Martin, "The Creative Experience of Arthur Miller: An Interview," *Educational Theatre Journal* 21, 3 (October 1969), 310.

know anything else. But that doesn't mean I was at bottom simply a realistic playwright.[2]

Miller, of course, had written one realistic play, "a family play," even before *All My Sons*.[3] Designed for the box-set mechanisms of fourth-wall illusionism, *The Man Who Had All the Luck* (1944) tells the story of seemingly Blind Fortune in small town America. In this early work Miller asks a question his work will pose again: do individuals in our society get what they desire or are they helpless victims of some cold, indifferent force?[4] Miller's man with all the luck finds success in business, romance, and family while his hapless friends fail through "bad luck." But the realization that an inhuman abstraction like fate decides who shall live and who shall die slowly begins to drive this "lucky" man insane. He tempers his uneasy consciousness by trying to understand how his own ability and actions are responsible for the good fortune life brings his way. Although Miller's device for exposing the dark side of an American success story is far too obvious to make us believe this is indeed a true slice-of-life, *The Man Who Had All the Luck* nevertheless demonstrates his growing fascination with the apparatus of realism. Despite the heavy-handed intrusion of determinism in this sometimes awkward parable of fate in the Midwest, Miller's manipulation of the realistic technique remains, nonetheless, very much intact.

By the time of *All My Sons* (1947), Miller's skill in rendering a realistic tableau more expertly accommodates a theme of human responsibility in a social sphere. With the writing of this play Miller moves from fable to social realism—or rather in this case, as in Ibsen, the one is subsumed within the other. Although *All My Sons* has usually been taken as an example of theatrical realism at its most conventional, Miller's style here is somewhat more complicated than we may have been led to believe. In the "August of our era," the set for this famous play exposes the heartland of postwar domesticity:

> The stage is hedged on right and left by tall, closely planted poplars which lend the yard a secluded atmosphere. Upstage is filled with the back of the house and its open, unroofed porch which extends into

[2]Josh Greenfield, " 'Writing Plays is Absolutely Senseless,' Arthur Miller Says, 'But I Love It. I Just Love It,' " *New York Times Sunday Magazine,* February 13, 1972, p. 37.

[3]Martin, "Creative Experience," p. 310.

[4]Eric Mottram, "Arthur Miller: the Development of a Political Dramatist in America," in *American Theatre,* eds. John Russell Brown and Bernard Harris (London: Edward Arnold, 1967), p. 131.

the yard some six feet. The house is two stories high and has seven rooms. It would have cost perhaps fifteen thousand in the early twenties when it was built. Now it is nicely painted, looks tight and comfortable, and the yard is green with sod, here and there plants whose season is gone. . . . Downstage right is a small, trellised arbor, shaped like a sea-shell, with a decorative bulb hanging from its forward-curving roof. Garden chairs and a table scattered about.[5]

The "secluded atmosphere" of *All My Sons* allows us to study in some detail the currency of corruption that exists beneath the comfortable façade of Keller's family life. This house, we soon learn, has been built on sand; this garden has been cultivated by the wages of sin. Miller's set foreshadows disaster, the transgression of a firm moral code, the crimes a man must pay for when he eats forbidden fruit: downstage "stands the four-foot high stump of a slender apple tree whose upper trunk and branches lie toppled beside it, fruit still clinging to its branches." What is important to notice about the set for this play is that all of its symbolic baggage has been formally integrated within the structure of one naturalistic set. Miller has finally designed a play whose allegory rests comfortably within the contours of fourth-wall realism.

Yet, for all its appeal as a believable portrayal of moral conflict (made all the more accessible in the screen version starring Burt Lancaster as Chris and Edward G. Robinson as Keller), *All My Sons* is not without some limitations. Not all of Ibsen's methods have been used well. Miller's play, like Lillian Hellman's *The Children's Hour*, is burdened by a contrivance that violates the illusion of reality the play has been striving so hard to sustain. Instead of integrating directly into the action the results of those tensions the drama places so effectively in motion, the playwright falls back in the final scene on a letter written by Keller's dead son to hasten the denouement. Unlike Hellman's, it should be noted, Miller's curtain in *All My Sons* has not been unnecessarily delayed: recognition follows quickly upon revelation, the gun goes off, mother-son embrace, the curtain falls. If Miller, still a novice to the realistic technique, tries to slip us a letter in the last act of *All My Sons* (as Ibsen himself had occasion to do in *A Doll's House*), at least he has used it in a swiftly paced finale where moral intent coincides with dramatic impact. The final scene, however, presents us with a more serious structural problem:

[5]*All My Sons* in *Famous American Plays of the 1940's*, ed. Henry Hewes (New York: Dell, 1960), p. 201.

Mother. Why are you going? You'll sleep, why are you going?

Keller. I can't sleep here. I'll feel better if I go.

Mother. You're so foolish. Larry was your son too, wasn't he? You know he'd never tell you to do this.

Keller (Looking at letter in his hand). Then what is this if it isn't telling me? Sure, he was my son. But I think to him they were all my sons. And I guess they were, I guess they were. . . . *(Exits into house.).* . . .

Mother (Of Larry, the letter). The war is over! Didn't you hear?—it's over!

Chris. Then what was Larry to you? A stone that fell into water? It's not enough for him to be sorry. Larry didn't kill himself to make you and Dad sorry.

Mother. What more can we be!

Chris. You can be better! Once and for all you can know there's a universe of people outside and you're responsible to it, and unless you know that, you threw away your son because that's why he died. *(A shot is heard in the house. . . .)*[6]

Although Miller has set us up from the very beginning to embrace the ultimate justice in Chris's ideological stance, somehow we wish the poignancy of this dramatic moment had relied less on direct statement and more on implication. Chris's rhetoric can be stirring in performance, but on stage it can also border perilously close on the melodramatic.

In *Death of a Salesman* (1949), however, Miller succeeds in creating a realism that is at once human in scale yet larger than life.[7] Both *All My Sons* and *The Man Who Had All the Luck* had demonstrated the playwright's impatience with what so often becomes in the naturalistic mode the picayune illusionism of everyday life. Miller knew very well how a strict fidelity to scenic and structural detail could, in the theater, obscure any confrontation with reality itself. Deceiving the audience into thinking it had seen the truth when it had merely been exposed to a series of facts, the realistic tableau needed to find a stage device capable of embodying the symbolic texture that helps to explain the present. "It isn't a question of reporting something," Miller said, referring to the construction of this work. "It's a question of creating a synthesis that has never existed before out of common materials that are otherwise chaotic and unrelated."[8] Integrating new stage mechanics into the set designed by Jo Mielziner, *Death of a*

---

[6]Ibid., pp. 287–88.

[7]Martin Gottfried, "Our Sometime Intellectual Superman," *Saturday Review,* September 29, 1979, p. 40.

[8]Martin, "Creative Experience," p. 312.

Salesman makes the past literally simultaneous with the present. Above and beyond formalism, here is the practical stage solution Miller's flirtation with realism has been searching for. The staging of Willy Loman's psyche, his frustrated hopes and his unfulfilled dreams, could now strike Miller's audience with astonishing immediacy and clarity. The plot is naturalistic, but the tone is everywhere symbolic; realism in this play reveals the substance of myth. "Chasing all the things that rust," Willy Loman is the American Everyman somewhere between the pathetic and the tragic.[9] Miller's realistic style has therefore been established to show us life, not a slice-of-life. Staging can no longer be divorced from thematic overtone.

"How may a man make of the outside world a home?" is the universal question Miller ponders in this play—and he ponders it in universal terms.[10] When the curtain rises on this drama, "A melody is heard, played upon a flute. It is small and fine, telling of grass and trees and the horizon." Miller's set suggests rather than completes the realistic tableau, for his staging makes highly selective use of the props of everyday life. In so doing, Miller liberates himself from a too careful literalism that might dwarf the symbolic texture of his play. "The entire setting," we see, "is wholly or, in some places, partially transparent." Yet, into this staged transparency Miller introduces those elements of tragedy that become in the course of this drama painfully real:

> Before us is the Salesman's house. We are aware of towering, angular shapes behind it, surrounding it on all sides. Only the blue light of the sky falls upon the house and forestage; the surrounding area shows an angry glow of orange. As more light appears, we see a solid vault of apartment houses around the small, fragile-seeming home. An air of dream clings to the place, a dream rising out of reality.[11]

In a very basic sense, the set *is* Miller's play. The tiny frame house clings desperately to its frail life-line beneath inhuman towers blocking out the sun and stifling its precarious existence. Willy's world has been passed by and somehow nobody noticed. Into this somber lyricism enters tired humanity in the person of Loman the Salesman,

[9]"Arthur Miller on Home Ground," produced, written, and directed by Harry Rasky. A Canadian Broadcasting Company documentary in the Spectrum series, broadcast October 24, 1979.

[10]Arthur Miller, "The Family in Modern Drama," in *The Theater Essays of Arthur Miller,* ed. Robert A. Martin (New York: Viking, 1978), p. 73.

[11]*Death of a Salesman* (New York: Viking, 1949), p. 11.

"carrying two large sample cases. The flute plays on. He hears but is not aware of it. He is past sixty years of age, dressed quietly. Even as he crosses the stage to the doorway of the house, his exhaustion is apparent."

The stark visual contrast between a highly symbolic set and the behavior of highly realistic characters is what adds such dramatic resonance to the themes Miller pursues. What happens here on the level of everyday life is performed on a set that has been delicately built to play a metaphorical supporting role. The actions and reactions of the Loman family, therefore, gain a density of meaning above and beyond what we normally expect from the conventions of fourth-wall realism. The play, in fact, carefully builds its conflicts from the interaction of its two separate levels of stage presence, the symbolic and the naturalistic. The careful orchestration of this scenic device prepares us for the thematic conflicts that will take place on this set and makes possible that conflict of ideas, which, in Miller's own terms, "embraces both determinism and the paradox of will."[12]

The carefully controlled staging of *Death of a Salesman* thus makes it something more than an old-fashioned naturalistic drama with symbols of the kind Miller had tried to write in *All My Sons*. In the earlier play Miller had been locked into the strict limitations of his four walls: when he seeks range and depth in Chris's final speech, the conclusion of his tale sounds far too much like speechifying to make for thoroughly satisfying dramatic closure. Rather than allowing the play to speak to us on its own terms, the playwright upstages the play itself—Miller's moral weight is preaching at us through the voice of Chris. *All My Sons* follows the same pattern Ibsen displays in *An Enemy of the People* (the five-act play Miller pared down to three acts during the McCarthy period): the thesis play with a tagged-on moral.

> *Dr. Stockmann.* Drive me away! Are you stark raving mad, Katrine? I'm the strongest man in the town! Don't you know that?"
> *Mrs. Stockmann.* The strongest—? You mean, *now*?
> *Dr. Stockmann.* Yes! I'll even go so far as to say that I'm one of the strongest men in the whole world!
> *Morten.* Are you really, Father?
> *Dr. Stockmann (Dropping his voice).* Hush! You mustn't say a word about it yet; I've made a great discovery, you see.
> *Mrs. Stockmann.* Not another, Tomas, dear!
> *Dr. Stockmann.* Another, yes—another! (*Gathers them round him and speaks in*

---

[12]"Introduction to the *Collected Plays*" in *Theater Essays*, p. 170.

a confidential tone) And I'll tell you what it is: the strongest man in the world is the man who stands alone.
Mrs. Stockmann (Smiles and shakes her head). Oh, Tomas, dear—!
Petra (Grasps his hands and says with eyes full of faith). Father!
Curtain[13]

But by the time of *Death of a Salesman,* Miller shifts his emphasis from "what ought to be" to "what is."[14] In order to accomplish this goal, Miller needed to free himself from the constraints of Ibsenism with which he was never completely comfortable. The playwright could now develop in his own stage terms "the unsingable heartsong the ordinary man may feel but never utter."[15]

Having opened up his set to accommodate the fundamental as well as the surface in "a structure that has stood instead of collapsing," Miller can now move on from literal to emblematic realism.[16] In the process he has discovered a new way to show the impact of the past on the present. Originally entitled *The Inside of His Head, Death of a Salesman* features a protagonist who can no longer distinguish between memory, imagination, reality, and desire.[17] Instead of reshuffling those old techniques the realistic theater had developed for evoking the consequences of past behavior on present action—the neat exposition of earlier events in parenthetically pointed commentary, the unexpected arrival of a confidante on the scene, and, worst of all, a letter from a "knowing" offstage character— Miller can now abandon these tricks completely. On this new stage, Willy's interior life can now be blocked on the same plane defining his life in the present. Through the use of lighting and careful orchestration of music, Miller's strategy here allows him to be infinitely more flexible and spontaneous. As Willy, "trying to write his name on ice on a hot July day," recoils from the present and retreats even further into the past, the play can move with him into his own disintegration.[18] Willy talks to himself; and so the soliloquy, the *noli me tangere* of naturalism, is once again possible. Miller adapts it skillfully to signal shifts from past to present: a statement uttered to a character only Willy—and sometimes we—can see is suddenly

[13]*Six Plays by Henrik Ibsen,* trans. Eva LeGallienne (New York: Modern Library, 1932), pp. 254–55.
[14]Greenfield, "Writing Plays," p. 38.
[15]"The American Theater" in *Theater Essays,* p. 50.
[16]"Arthur Miller on Home Ground."
[17]"Introduction to the *Collected Plays,*" p. 135.
[18]"Arthur Miller on Home Ground."

overheard and misinterpreted by someone in the present. Past and present become one as we are startled into recognition by the play's unpredictable exposition. On stage these shifts are accomplished simply and, in those moments when they are accompanied by the muted tones of a flute, very eloquently indeed. The poetic suddenly rises from what in other stage terms might have been strictly prosaic. Dialogue can now reach a lyrical pitch, which would be entirely inappropriate on a naturalistic set. This is no longer the semblance of "dialogue caught through a keyhole—it's written, composed."[19] Dramatic language can now achieve that range and depth so elusive to Miller when recited on his more conventional sets:

> I don't say he's a great man. Willy Loman never made a lot of money. His name was never in the paper. He's not the finest character that ever lived. But he's a human being, and a terrible thing is happening to him. So attention must be paid. He's not to be allowed to fall into his grave like an old dog. Attention, attention must be finally paid to such a person. You called him crazy—. . . . a lot of people think he's lost his—balance. But you don't have to be very smart to know what his trouble is. The man is exhausted. . . . A small man can be just as exhausted as a great man.[20]

Linda's Act One speech disturbs no surface texture of naturalism because she is a character in a work conceived on an entirely different stylistic basis. Miller can now get away with the "summing up" that seemed so intrusive before in a work like *All My Sons*.

If his abandonment of literal realism means Miller's characters can now make a "statement" without necessarily violating the spirit of the mise-en-scène previously established, it also allows them to become poetic in places where it would have been unsuitable before. Because we have lived with a character whose grip on reality is slipping away before our very eyes, because we have walked with him into his dreams and found them more delicate than anything his world can offer, and finally because we recognize that the story he tells us is not merely his own, we no longer expect him to deliver lines in the cadence of everyday speech. For though Miller's plot involves an everyday problem, this is not an everyday character and this is not an everyday setting. Willy's emblematic situation demands a special language. Miller has invented one for him, for this particular pro-

[19]Ralph Tyler, "Arthur Miller Says the Time Is Right for 'The Price,'" *New York Times,* Sunday, June 17, 1979, sec. 2, p. 6.
[20]*Salesman,* p. 56.

letarian man rises to new heights of lyricism when he remembers a past that exists only in his own imagination:

> ... my father lived many years in Alaska. He was an adventurous man. . . . I thought I'd go out with my brother and try to locate him, and maybe settle in the North with the old man. And I was almost decided to go, when I met a salesman in the Parker House. His name was Dave Singleman. And he was eighty-four years old, and he'd drummed merchandise in thirty-one states. And old Dave, he'd go up to his room, y'understand, put on his green velvet slippers—I'll never forget—and pick up his phone and call the buyers, and without ever leaving his room, at the age of eighty-four, he made his living. And when I saw that, I realized that selling was the greatest career a man could want. 'Cause what could be more satisfying than to be able to go, at the age of eighty-four, into twenty or thirty different cities, and pick up the phone, and be remembered and loved and helped by so many different people? Do you know? when he died—and by the way he died the death of a salesman, in his green velvet slippers in the smoker of the New York, New Haven, and Hartford, going into Boston—when he died, hundreds of salesmen and buyers were at his funeral. Things were sad on a lotta trains for months after that. . . . In those days there was personality in it. . . . Today, it's all cut and dried, and there's no chance for bringing friendship to bear—or personality. You see what I mean? They don't know me anymore.[21]

Miller, of course, has saved his best poetry for the Requiem. Something more than a Coda, this short scene justifies the overall design of the play. *Death of a Salesman* reflects the shape of a lopsided arch, the peak of which occurs near the end of Act Two. But the curtain is not quite ready to fall here. The Requiem permits a swift drop in dynamic level and tension, but not in dramatic intensity. Linda is now ready to deliver her parting words as the "flute begins, not far away, playing behind her speech":

> Forgive me, dear. I can't cry. I don't know what it is, but I can't cry. I don't understand it. Why did you ever do that? Help me, Willy, I can't cry. It seems to me that you're just on another trip. I keep expecting you. Willy, dear, I can't cry. Why did you do it? I search and search and I search, and I can't understand it, Willy. I made the last payment on the house today. Today, dear. And there'll be nobody home. *A sob rises in her throat.* We're free and clear. *Sobbing more fully, released:* We're free. *Biff comes slowly toward her.* We're free . . . We're free. . . .[22]

[21]Ibid., p. 81.
[22]Ibid., p. 139.

Although one might have thought it impossible to write dramatic poetry about broken refrigerator fan-belts, this is precisely what Miller has accomplished in this play. This has been all along, we should remember, "a dream rising out of reality." And in dreams anything is possible, even poetry. But the most lyrical moment in this play takes place without the intrusion of any words at all. The set is finally allowed to speak to us in its own special language. As the characters slowly exit, Biff lifting Linda to her feet, followed by Charley, Bernard, and finally Happy, only the music of the flute is left on Miller's "darkening stage." Over Willy Loman's house "the hard towers of the apartment buildings rise into sharp focus." The curtain falls. Unlike the crowd who attended Dave Singleman's funeral, hardly anyone at all has bothered to see this salesman off.

Something more needs to be said here about Miller's use of music in this play. For music in *Death of a Salesman* is far more central to its appeal in production than the term "incidental" would seem to imply. As opposed to the naturalistic style, where the playwright is obliged to invent any number of realistic excuses for the incorporation of musical elements to enrich, highlight, or pinpoint a significant moment, *Salesman* calls upon music to create meaning on its own. Once it has been established, for example, that Willy's father not only sold flutes all over the country, but made them as well, the sounding of this instrument on Miller's stage evokes the whole spirit of an unobtainable past. The flute, therefore, is a principal organizing force: opening the curtain and closing it, the flute establishes the play's proper atmosphere. When we first meet Willy Loman, he "is at that terrible moment when the voice of the past is no longer distant but quite as loud as the voice of the present."[23] The main role of the flute, then, is to inform the audience that the past is about to merge with the present. But the situation is not so clear-cut as that. Each "flashback" (a term disliked by Miller, but useful in this context nonetheless) is somewhat different in shape.[24] When Willy moves from the kitchen, to Linda and the boys, to the Woman, back to Linda, and then to Happy and Charley in the kitchen, he actually takes a double trip into the past before returning to the present. Later, when Biff and Happy return home after having stranded their father in a restaurant, we hear the flute but do not see Willy. As the

[23]"Introduction to the *Collected Plays,*" p. 138.
[24]See Miller's introduction on the cover notes to the Theatre Recording Society Production Folio version of *Death of a Salesman.*

following scene shows, he is digging in the garden and talking to his brother Ben about his upcoming suicide—a plan involving a character from the past with future events. Finally, it is Linda who has the flute behind her voice as she talks to her dead husband as though he were still alive: her speech in the Requiem combines past and future in an empty present.

Other kinds of music can be similarly strategic. Ben's music is "idyllic." When Ben and Willy reminisce about their father, we hear "some kind of high music" followed by a high, rollicking tune. Biff and Happy have a music of their own. When the Game is being planned, when Willy talks to Ben about past camaraderie with his sons, and even when the boys have left home and only the smell of shaving lotion lingers, their cheerful "boys' music" rings in the air. Charley's deprecating remark about Biff's big game at Ebbets Field results in a wild explosion of sound caused by a rising intensity of this same music. But only the audience and Willy hear it—the music is all inside his head.

Whistling—or singing, as in Linda's case—is another kind of music this play uses to build meaning, and the working-class Lomans are great whistlers. Willy whistles, even in elevators. So does Biff, but he is reprimanded for it. Biff says that carpenters can whistle when they work and that perhaps this is exactly the job for him—a manual skill inherited from his father far more suitable to his personality than salesmanship. But much more than whistling in elevators—or saying "gee" (another Loman trait)—is responsible for Biff's "failure." In this play many "important" people whistle. Howard and his daugher whistle on tape; even Bernard whistles as he waits to go off to Washington to argue a case before the Supreme Court.

Music, therefore, creates the atmosphere appropriate to the individual scenes in which it plays so crucial a part. In the restaurant there is raucous music until it is interrupted by one blast from a trumpet. In Boston there is raw, sensuous music as the Woman unbuttons Willy's shirt; when Biff enters the hotel room, the music stops dead. And as Willy drives to his death, a single pulsating cello note sounds, leading into a dead march and finally the grave scene with flute. In the context of *Death of a Salesman*, none of this is artificial. Music works in this play because it brings to Miller's moral weight a sense of poetry. In order to achieve this scope and depth, Miller has had to use music in a highly symbolic way, abandoning the facts of realistic literalism and aiming for the truth instead. "A worship of fact," he once said, "is always an obstruction if one is looking for truth. There's a difference between the facts and the truth; the truth is a synthesis of facts."[25] In *Salesman*, Miller's emblematic realism therefore, holds the naturalistic and the symbolic in perfect equilibrium. And in this way his people are transformed into archetypes.

In *Death of a Salesman*, Miller presents us with a realism concerned far less with what happens than why. "A totally articulated work instead of an anecdote," the play has made highly selective use of expressionistic techniques only to reveal more clearly the pattern of life itself.[26] "I've become aware now that I was dealing with something much more there than Willy Loman, the tactile quality of the experience of one particular character."[27] The very special theatrical style of this work, therefore, has much to tell us about the structure of realism in light of what John Gassner once called its "multivalent and relativistic character."[28] Realism, concerned in Miller's hands with the family and, by extension, with the family of men, can be the most symbolic dramatic style of them all.

[25]Martin, "Creative Experience," p. 314.
[26]Tyler, "Arthur Miller," p. 6.
[27]Greenfield, "Writing Plays," p. 37.
[28]John Gassner, "Realism in the Modern American Theatre," in *American Theatre*, p. 11.

The Crucible: "This Fool and I"

by Walter J. Meserve

Giles Corey speaks the line just before the Reverend Hale enters the scene in Act One of *The Crucible*. He has just indulged his irascible nature by joining Proctor in an argument against Thomas Putnam over lumber that Proctor has cut. It is a real but petty argument, typical of the real but petty problems that trouble the people of Salem, and it reflects the early tone of the drama.

When the play opens, Reverend Parris is with his niece Betty in an upstairs bedroom, panic-stricken that his reputation and job will be lost because she and some other girls had danced in the woods and become hysterical when he discovered them. His immediate problem is the group of people downstairs waiting for his explanation. Finally, he goes down to them. The girls, left alone, try to figure out how they can explain their activities without revealing too much or getting into even greater difficulties. After they have scattered without arriving at a satisfactory solution and Proctor and Abby have had their brief talk, the adults gather in the upstairs room. The problem, raised by Betty's behavior, remains unexplained. Being ordinary people they have limited constructive comment, and the sensible things they say go unrecognized. Quickly, the plight of Betty and the suspected witchcraft—already exposed by the girls as "sport"—evolves into petty adult arguments over church-going, the minister's salary, his demands for deeds and firewood, the church factions, and the greedy actions of certain parishioners. The scene climaxes in the argument over lumber. There were the Putnams, greedy and self-righteous, who would happily ride roughshod over their neighbors, and there were the stubborn few, like Corey and Proctor, who for different reasons rebelled against such people. In a cause that stimulates his sense of justice, Corey is contentious and eager to join

"*The Crucible:* 'This Fool and I' " by Walter J. Meserve appears in print for the first time in this volume, with the author's permission.

Proctor: "Aye," he responds quickly to Putnam's threatened legal suit, "and we'll win too, Putnam—this fool and I."

And there the matter might have ended as Corey and Proctor headed for the door. But the Reverend Hale had been called, and with his appearance a new set of situations and actions are created. Corey's phrase, however, appears more representative and symbolic than the situation suggests. There is, of course, the touch of irony, but there is also sentiment in this good-natured name-calling, a sense of courageous comradery that invites the audience to share their feelings and sympathize with their actions. There is no fear at this point, but changes will occur that lead "this fool and I" not into the courts disputing the ownership of a wood lot, but to death.

There is folly in Proctor's attitude, which even Corey does not understand. Proctor is no saint. This he admits, and this Corey can understand. But there is a stubborn sense of reason in him, which, during a social upheaval such as the one about to strike Salem, makes him incapable of dealing with life around him. A reasonable man in a time of unreasonable action by his fellow men, he appears the fool. A man of beliefs about himself and his god, he may not indulge himself in the fantasy that the kingdom of God can be recreated on earth—particularly through the men he sees administering God's Word—but his thoughts have been directed by church dogma for many years, and he can reveal an honest naivete that will be his undoing. He is that common man who frequently lacks good judgment and acts the fool that all men who contend honestly with life suffer and understand, becoming finally a wiser man than he realizes, one who can be mistaken for a heroic figure. There have been more fools than wise men through the ages, and it is sometimes difficult to tell the difference.

The structure of *The Crucible* supports the confusion that makes that difference difficult to determine. It is consistently based on lies and confessions—lies that show the Devil's world and confessions that are associated with God and mercy or courts of law and justice. The climax of every act builds upon the idea of a confession, true or false, forced or withheld. The first act closes upon the lying confessions of the hysterical girls made more horrible when mingled with Hale's naive "glory to God!" and Parris' self-indulgent and relieved prayer of thanksgiving. The climax of Act Two shows Proctor forcing Mary Warren to agree to confess her lies in court. Condemned as the "Devil's man" at the end of Act Three, Proctor will not confess.

Again, at the end of the play, it is Proctor's refusal to confess to a lie that creates the climax.

Lies are vital to the development of the play. They establish character, dramatize differences between people, reveal ironies, move the plot, and underscore the theme. Abigail lies easily; Tituba and the other girls lie under duress; Elizabeth cannot lie, according to Proctor, but she can. Rebecca cannot confess to a lie, but Proctor can. Mary Warren's forced decision to confess her lie in court leads to the major crisis of the play. Hale's pleading that Proctor be allowed to "give his lie" and Danforth's statement that he will not accept lies skillfully dramatize the deep ironies that make the play a penetrating comment on people and society. Lies always lead to confusion; lies juxtaposed to confessions may make that line between folly and wisdom even more indistinct.

John Proctor is not a difficult man to know, and yet there is a complexity in his character, which, broadly viewed in the first act, becomes more sharply focused as the play develops. The sense of authority, for example, against which he rebels in the posture of Parris is a strong part of his nature. It is, in fact, his strength as well as his weakness, and Abigail recognizes it as soon as he enters the scene. Mary Warren feels the force of it most as she flees from it in Act One and because of it agrees to a humiliating scene of self-condemnation in Act Three before she succumbs to another authority, which will allow her a sense of self-preservation. Proctor believes in and respects authority. As much as he dislikes and fears the court, he appeals to its authority in the accepted fashion: he presents his deposition to Danforth. Correct in his feeling that "authority" is at the root of their problems in Salem, Proctor's ambivalent attitude toward it allows the "fever" to run its course.

It is commonplace to refer to Proctor as an honest, straightforward, and reasoning man; and to a certain extent he is described accurately. He is basically honest—to himself as well as to others—and when he has not been honest, he suffers accordingly. His guilt feelings, which emerge dramatically in the first scene of Act Two, are a painful reminder of his human frailty. From this point until his final decision in the play, his sense of guilt and dishonesty toward Elizabeth direct his actions—his early uneasiness toward Hale, his violence at Elizabeth's arrest, his anger at Mary Warren, his appearance at court, and the pleading, arguing, and damning that its activities excite in him. Yet, he is, withal, an honest man. Lies disturb and anger him, and it is a masterful stroke by the dramatist that he structured his play around lies to more forcefully reveal the character of his protagonist. Proctor is ever mindful that God damns the liar even if under stress he can lie to save his own neck from the hangman's noose. The "marvel" that he exclaims when he makes his decision between life and death is as much a marvel to him as he expects it to be to the others. It is also the ultimate revelation of the basic honesty that has characterized Proctor from the first act. Fraud and falseness are anathema to Proctor, and whenever he is aware of their existence, he points out the fact—in Abby, in Putnam, in the girls, in Hale, and in the court. It is a powerfully positioned irony that the falsehood of Elizabeth, so kindly meant, starts the events that condemn Proctor, when the truth might have set him free.

Honesty and goodness, however, may not be parallel virtues. The honest whore and the high-minded thief people both history and fiction. Readily admitting that to go to the gallows as a saint would be a fraud for him, Proctor recognizes his limited goodness—which is why his final decision excites him as it does. Perhaps his most revealing and heartrending cry is his response to Francis Nurse's horrified rejection of Proctor as a lecher: "Oh, Francis, I wish you had some evil in you that you might know me!" Absence from church services or plowing on Sunday are not severe moral problems for modern society; even allowing one's children to go unbaptized does not place one among the sinful. Seducing a seventeen-year-old girl is another matter. In most plays and in most lives such an act would condemn the seducer. It is a tribute to the dramatist's skill that Proctor can demand the audience's sympathy after his initial scene with Abby.

This scene has all of the elements of melodramatic sentiment in which the confident and aloof seducer coolly rejects the young and beautiful orphan. Knowing her effect upon him and reacting to his smile, Abigail pleads for "a word, John. A soft word." But he is distant and firm in avoiding her advances. He is "no wintry man," however, as Abigail well knows, and he admits to having looked up at her window. But when "she clutches him," he reacts with patronizing hardness and calls her "child." Elizabeth was right when she told her husband: "You have a faulty understanding of young girls." Nowhere in the play is that more clear than at this moment, and Abigail's righteous indignation strikes back with bitter anger—at Elizabeth, that spot in Proctor's soul that is most sensitive to pain. To this, Proctor responds with the threat of a whipping, which only reemphasizes his attitude toward her as a child. Even as Abby breaks into tears and tries to explain what their love has meant to her, Proctor is unmoved. Clearly, there is desperation in Abigail's words, but there also appears to be more honesty than design. Her final pleading cry, "John, pity me, pity me!" goes unanswered. [Although the wood scene between Abigail and Proctor, later added to introduce Act Three, softens Proctor's attitude as he warns her of what he will do in court, it shows that Elizabeth is right—Abigail has "an arrow" in him yet—and creates serious problems for the audience trying to understand the "goodness" he finally sees in himself. The scene is unnecessary dramatically and only confuses Proctor's character.]

In ordinary circumstances a scene such as this in a theater would have riveted the audience's emotions at obvious poles. In this instance, of course, Miller has carefully prepared the audience in the immediately previous scene to accept Abigail as a dissembling, designing, and even coarse and violent girl [as she "smacks" Betty "across the face"] who deserves the callous rejection Proctor gives her. (It is interesting that a French adaptor of Miller's play had difficulty accepting Proctor's behavior and the lack of sympathy allowed Abigail.) Proctor, however, remains the guilty seducer who has enjoyed Abby's love more than once, the lecher in the eyes of the community whose ungodly acts must be accepted as humanizing qualities of the common hero. They are also startling illustrations of the lack of good judgment that all "fools" to society occasionally exhibit.

A facet of Proctor's character, which undoubtedly helped his standing among members of his community, is his sense of humor. Interwoven among the strands of his contempt for a paranoid minister and his belligerence toward the embittered and vindictive Putnam, there is an attitude that allows him to see some lightness and frivolity in society. Granted this disposition toward humor turns bitter and disappears soon after the action in Act One, but it helps to define his character in the early scenes. There is also both light and black humor throughout the play, which Miller uses skillfully to change the pace of his revelation—Corey's adamant defense of his legal rights, his conscious and unconscious humor ["I am asked the question," Corey spits at the interrupting Parris in the opening scene of Act Three, "and I am old enough to answer it"], the drunk scene, which opens Act Four as Sarah Good and Tituba mistake His Majesty the Devil for a "bellowing cow," and the grotesque misconceptions of adults who take seriously the sporting of young girls in the "silly season." Parris also has his unconscious humor, especially when he asserts in great embarrassment that he never saw the girls naked; and Abigail's creative response to the contents of the boiling pot attests to a certain lightness.

Proctor, however, is the only character in the play with an ability to appreciate fully the silly side of people—more evidence of the fool he is to this serious society. He may well be the only one in the play who laughs and smiles in happiness and wonder. As soon as he has routed Mary Warren, at his appearance in Act One, he approaches Abigail with a "knowing smile": "What's this mischief here?" His teasing attitude continues and his smile widens: "Ah, you're wicked yet, aren't y'!" There is a light touch in their closeness, and she answers him honestly, explaining the girls' silliness. Then the mood changes. In the following scene among the adults, both Corey and Proctor exercise their wits to sharpen the edge of the growing confrontation with Parris. Corey notes Parris' expertise in arithmetic, while Proctor humorously compares his sermons to an auction, so much does he concentrate on deeds and mortgages. Proctor can make fun of Parris' assertion that there is a "faction and a party" in the church opposed to him, followers of Proctor. "What say you," he asks Corey with a smile, "let's find the party" and join it. He can also make fun of Corey and laugh not only at the old man's idiosyncrasies, but also at his own expense in dealing with them.

In this first act, Proctor shows his good humor as well as his solemn temper toward those for whom he holds no respect. He is too quick to accuse, of course, but this readiness comes from his intolerance of stupid people. Because he does not understand the seriousness of the situation, he can make jokes, and because he has heard that Hale is a sensible man, he can leave without fear for the future. As Act Two opens, he is still in a good mood as he talks with Elizabeth, but this mood changes. He is astonished and unable to grasp the reported activity at court. When he becomes defensive toward Elizabeth's judgments, his language shows the side of life he can enjoy, but his tone has changed: "Oh, Elizabeth, your justice would freeze beer!" From this point on he finds no joy in life. He tries to smile at Hale in the next scene, but the smile sinks within him.

The no-nonsense approach to life, buoyed by a good sense of humor, characterizes Proctor in Act One and contrasts with the attitude of the other adults (with the exception of Rebecca), but it also reflects the realistic atmosphere that permeates this act. As Proctor bursts upon the scene, he is a man to be dealt with. The girls recognize this instantly, just as he recognizes and dismisses their mischief as insignificant in the long run of things. When there appears to be no reason why Betty should scream, he is unnerved: "Girl, what ails you?" But Rebecca's explanation of young girls in their "silly season" satisfies him completely. Parris, he argues, had no business sending for someone to look for devils: it was not necessary. Children dying? "I see none dying," he says. His part in the argument with Parris shows him to be a hard-working, god-fearing man who expects others to be the same. If they do not measure up, he will tell them. To such self-serving and vindictive hypocrites as Parris and the Putnams, he is a world apart, and he cannot be in the scene when Hale infects their superstitions with his eager desire to confront the devil. The other reasonable person must also depart, and Rebecca leaves with the disturbing suggestion that neither Parris nor Hale distinguish between God and Satan with a convincing certainty. Then, immediately, the adults undertake to solve the problem, in Parris' ironic metaphor, to "open up the boil of all our troubles."

It is vital to the developing character of John Proctor that all of the actions in Act One have a perfectly rational explanation. Abigail lies easily; she is accustomed to looking out for herself, and lying comes naturally to her. She is also a strong person with a fierce control over the other girls, which she exercises whenever she finds it necessary; Betty, terrified on being discovered in the woods, is completely in her control. Goody Putnam is a superstitious, "twisted soul." Unable to reconcile her problems with events in the natural world, she unashamedly searches the world of the supernatural, becoming a ready tool for God or the devil. Abigail has an easier time lying to her uncle than she does to Hale, but she asserts her control when she understands what he wants and even invents a frog for the soup. When the going gets rough, she naturally blames someone else—Tituba. It would appear a hollow victory for Hale to force a confession from a poor, ignorant, superstitious black woman, but he rejoices in such accomplishments. Once Abby sees what is happening, she starts to play this game that seems to fascinate the adults. She helps Hale with more lies—realizing fully, in a way that shows her malicious character, that a condemned Tituba will solve her problems. All that Putnam has to say is that Tituba must hang, and she confesses with the rich imagination that her Barbados upbringing and superstitious nature make possible. The power of suggestion is strong upon her.

Combine this with her experience as a conjurer and her terrified determination to please these people who want to hang her and she would confess to anything. Excitement builds as the tension rises. As a person who wants to believe in conjuring and who enjoys the thrill of sporting naked in the woods, Abigail now sees another way of staying on the right side of those who seem to be in power. Betty, too, joins the chanting as she senses a way out of their situation. She is relieved, as the stage directions explain. So, too, is Parris who has been under tremendous pressures of anxiety since the opening of the act. Given the people, their particular characters, and the situation, everything has happened in a manner that can be logically explained. The utter chaos of man's mindless response comes later, and then Proctor must act.

As he tears and crumples his confession in the final scene of the play, Proctor makes a decision that is not easy to interpret with certainty. He says that he sees "some shred of goodness in John Proctor," and Elizabeth echoes this statement: "He have his goodness now." By such reasoning his choice reveals dignity and perhaps tragic stature, but there are other reasons of less than noble quality to consider. Proctor requires a sense of personal dignity, which he associates, symbolically, with his name; it is interesting that Abigail, in Act One, argues for her name in the same fashion. Proctor's sense of dignity, however, is based not so much on what he believes, as on what he sees other people thinking of him. He is angry with Elizabeth that she judges him harshly and angry with himself that she has the evidence to think as she does. He will not trade his condemnation of Danforth's court for Elizabeth's life: "These are my friends," he says, "their wives are also accused—" This strong decision by Proctor shows both his "goodness" toward society as well as society's pressure. Later, rationalizing that he is no saint, he decides to lie in order to live, but he is cut to the quick when he must repeat his lie before Rebecca who has only pity for him. He can confess, but his back stiffens when he learns that others will see his name: he will not be used.

Essentially, Proctor can be false to himself and before God, but not before his neighbors. His choice, then, is made under pressure from a force outside himself in the manner of melodrama. Hale sees it in yet another way and describes it bluntly: "It is pride, it is vanity." In other words, Proctor is a fool to so waste his life when it is not necessary in such corrupt circumstances. Does he, therefore, choose to be a martyr and sin once more? Does he, like Willy Loman, choose a meaningless death for the wrong reasons? Or is he truly enlightened by a personal discovery? There is room for argument.

However it came, Proctor's decision had immediate consequences. It also bore the imprint, directly or indirectly, of all the forces in society that he had been contending against since he first discovered Abby: evil, superstition, gossip, vengeance, malice. This was the society, the people whose "moral size" attracted the dramatist. Anyone of several could have been the protagonist of a play. Elizabeth, saved from the gallows by a discovered pregnancy, would have been the heroine of a nineteenth-century melodrama. Rebecca's story is that of the staunch Christian martyr—a lesson in Christian dogma there. Corey, as a stubborn man, became the central figure in a melodrama by Mary Wilkins Freeman, *Giles Corey, Yeoman* (1893). Mary Warren is that guileless, lonely girl who knows what is right but can be led to her own destruction. Although it might be difficult to make either Parris or Danforth the hero of a play, both have the potential for character conflict.

The Reverend Hale is one of the most substantial figures in *The Crucible* and can easily absorb the interest of the audience measuring the parallel action of the "fall" of John Hale with the "rise" to glory of John Proctor. Inasmuch as Proctor is concerned with the natural, visible world, Hale is concerned with the supernatural and spiritual world. In the beginning, like the Reverend Ravensworth in James Nelson Barker's *Superstition,* Hale mistakes his own eager certainty for the voice of God. But whereas Ravensworth remains a villain concerned only for revenge on the heroine who has not attended his church, Hale changes. Proctor's final decision comes as a surprise, but Hale reveals his change step-by-step and finally acts upon his discovery, which involves a reversal of fortune in good Aristotelian style. After asking the question in Act Two—"Is every defense an attack upon the court?"—Hale goes on to acknowledge the expressed fear of the court, to argue for Proctor and his deposition, to show his disdain for Abigail's games, and as the act ends to denounce "these proceedings" and quit the court. Although Proctor's condemnation is the main line of action during the scene, Hale's decision is more climactic and more dramatically placed than Proctor's cry that "God is dead." Proctor's words are also less meaningful to the audience and become merely a supportive statement to Hale's carefully dramatized change of view and momentous condemnation.

By Act Four, Hale is a completely changed man, a guilty man "steeped in sorrow," concerned only with trying to save those he has condemned by urging them to lie and confess a partnership with the devil. A great guilt has so perverted this man, no longer a man of God, that to ease the agony of his own soul he will urge others to sell theirs. His "moral size" also fascinates. Although Miller did not choose to dramatize his story completely, Hale's moral disintegration figures prominently in the final tableau of the play as he "weeps in frantic prayer" and is perhaps a more compelling vision for the audience than the apotheosis symbolized by the sun shining upon Elizabeth's face. Proctor was wrong; Hale was not a coward and, indeed, showed more strength than he—even in defeat while Proctor rose victorious. Neither, however, had particularly noble motives.

Whatever the possibilities presented, Miller chose not to dramatize the defeat of man but to assert, as he stated, "a positive kind of value." Proctor is his vehicle, this common man who acts neither the saint nor the hero, but speaks his mind when he feels he must. He would be an easy-going man if both he and other men measured up to his standards. Because his strong sense of pride has been chipped away by his guilt feelings, he is subject to social and personal pressures that make true nobility difficult to achieve. He is as reluctant to confess to lechery, which is true, as he is to confess to witchcraft, which is false. Yet both become real possibilities to him. Stating that he is not fool enough to get involved with a court that would suspect such a good woman as Elizabeth, he has been fool enough to get involved with a desperate and vicious girl and to antagonize the authoritative and powerful men of the community. And he is, eventually, fool enough to appear before the court in the manner of the court's choosing and under conditions that will not allow him to win. Obviously, the play has a positive value. Proctor's rise to "glory," by whatever interpretation one wishes to give it, asserts a positive statement. Yet, the evil social forces against which Proctor must contend are important in revealing the character of the man whose act symbolizes that statement.

It is a play of vengeance in which the lines of action are clearly and simply stated. Rejected by Proctor in Act One for a "cold, sniveling woman," Abigail takes her revenge. Except for the appended night scene in the woods, Abigail and Proctor never speak again as friends. The weak and despicable Parris sees an opportunity to avenge his pride toward those who do not attend his church and to protect his crumbling reputation. He is a small man who excited little sympathy from anyone and deserved little. Clearly, vengeance was "walking" in

Salem, and Thomas Putnam was part of that mysterious force. So, too, were the men of presumed good will, taking vengeance against the devil in the name of the Lord and mistaking the twitching of their own egos for the Word of God. In every instance that vengeance is turned upon Proctor.

It is a play in which private feuding erupts into controversies that overwhelm an entire community. This view supports Miller's idea that the problems of a single man are not sufficient to "contain the truth of the human situation." Yet a play must focus upon individuals whose discoveries and decisions determine both its actions and its theme. In this instance the object of the dramatist is to show the whole man—therefore, man as individual in conflict with himself (tragic possibilities) and the society (melodramatic possibilities). The initial situation of the play is well devised to present the social forces that in Act Two provide the major conflict for Proctor as he becomes aware of the court and reveals his temper, his strengths, and his failings. It would appear in Act Two that evil may win over a typically blind justice. Neither a Job nor a Lear, Proctor is a prideful and strong man who, in folly, both causes and curses his fate. As in any effective melodrama, the relentless forces of evil must appear inevitable. For this play these forces involve the theocratic processes run amok. That balance that once existed between order and freedom in that society—illustrated in the play by the character of Proctor as revealed in Act One—is being destroyed. Both social and personal conflicts are dramatized in the destruction of a man by deadly fraud and by a self-imposed hypnotism on the part of a society in panic. Symbolically, the climax suggests the end of an era, the waste of human lives, and the confused state of man as either a tragic figure whose personal disaster shatters the balance of the world or as a melodramatic hero whose committed choice for personal sacrifice and death returns order to the world.

Throughout the play it is Proctor who responds to situations and incites the action that determines the plot of the play. It is his story that is told after the exposition of Act One, as the petty problems supporting the theme of vengeance running through the play underscore the moral "rise" of John Proctor. A desperate and ironic tone, set at the beginning in a stage direction, is repeated at the end of the play: there is prayer and weeping, first by Parris and finally by Hale. Underlying this tone and fusing the real problems with the theme of vengeance are the paradoxes of life for which people like John Proctor have no defenses. The land that sustains the people is also a source for rivalry in which unaccommodated zeal may bring disaster; religion, a guide for spiritual peace and a satisfying social existence, has that explosive quality that in some people can destroy what it is supposed to create. As Proctor struggles to assert some control over individuals, he slowly determines his own fate, becoming both a victim of a social situation and a hero in his own mind.

Some people consider Proctor a fool because he did not choose to save his life, no questions asked. Be that as it may; it is an argument in which only a certain kind of person can find interest. The Proctor of this play could not have done so. But Proctor was a fool of his society long before he thought of having to make that choice. Consciously or unconsciously, Corey recognized the fact. That man who has the conviction and the courage to say what he thinks but is not consistently blessed with the best judgment in the creation of his thoughts—that man will be considered either a fool or a hero by society and sometimes both when he properly deserves to be neither. I write about myself and you—and John Proctor.

Why *A View from the Bridge* Went Down Well in London: The Story of a Revision

by J. L. Styan

I saw the first production of the revised two-act version of *A View from the Bridge* in London in 1956. It is generally known that Arthur Miller first wrote the play as a long one-act to go along with another, *A Memory of Two Mondays*, on the same bill. The two plays are quite different, the latter being his most Chekhovian, but in their subject both were reflecting the ugliness of the McCarthy period, in which "friendly witnesses" could betray their former friends to the Un-American Activities Committee, by reaffirming that communal human relationships were still at the root of social life. In Miller's words, they were written "at a time, in 1954, when it seemed to me that the very notion of human relatedness had come apart.... Whatever both plays are, they are at bottom reassertions of the existence of the community."[1] The program was altogether immensely relevant and significant and as it should be. Nevertheless, the production by Martin Ritt at the Coronet Theatre in New York on September 29, 1955, with Van Heflin as Eddie Carbone and J. Carrol Naish as the lawyer Alfieri, was unsuccessful. It ran for only 148 performances, which by any other standards than those of Broadway would be seen as a grateful achievement, but which in New York is close to a disaster.

For the original Viking edition of the two plays in 1955, Miller wrote a challenging preface entitled "On Social Plays," an essay that was preoccupied with the Greek idea of *polis*, the tribal and city unit of Greek society by which people organized their lives and to whose laws they adhered. "Social drama," Miller argues, was not primarily

"Why *A View from the Bridge* Went Down Well in London: The Story of a Revision" by J. L. Styan appears in print for the first time in this volume, with the author's permission.
[1]"What Makes Plays Endure?," in *The Theater Essays of Arthur Miller*, ed. Robert A. Martin (New York: Viking 1978), p. 260.

written as an attack on society in the manner of some plays of Ibsen and Shaw: it was historically an expression of a people's fate, or will, or destiny, and it "rises in stature and intensity in proportion to the weight of its application to all manner of men."[2] This preface, written before the final two-act version of *A View from the Bridge*, is central to the thinking behind much of Miller's early drama, and it unwittingly tells us a good deal about the play's failure in New York.

Miller believed his one-act play to be almost full-length, "needing only the addition of a little material to make it obvious as such," but that little material—what he elsewhere calls "ornamentation"—was exactly, he decided, what the play should *not* have. He has offered a variety of reasons for his astringency. There was no point at which the act curtain could naturally drop. He had exhausted his knowledge of the subject. It was his sense of form that the skeletal simplicity of the story should be preserved and the characters be seen only in relation to the theme of the play. Nothing else in Eddie's life was worthy of notice. He felt he had chanced upon an essentially mythological subject, "a sense of having somehow stumbled upon a hallowed tale," and he wanted to avoid "psycho-sexual romanticism."[3]

In spite of all this, Miller intimated that he had much more that he could have said:

> This is not to say that there is nothing more I could tell about any of the people involved. On the contrary—there is a great deal—several plays' worth, in fact. Furthermore, all the cues to great length of treatment are there in *A View from the Bridge*. It is wide open for a totally subjective treatment, involving, as it does, several elements which fashion has permitted us to consider down to the last detail. There are, after all, an incestuous motif, homosexuality, and, as I shall no doubt soon discover, eleven other neurotic patterns hidden within it, as well as the question of codes. It would be ripe for a slowly evolving drama through which the hero's antecedent life forces might, one by one, be brought to light until we know his relationships to his parents, his uncles, his grandmother, and the incident in his life which, when revealed toward the end of the second act, is clearly what drove him inevitably to this disaster.[4]

The antecedent life forces mentioned here are, of course, those very ones that Ibsen, Strindberg, and Chekhov worked so diligently at

---

[2]"On Social Plays," in *Essays*, p. 54.

[3]Ibid., p. 67. "Psycho-sexual romanticism" comes from Miller's introduction to the two-act version of the play (*Essays*, p. 219).

[4]Ibid., p. 66.

disclosing. But Miller assumed that his audience wanted to see only "a fine, high, always visible arc of forces *moving in full view* to a single explosion" (author's italics).

He was quite wrong. When the play was modestly revised and moderately enlarged as a two-act piece for the British production, directed and designed by Peter Brook (no less) for a "club" performance at the Comedy Theatre, London, on October 11, 1956, the London audience was taken by storm. It had a particularly strong cast, with a volcanic Anthony Quayle as Eddie, Michael Gwynn as a very dry Alfieri, Mary Ure and Megs Jenkins as the women, and Ian Bannen and Brian Bedford as the "submarines." The press notices made much of the sexual ingredients, probably because of the play's tussle with the censorship of the Lord Chamberlain's office. But I like to think that the play's success was due to its humanity. Jean Gould believes that "British audiences were spellbound by the complex emotions laid bare in a tale of the outwardly simple, hard-working lives of longshoremen"[5]—however that may be, British audiences certainly knew little, and perhaps cared less, about the activities of Senator McCarthy's committee. Miller himself reported that when he asked Peter Brook whether British audiences would understand the play, Brook replied:

> They may find it bizarre, but they like that sort of thing. What may put them off, though, is its logical inevitability. The British are terribly disturbed by any suggestion that the future is so closely determined by the present. If that were so, you see, we should have to blow our brains out. Of course, this is all happening in Brooklyn, and they may allow it there.[6]

Doubtless, Brook was here expressing a sly comment on the play he was directing, but he was also glancing at the dangers ever present in the too-logical form of tragedy, in which tragic inevitability can be as false to human experience as the world of farce. (Miller also reported that in France the logic was taken for granted, with the reason, or the result, that it became a tale of sexual passion: it ran in Paris for two years.)

But perhaps Brook was also making a comment on that side of Ibsen's social plays, and on that streak in Arthur Miller, which can be so preachy and destructive of a lively performance, inhibiting the necessary rapport between stage and audience, striking at the roots of

---

[5]*Modern American Playwrights* (New York: Dodd, Mead, 1966), p. 257.
[6]"What Makes Plays Endure?," in *Essays*, p. 261.

strong, expansive immediacy in the theater. At all events, Miller recognized that the London production was in "a different mood, a different key"—because it had a different purpose.

It is clear from reading Miller's comments on *A View from the Bridge* over the years (in the preface to the one-act 1955 edition, "On Social Plays," the introduction to the *Collected Plays* of 1957, the interview with Phillip Gelb for the *Educational Theatre Journal* of October 1958, the preface to the two-act version published in 1960, and a piece for the *New York Times* of August 15, 1965, "What Makes Plays Endure?") that the playwright has been worrying at the issues behind the play's composition, as well as behind the reception it has had at different times and places. If you believe, as I do, that a play is only beginning its life and being as a work of art at the time of its writing or publication, that some sense of its growth and power and true nature can only emerge as it demonstrates itself in performance under a variety of circumstances and conditions, it was entirely proper on the playwright's part to confront such problems as had evidently arisen in the case of *A View from the Bridge*.

To begin with, it seems that Miller is still not entirely certain in his own mind that he did the right thing in revising the play. The original one act he considered to have been appropriately telegraphic and unadorned. "Nothing was permitted which did not advance the progress of Eddie's catastrophe in a most direct way," and he wanted to write a more self-aware, intellectual drama, since "to bathe the audience in tears, to grip people by the age-old methods of suspense, to theatricalize life, in a word, seemed faintly absurd to me if not disgusting."[7] One can hear in this the voice of the reformer who knows he is tempting failure by kicking against the time-tested methods of putting an idea across in the theater.

So it was that the chorus-figure Alfieri and other characters were made to speak in verse, and the characters in Eddie's background, particularly his wife and niece, were drawn sparely and were deliberately undeveloped. Such characters were made to serve only the catastrophe. To match this, the set seemed bare and expressionistic:

> Like the play, the set is stripped of everything but its essential elements . . . [The room] is slightly elevated from the stage floor and is shaped in a free form designed to contain the acting space required, and that is all. At its back is an opaque wall-like shape, around whose right and left sides respectively entrances are made to an unseen kitchen and bedrooms.

[7]Introduction to the two-act version, in *Essays*, p. 219.

Even the acting was necessarily less realistic when the detail of setting and characterization were trimmed in this way. In a word, the mode of the play had become *abstract*, and something of ritual drama had begun to usurp the peepshow theater of the proscenium arch, but with none of the ritual preparation and expectation of the ancient audiences, and none of the form, finally, of a drama that involved the participation implied in the ritualistic inclination of the play's theme and its treatment. But it did not work. Had Miller created some actor's monster in Eddie Carbone? The author confessed that he and the New York company were aware that a strange style was called for, which they could not provide. The fact that *A View from the Bridge* readily lent itself to adaptation into so abstract a form as opera—and Renzo Rossellini's *Uno sguardo dal ponte* of 1961 appears to have been well received everywhere—suggests that the appropriate style might have been lyric.

Miller believed that the play, like *Death of a Salesman*, was a compound of expressionism and realism. I suppose he was thinking of the superficial elements of episodic scene construction, flashback, and choric speech. My sense is that both of these plays are far removed from the essential expressionism of its German ancestry. Prototypical expressionism may be seen as one of the basic modes of seeing and revealing human life, a defiantly subjective form of art in which the artist sought to impose his own intense, and often eccentric, view of the world on his subject and on his audience. The form of an expressionistic play "expressed" its content traditionally as a protest against authority and was particularly applicable to the per-fervid movement that gripped the German theater at the time of *Das junge Deutschland* in the 1910s and 1920s. But none of the characteristics of basic expressionism are seen in our play, the nightmarish atmosphere, the visual distortion, the stark decor, the disjointed and tableaulike scene structure, the dreamlike sequence of events, the total impersonality of the characters, the staccato, rhapsodic dialogue, the grotesque and mechanical acting of the expressionistic actor "externalizing" his thoughts and feelings.

By contrast, *A View from the Bridge* depends absolutely on its realistic content—the actual event of breaking the immigration laws and telling the whole truth about it. It is necessary to convince its audience with a plain story told in the authentic atmosphere of the Brooklyn dockland, and it has to speak through credible characters. The play obeys the laws, not of Greek tragedy nor of the German subjective expressionism, but, with no surprise, of nineteenth-century naturalism, whereby, at his best, the playwright encourages the audience to believe, to recognize, to respond in modestly human ways, to feel affinity with the activity on the stage by its small details of speech and behavior, in order that the drama can make the earth shake and the sky light up.

In London, the British actors could not handle the Brooklyn Italian-American dialect (not that Miller himself entirely shed a Jewish quality in the quasi-Sicilian lines, and Ruby Cohn quotes one like "You're savin' their lives, what're you worryin' about the table-cloth?" as a nice sample[8]). Miller consequently felt that "already naturalism had evaporated by this much," and that "the characters were slightly strange beings in a world of their own"[9]—although, of course, very few in the London audience could tell the difference between one American accent and another. There is a kind of British stage-American that serves well enough in a multitude of cases, a kind of mid-Atlantic, if not Sargasso Sea, blur. But the British Equity pay scale allowed a cast of twenty or more supers to represent the Sicilian community in Brooklyn, for whom Peter Brook proceeded to design one of those characteristic Jo Mielziner frame sets of apartment buildings with iron fire escapes and a maze of walks and alleys that served Tennessee Williams so well in *The Glass Menagerie* and *A Streetcar Named Desire*. Such a set seems to expose the characters' souls, like taking the lid off a pot of stew, in a way that no bare stage ever could.

Miller also believed that the British actors were able to assume a representative, larger-than-life attitude because they were accustomed to playing Shakespeare. This flatters them, although it is probably true to say that at that time few of them had been cramped by the reductive sort of acting demanded by the film and television camera. The British actors were acting their hearts out to convey the world of Brooklyn longshoremen.

The revision gave more time to the lives and motives of the characters that the first version had excluded, particularly those of Beatrice, Eddie's long-suffering wife, who feels that she has lost him to their niece. The physical details of the home were filled in, with a Christmas tree to add color and, let it be said, sympathy. Then, not surprisingly, "once Eddie had been placed squarely in his social context, among his people, the mythlike feeling of the story emerged of itself, and he could be made more human and less a figure, a

G. 79

[8]*Dialogue in American Drama* (Bloomington: Indiana Univ. Press, 1971), p. 83.
[9]Introduction to the two-act version, in *Essays*, p. 221.

force."[10] The paradox was this: when the stage and its actors were more real, the representative element of Eddie's story grew stronger. The play acquired, not blunted, but sharper edges from what might at first glance seem merely fussy. The drama, the conception behind the play, took on life and began to work. Even Eddie, who has been considered bestial for his incestuous feelings toward Catherine, and who is certainly as obtuse and inarticulate as any in the famous line of American dumb oxen after O'Neill's Yank, managed to endear himself to the sophisticated bourgeois audience in London's West End. The audience, even at a considerable distance both in space and experience, could understand and appreciate him.

Look again at the story. A Sicilian longshoreman working on the New York waterfront shelters two of his wife's relatives as illegal immigrants; when one of them wants to marry his niece, the longshoreman, in an incestuous rage, informs on them to the Immigration Bureau, but in doing so breaks the Sicilian code of honor and is consequently killed by the other. The parts of this story that do *not* require explanation, even to audiences who have never been to Italy or America, are those that touch the *natural* relationships—the ties of family, the bond between the man and his wife's relatives, the relationship between the man and his wife insofar as it is usual, their affection for their niece. Of course, these ties and bonds and relationships must be recognizably present in the signals of speech and behavior on the stage. The parts that *do* require explanation are the *unnatural*, the eccentric, the individual issues—the man's desire for his niece, his impulse to inform on his kin. These are the areas where the playwright and his team must work hardest to convince us of the reality of what we are seeing. They also happen to be the rather less successful elements in the play, although by no means destructively so. That today *A View from the Bridge* touches a sensitive nerve in its audiences everywhere suggests that Miller has solved his problem.

In the revised version, much more time is given to the women. Catherine not only threatens to take a job, she does so. That Beatrice now has no children makes Eddie's attitude toward Catherine a little less unnatural. Beatrice and Catherine are allowed to be more awake to their sexual dilemma by the addition of a whole new episode. It is in such matters that Miller moved away from the Greeks and their ritual symbolism, away from the social drama, away from the Ibsen of the social plays—perhaps toward Chekhov. The success here, in

[10]Ibid., p. 222.

Miller's words, was "to present rather than to represent an inter-pretation of reality."[11] It had nothing whatever to do with whether there was a detached chorus figure or not, or whether the characters spoke in a distancing verse or an intimate prose (in any case, the lines in both versions use most of the same words, even when they had been printed as verse). The lesson of naturalism insists that the tension at the heart of this play, that between the public social code and the private and individual psychology of the central character, be felt as real through convincing detail. Even when Ibsen wishes to reveal the condition of society, he examines the individual soul, Nora's, Mrs. Alving's, Hjalmar Ekdal's. Even when Brecht wishes to recite a universal parable, he tells the detailed story of one man's or woman's survival, Mother Courage's, Galileo's, Grusha's, Shen Te's.

So, in my view, the best parts of *A View from the Bridge* as we now have it could be those in the early part of the play, when fine detail and understatement are holding the stage and eliciting our new responses. Of course, the physical incidents that catch our attention are unforgettable, the sparring between Eddie and Rodolpho, Marco's threat with the chair held aloft, Eddie's angry kisses, first on Catherine's mouth and then on Rodolpho's, Marco's inevitable spit in Eddie's face—incidents fraught with the excitement that comes from their meaning. But they are only as effective as they are because of the many fine strokes and insights into human behavior that precede them and often stand in counterpoint with them. These are the strokes and insights that make Miller a major writer and lend an exact and authentic flavor of life to the stage action.

I think of Catherine's primping her hair at another longshoreman, Louis, and smoothing her skirt before Eddie.

> *Catherine.* I just got it. You like it?
> *Eddie.* Yeah, it's nice. And what happened to your hair?
> *Catherine.* You like it? I fixed it different. (*Calling to kitchen*) He's here, B!
> *Eddie.* Beautiful. Turn around, lemme see in the back. (*She turns for him*)
>   Oh, if your mother was alive to see you now! She wouldn't believe it.

I think of Eddie's reaching in his pocket for money to buy a new tablecloth to impress the submarines, after he had previously thought it unnecessary.

> *Beatrice.* . . . I didn't even buy a new tablecloth; I was gonna wash the walls . . .

---

[11]Introduction to the *Collected Plays*, in *Essays*, p. 164.

> *Eddie.* Listen, they'll think it's a millionaire's house compared to the way they live. Don't worry about the walls. They'll be thankful. (*To Catherine*): Whyn't you run down buy a tablecloth. Go ahead, here . . . (*He is reaching into his pocket*)

I like the way this is picked up by Catherine as she plans how she will spend her first pay packet.

> *Catherine.* . . . (*Bursting out*) I'm gonna buy all new dishes with my first pay! (*They laugh warmly*) I mean it. I'll fix up the whole house! I'll buy a rug!

It is a happy longshoreman who offers to bring home a supply of coffee from the hold of the ship he is unloading, and who teases his wife with the thought of a spider in the goods—indeed, they tease each other:

> *Beatrice.* Just be sure there's no spiders in it, will ya? I mean it. (*She directs this to Catherine, rolling her eyes upward*) I still remember that spider coming out of that bag he brung home—I nearly died.
> *Eddie.* You call that a spider? You oughta see what comes outa the bananas sometimes.
> *Beatrice.* Don't talk about it!
> *Eddie.* I seen spiders could stop a Buick.

And I think of the Catherine who brings and lights her uncle's cigar, with his concern that she might be holding the match too long:

> *Catherine.* Here! I'll light it for you! (*She strikes a match and holds it to his cigar. He puffs quietly*) Don't worry about me, Eddie, heh?
> *Eddie.* Don't burn yourself. (*Just in time she blows out the match*)

This moment is nicely set against her later gesture in sugaring Rodolpho's cup as Eddie watches them. It is such moments as these that paradoxically permit Eddie to die a representative, a symbolic, even a tragic figure. These are all additions to the original text, and some of the great moments in the play that appealed to the London audience in 1956 and to other audiences since. They are the Chekhovian moments.

Now, in fact, there were many such touches of Chekhovian poetry in the first version, too, and wisely carried into the second: Eddie's pleasure at the smell of the coffee in the hold ("it's like flowers, that smell") and Rodolpho's wonderment that there were no fountains in Brooklyn. The brilliant lines about the sardines in the ocean, and about oranges and lemons growing on trees, are not new. They are characteristic of Arthur Miller's more profound moments as a dramatic poet, when he leaves his medium to take care of his message. When he saw the New York revival of the play by Ulu Grosbard in 1965 (with Robert Duvall and Jon Voight as Eddie and Rodolpho), it was performed to the different responses of the mid-1960s. Laughter then at Catherine's prospect of earning fifty dollars a week, at wanting to buy a rug with her first pay. Laughter at her treasured virginity. The McCarthy years had been forgotten, the agonies of the immigration quotas unknown. But it was still the naturalistic detail that brought the play alive. As Miller reported, Eddie entered the play "not like a tragic character but a longshoremen scratching himself after a long day on the ships."[12]

We may, indeed, conclude that the extra lines were far from being "ornamentation." And it is not really surprising that Londoners and New Yorkers find good drama in the same play. When Miller displays dramatic insight beyond mere literacy, he is irresistible.

[12]"What Makes Plays Endure?," in *Essays*, p. 262.

A *Memory of Two Mondays:* Remembrance and Reflection in Arthur Miller

by Benjamin Nelson

"The play is memory."

So says Tom Wingfield of the story he is about to unfold in Tennessee Williams' *The Glass Menagerie.* So, too, might Bert say of the tale he tells in *A Memory of Two Mondays.* The similarity between the two dramas is striking. In both plays the characters are caught in the most ordinary and awful of human situations: attempting to exist meaningfully in a world which allows them no sensible reason for either existence or meaning.

Each play is about hope attempted and deferred, and in each, one character manages, however dubiously, to break out of the trap of deadening routine. But the break is neither conclusive nor complete, and both escapees, Tom Wingfield and Bert, carry their memories with them, more faithful—as Tom reminds himself—than they thought they would be. Each returns to his past in memoriam and with love, and each offers a final, mournful salute, as Tom's sister Laura blows out her candles and Bert's friend Kenneth concludes his song.

Moreover, each narrator speaks in great part for his author. Although Bert is no more an unerring autobiographical portrait of Miller than Tom is of Williams, both characters recall events based upon the playwrights' lives. Tom Wingfield remembers a family conflict similar to Williams' in St. Louis during the Depression, and Bert evokes the memory of the year and a half Miller worked in an automobile parts warehouse in Manhattan during the same bleak decade.

Like Miller, Bert is working in the warehouse to earn enough money to get to college. Like Miller, he becomes attached to the people with whom he works, gradually coming to know them and sharing their troubles, joys, hopes, and disillusionments. And then, following his author's footsteps, he leaves. On the morning of his departure he expects some kind of significant moment, a sign perhaps that his presence has meant something to his friends; but lost in their personal problems and the deadening morass of routine, they barely notice him. Bert steps out of one existence and into another without a single clarion call heralding the momentous event. And the play is over.

Because *A Memory of Two Mondays* is shaped by Bert's memory, the play is not wholly realistic. The recollections of the warehouse and its inhabitants are not as feverishly subjective as those which flicker through Willy Loman's distraught mind, but characters and incidents are dramatized as they are impressed upon Bert's consciousness; and when he chooses to stop the flow of memory and comment upon it, he simply does so, once in the middle of the play, as an interlude between the two Mondays he is recalling, and again toward the end of the drama, as a kind of premature coda. And since the play is memory, it advances less by plot than by a series of seemingly random incidents and casual relationships. But its apparently loose form is deceptive. *A Memory of Two Mondays* is no more an arbitrary collection of characters and events than are *Uncle Vanya* and *The Cherry Orchard*.* Beneath the outward aimlessness of its action is a tight, carefully conceived structure.

Although the first Monday is set in midsummer and the second in winter, their chronology is blurred. We do not know if the winter belongs to the same year as the preceding summer or to the following year. The two days are structured laterally, set parallel to each other like two railroad tracks, never touching yet integrally related as they move off toward eternity. The time sequence between them is not measured in hours or weeks but in the period it has taken Bert to earn his first semester's tuition at college. The transition is made as the first Monday draws to a close.

Bert and Kenneth decide to wash the incredibly filthy windows of the warehouse. As they do, summer light flows into the room, followed gradually by the harder and colder light of winter. While

---

*A Memory of Two Mondays is the most Chekhovian of Miller's plays. In its arrival-departure structure it is quite similar to the time pattern of Chekhov's dramas. And even more significantly, in its consideration of human attrition in the ceaseless ebb and flow of time it strikes a thematic chord that reverberates in all four of Chekhov's major plays.

Kenneth continues to wipe the windows, Bert moves out of the action for a moment and soliloquizes about the awesome eternality of the lives that surround and affect his:

> There's something so terrible here!
> There always was, and I don't know what.
> Gus, and Agnes, and Tommy and Larry, Jim and Patricia—
> Why does it make me so sad to see them every morning?
> It's like the subway;
> Every day I see the same people getting on
> And the same people getting off,
> And all that happens is that they get older. God!
> Sometimes it scares me; like all of us in the world
> Were riding back and forth across a great big room,
> From wall to wall and back again,
> And no end ever! Just no end![1]

Bert's lyrical contemplation signals the interlude between the two Mondays, and also provides the central image of the play while illuminating its meaning. Much less pertinent is the young man's second verse soliloquy toward the end. Although it exhibits Bert's adolescent self-consciousness ("Gee, it's peculiar to leave a place, forever! . . . They'll forget my name, and mix me up with another boy who worked here once, and went. Gee, it's a mystery!"), it too bluntly reemphasizes what the entire movement of the drama has already clarified. Like Linda Loman's little-men-also-suffer speech, it is sentimental but superfluous.

If, at the conclusion, Bert's departure remains unheralded, it is nevertheless the most positive action in the drama. It is both an escape from calcification and a movement toward an objective. From the beginning of the play, Bert is differentiated from the others by his youthful aspirations and his unassuming persistence in seeing them realized. Kenneth points to these differences when he conjectures that Bert must have "some strong idea in his mind."

"That's the thing, y'know," he affirms in the poignant awareness of his own weakness. "I often conceive them myself, but I'm all the time losin' them, though. It's the holdin' on—that's what does it. You can almost see it in him, y'know? He's holdin' on to something."[2]

Unobtrusively, even shyly, Bert is doing just that. He is stronger than the rest of them. He has his goal, and the play traces his approach

---

[1]Miller, *A Memory of Two Mondays, Collected Plays*, p. 358.
[2]Ibid., p. 341.

toward it by contrasting him with the others who "often conceive" goals, but are "all the time losin' them."

In one respect Bert resembles other Miller protagonists: he is on a quest for knowledge. Its literal manifestation is the college education for which he is working, but his instruction has already begun in the warehouse to which he has become so ambivalently attached. Bert's is the story of a boy's initiation into maturity, the bumpy voyage from the deceptive surety of innocence to the doubt and anguish bred of experience.

In another respect, Bert is markedly dissimilar to the usual Miller hero. The knowledge he gains is not so much an understanding of himself as it is the most tentative kind of intuition into the lives of the people with whom he has spent the past year. It is entirely fitting that at the end of the play Bert should come to no conclusions or resolutions about life, other than the realization that it is indeed a mystery. He leaves appropriately bewildered, and yet in his confusion he has quietly but emphatically taken the first important step in his education.

Interestingly, Miller has expressed astonishment that *A Memory of Two Mondays* was interpreted by many viewers as "something utterly sad and hopeless as a comment on life." Although he acknowledged the raucous despair of most of Bert's co-workers, the playwright nevertheless pointed to his protagonist as a manifestation of the affirmative in man.

"After all, from this endless, timeless, will-less environment," he argued, "a boy emerges who will not accept its defeat or its mood as final, and literally takes himself off on a quest for a higher gratification."[3]

Even though Miller's point about Bert is well taken, with respect to the play as a whole it is somewhat misleading. He may want us to focus our attention on Bert, but it is difficult to do so. The shyness, unobtrusiveness, and bewilderment which render the boy such a perfect evocation of youth on the verge of maturity, simultaneously mitigate his dynamism as the protagonist. For all his genuine strength and promise, he is dramatically the most passive character in the play.

Consequently, it is not so much the affirmation implied in Bert's escape which remains imprinted on the audience's memory, as it is "the endless, timeless, will-less environment" and the despair of those frustrated souls who stumble through it. We remember the

---

[3]Miller, "Introduction," *Collected Plays*, p. 49.

departing Bert, but we recall even more clearly and poignantly those who stay behind: Gus and Larry and Kenneth and Tommy and Agnes and Jimmy and Patricia and Raymond.* Together, like the denizens of *The Lower Depths*, they are the protagonists of *A Memory of Two Mondays*, and through them the play speaks sadly and humorously of change and inertia, hope and despair, life and death—all the aspects of the supreme mystery that Bert is only beginning to comprehend.

The two Mondays which the young man remembers are deceptively similar. The same characters are at the same jobs; their conversations are dotted with the same bits and pieces of repetitious dialogue; some of their jokes and most of their complaints are unchanged; even their wariness of the employer who comes to check on them each of these Mondays has not abated. Nevertheless, changes have taken place, and in two of the relationships they are readily recognizable.

The relationship between Kenneth and Tom Kelly almost completely reverses itself between the two Mondays. Kenneth, the sensitive, poetic young Irishman of the first scene, has begun to deteriorate in the second. He is still sensitive, compassionate, and appealing; but he is now slipping into alcoholism. It is not a marked dissipation, but his constant complaint that he can no longer remember the snatches of poetry which he formerly delighted in reciting is a painful indication of his slow but remorseless descent.

On the other hand, Tom Kelly has risen. The seemingly hopeless drunk of the first scene, teetering on the brink of expulsion from his job, has by some incredible exertion of will pulled himself together and become a respectable teetotaler. There is no precise correlation between the changes in the two men. They are not particularly close friends and there is no indication that they have influenced each other. Nonetheless, emerging out of their reversals is the element that defines each of them and most of their co-workers: a sense of loss.

Kenneth's charm and spontaneity have all but dissolved in a drunken torpor, and Tom, although he has apparently straightened himself out, has become somewhat unbearable, puffed up with an unattractive self-righteousness that contrasts ironically with the

---

*Tom Wingfield of *The Glass Menagerie* parallels Bert on this score, too. Although he is the narrator and the individual who has at least literally escaped from the trap his home has become, Tom is etched less clearly in the viewer's memory than the defeated mother and sister who remain eternally behind.

inebriate affability of his former self. Larry cuts to the heart of the change when he reminds Tom that he liked him better as an alcoholic.

"I mean it," he asserts. "Before, we only had to pick you up all the time; now you got opinions about everything."

Larry is also a study in loss, and his relationship with Patricia, the girl who works in the outer office, again emphasizes this motif and mood. On the first Monday Larry has just rebelled against his claustrophobic existence by buying a car he cannot afford. He has done so as an act of self-assertion over the protests of his wife, and his brother and sister who are both in debt to him but who never hesitate to remind him of his responsibilities. His casual invitation to Patricia to go driving is a further attempt to reassert his independence, and this new feeling of assurance reaches a peak when Larry rises majestically to the greatest challenge existence in the warehouse has to offer: finding a replacement for an obsolete truck part.

Locating the piece of machinery becomes a mock-heroic quest, and as Larry tells Bert how to find it, the rest of the workers group around him in open-mouthed wonder and respect. For a brief moment, man has chosen to do battle with the mechanized, deterministic jungle around him, to assert his will and conquer the forces that have victimized him.

> Get the key to the third floor from Miss Molloy. Go up there, and when you open the door you'll see those Model-T mufflers stacked up. . . . Well, go past the mufflers and you'll see a lot of bins going up to the ceiling. They're full of Marmon valves and ignition stuff. . . . Go past them and you'll come to a little corridor, see? At the end of the corridor is a pile of crates—I think there's some Maxwell differentials in there. Climb over the crates, but don't keep goin', see. Stand on top of the crates and turn right. Then bend down, and there's a bin—No, I tell you, get off the crates, and you can reach behind them, but to the right, and reach into that bin. There's a lot of Locomobile headnuts in there, but way back—you gotta stick your hand way in, see, and you'll find one of these.[4]

This is part search for the Holy Grail, part voyage into the Heart of Darkness, and part descent into Jack Benny's vault. In recent drama its closest parallel is Willy Faroughli's ecstatic triumph over that glittering symbol of modern, mechanized society, the pinball

---

[4]Miller, *A Memory of Two Mondays, Collected Plays*, p. 351.

machine, in Saroyan's *The Time of Your Life*. It is Larry's victory over necessity, and the moment is shiningly his.

On the second Monday he is confronted only with defeat. The car has been sold, an affair with Patricia is sputtering to a dismal conclusion, and he is once more between the pincers.

Larry's defeat is also Patricia's. The bright, brassy girl of the first Monday has hardened; the brass has begun to tarnish. There will be more Larrys for her, but without his sincerity. Like Kenneth and Tom, Patricia and Larry have lost some charm, some warmth, and some belief.

The other characters in the play do not change perceptibly. They act on the second Monday as they did on the first. Raymond, the manager, dourly attempts to keep the operation running smoothly; Gus lecherously teases Patricia; Agnes continues her spinsterly giggles and blushes; Jerry and Willy still display their crude efforts at sophistication; Frank the truckdriver still arranges his route so he can stop over with various girl friends strategically interspersed throughout the five boroughs of New York; and Jim loyally and quietly looks after his friend Gus.

But even for those to whom the second Monday is a carbon copy of the first, some measure of defeat is evident. Like a carbon, the second day lacks a freshness and spontaneity, a vitality which marks Bert's first recollections. And although the workers have not undergone marked alterations, they have still experienced loss. They have all grown older, wearier, and more disillusioned. We see them finally by winter light.

Kenneth has cleaned the windows to better view the sky, but instead he has opened onto a neighboring brothel. No one objects to the new vista but Kenneth, and when he complains to his employer about the morally dispiriting effects of such a spectacle, he is told quite matter-of-factly that perhaps he should not have washed the windows. The alternatives in this situation clearly mirror the choices for most of the characters: they must either accustom themselves to the darkness or be prepared to confront the reversals that letting in any light might entail. The majority have already acclimated themselves to the darkness.

Miller has termed *A Memory of Two Mondays* a "pathetic comedy." Certainly the strongest effect of the play is the genuine sympathy it evokes for all those who remain behind after Bert's departure. But the pathos of the drama never degenerates into sentimentality. One of the compelling reasons we feel compassion for these people is because they do not ask for it; they do not feel sorry for themselves. Loudly and actively they affirm their existences in that musty community, laughing, crying, even sporadically raging against their woefully circumscribed destinies. And nowhere is this phenomenon more graphically personified than in the character and situation of Gus, the coarse, indomitable old lecher whose vigor and defiance attain almost heroic dimensions.

Gus is actually the man hit hardest by adversity. In the first scene, while he is carousing away a drunken weekend with his friend Jim, his ailing wife dies. In the second scene, although he still makes obscene remarks, chases the girls, and growls defiance at his employer, he is a changed man, racked by the guilt he feels for his wife's death. But although Gus is finally destroyed, he goes down riotously and uncompromisingly on a monumental spree of drunken self-assertion.

He begins by intending to visit his wife's grave, but he never gets there. Instead he buys two fenders to put on an old wreck of a Ford he has picked up somewhere, and he spends the whole weekend lugging them around, until he finally brings them to the warehouse. Then he lashes out in a final rebellion against the accumulated monotony of his life, and stalks out. Drawing all his money out of the bank, he goes on one last great bender, purchasing new clothes, picking up some girls, hiring three taxis (one for himself, one for Jim, and the other to bring up the rear in case of emergency), and making a rum-sodden pilgrimage to every bar he can find. He finally dies in his taxi, amid his girls, in a rather bizarre approximation of Oriental splendor.

However, for all his vitality, bravado, and rebelliousness, Gus is crushed by the tonnage of twenty-two years in the warehouse. His valedictory speech, in which he traces those years in the cars he has serviced, beautifully illuminates his character and the themes of the play. Referring to his boss, he calls out to Bert and the others:

> When Mr Eagle was in high school I was already here. When there was Winston Six I was here. When was Minerva car I was here. When was Stanley Steamer I was here, and Stearns Knight, and Marmon was good car; I was here all them times. I was here first day Raymond come; he was young boy; work hard be manager. When Agnes still think she was gonna get married I was here. When was Locomobile, and Model K Ford and Model N Ford—all them different Fords, and Franklin was good car, Jordan car, Reo car, Pierce Arrow, Cleveland

car—all them was good cars. All them times I was here.[5]

"I know," Bert says sympathetically, and Gus replies, "You don't know nothing."

To a great extent he is right. Bert cannot fully comprehend the terrible obsolescence the older man has described. He does not even know why he should be the one fortunate enough to escape Gus's grim inventory.

For all its flamboyance, Gus's death symbolizes the defeat of those who remain; and by contrast to his final blaze of defiance, their corporate demise is marked by its implacable ordinariness. Just as Bert's achievement is unheralded, so is their failure. And it is ironically apropos that their reactions to the young man's departure are even more dulled by the news of Gus's death.

At the end, Bert walks, slowly, almost unwillingly toward the door, while around him there is constant activity. Willy snatches an order slip from the hook; Kenneth wraps a package; Jerry enters, picks up a parcel, and leaves; Jim arrives, drops some goods on the table, and exits; Larry comes in with a container of coffee and checks through some orders; Patricia enters and ambles past Bert to get some fresh air at the window; and Tom bumbles through a pile of goods on the table, checking a package against the order slip in his hand.

Arrivals. Departures. Perpetual motion. And yet the overwhelming stasis as time and circumstance combine to make a mockery of all this effort. Things are sent out, things are received—but nothing is really accomplished, and as the activity continues, time slips away, slowly and imperceptibly narrowing the circumferences of the lives that comprise the existence of that large, pallid room. Only the boy, edging hesitantly and disappointedly toward the door, makes a movement that is not circular and self-defeating.

A Memory of Two Mondays does not fit into any plan that neatly traces the thematic development of Arthur Miller. An almost flawlessly structured play, it shows the dramatist in complete control of his form, but basically departing from the major themes and conflicts that had interested him in the past and would again preoccupy him in future endeavors. The play does not deal with ethical problems; it contains no strong moral conflicts nor does it present the need for self-recognition, free choice, or commitment. It is not about family strife; and it does not pattern itself after a court of inquiry or a trial. It does not advocate, condemn, polemicize, or even judge.

[5]Ibid., p. 370.

It is elegiac in both form and mood, evoking a tragicomic portrait of human existence as it vacillates between the interrelated poles of death and rebirth. At the conclusion a man dies and a boy sets out on a new life, while in the balance a dozen lives are suspended in a limbo of attrition. But ultimately Bert is not the only one who is resurrected. He promises Kenneth that he will return.

"I'll come back sometime," he vows. "I'll visit you."

The play is the fulfillment of that promise. Bert returns, in love and in sorrow, in respect, and with a certain wonder, with a hail and a farewell. And by so doing, resurrects them all.

"Nothing in this book," wrote Miller in the Introduction to his *Collected Plays*, "was written with greater love, and for myself I love nothing printed here better than this play."

Obviously.

Pessimism in *After the Fall*

by Stephen S. Stanton

After the premiere, on January 23, 1964, of Arthur Miller's *After the Fall* at the ANTA—Washington Square Theatre, New York City, the critical reviews and interpretations were quick to point out many technical flaws and the supposedly shameless—some said voyeuristic—exposé of the playwright's turbulent marriage to Marilyn Monroe. Although many of the play's defects are still evident after nearly two decades (and some also appear in varying degrees in his other plays), the sensationally autobiographical nature of the play made it impossible to see in 1964 that Miller had evolved a new philosophy of life—albeit a more pessimistic one than he had expressed in any of his previous works. This essay reviews briefly the critical record, summarizing some of the more provocative and more limited or erroneous assessments to date of *After the Fall*. The play reveals, in confessional monologue form, an attitude intensely pessimistic, and one should not be deceived by the seemingly lighter tone of Miller's most recent plays—*The Price, The Creation of the World and Other Business, Up From Paradise,* and *The American Clock.*

Questioned about the audience's seeing the original production of *After the Fall* simply as a shocking, tasteless, and too revealing *pièce à clef,* Arthur Miller responded: "The play was never judged as a play at all. Good or bad, I would never know what it was from what I read about it, only what it was supposed to have been."[1] Throughout the 1960s and, for the most part, up to the present, the press has continued to interpret it in terms of Miller's earlier plays of the 1940s and 1950s, written before the eight-year silence that separated them

"Pessimism in *After the Fall*" by Stephen S. Stanton appears in print for the first time in this volume, with the author's permission.

[1] Olga Carlisle and Rose Styron, "Arthur Miller: An Interview," from *The Paris Review* (Summer 1966), pp. 61–98. Reprinted in *The Theater Essays of Arthur Miller,* ed. Robert A. Martin (New York: Viking, 1978), p. 283. A later citation is by page number in the text.

from *After the Fall*. In these plays the fate of mankind was seen as
socially ordered since society was the center of human life, "a power
and a mystery of custom and inside the man and surrounding him,
as the fish is in the sea and the sea inside the fish, his birthplace and
burial ground, promise and threat."[2] But *After the Fall* reveals Miller's
new assessment of society in the 1960s, the ultimate destiny of which
is irrevocably shaped by the nature of man. Miller sees this destiny as
destructively predetermined in a world without God, despite individual acts of free will tentatively (perhaps futilely) undertaken out
of "the urgent need inside the [protagonist] to keep his spirit alive
against all odds, even if he has to embark on a self-destructive course
of action."[3] Although Alfred Schwarz is speaking here of Miller's
plays generally, he is accepting them (including *After the Fall*) on their
own terms rather than according to preconceived notions of what
they were supposed to have been.

Some of the first reviews of *After the Fall*, however, and even later
studies accused Miller of totally absolving his hero Quentin from
guilt. Quentin has become estranged from his first wife and has
indirectly contributed to his second wife's suicide. Robert Brustein
wrote in *The New Republic* (February 8, 1964) that Miller is dishonest
because Quentin hides behind a veil of guilt that dissolves, leaving
him blameless. Gordon Rogoff claimed that Quentin's self-justification is not a synonym for justice (*The Nation*, February 10, 1964). That
Quentin shares Adam's innocence before the Fall and is absolved
from guilt or responsibility is Henry Popkin's contention in *Vogue*
(March 15, 1964). Quentin's goal in life is passing the buck, says
Popkin, and Holga, Quentin's prospective third wife (a German girl),
ignoring her country's guilt in the mass annihilation of Jews in World
War II, is aggressively innocent. This early insistence on the innocence of Miller's hero is perpetuated as late as 1971. In her chapter
on Miller's dialogue, Ruby Cohn writes: "Confessing his guilt,
[Quentin] actually implies his innocence; . . . Quentin is, finally, . . . a
slave to his illusion about personal success in paying lip service to
guilt. Instead of suicide, however, [he] goes blithely off to his third
marriage, playing God with his final stage gesture."[4]

[2]Arthur Miller, Introduction to the *Collected Plays* (New York: Viking, 1957).
Reprinted in *The Theater Essays of Arthur Miller*, ed. Robert A. Martin (New York:
Viking, 1978), p. 143.
[3]Alfred Schwarz, *From Büchner to Beckett: Dramatic Theory and the Modes of Tragic
Drama* (Athens: Ohio Univ. Press, 1978), p. 166.
[4]*Dialogue in American Drama* (Bloomington: Indiana Univ. Press, 1971), p. 90.

If Miller made his hero guiltless, as implied by the above commentaries, that was certainly not his intention, according to an interview between Arthur Miller and Robert Martin:[5]

> It's a play [said Miller] which is trying to recreate through one man an ethic on the basis of his observations of its violation. [Quentin] says, in effect, "I see perfectly well that we all harbor in ourselves the destruction of each other. We all harbor in ourselves these murderous desires. We all harbor in ourselves this breach of faith." I can't accept that as his last word. Why? Because if I do accept it as his last word, life has no reason for me. . . . [Quentin sees] that unless by an act of will he insists . . . that he creates good faith and behaves with good faith, it will never exist. He has got to will it into existence. And why? Because otherwise we're doomed. Otherwise, we're serving death. And he knows this because it is in himself . . . (37). Quentin sees the potential of disaster in himself. . . . There it is, I can't close my eyes to it, because it's there and it came from me—that perversity. But . . . that isn't the whole thing. . . . There's something else in there . . . (39).

Miller creates in Quentin an awareness that he can resist this perversity in himself and in human nature.

> He makes a choice at the end [to marry Holga]: "I choose to go that way." And we're fully aware that this struggle will never end (39).

Earlier in the interview, Miller put his philosophy of life very succinctly:

> What I'm trying to assert—or reaching toward—is a humanistic, but nevertheless universal, potential, I suppose, which has for me a mystical quality (36). [Man is] born trying to preserve life. He's born on the side of life, and we gradually teach ourselves how to enjoy death and all its manifestations, and how to give ourselves to it (37).

It is basically a Rousseauistic stance: man is instinctively good but is corrupted by society and by an illusion that the real nature of people is to be unified with one another.

> Implicit in [*After the Fall*] is the idea of a primeval unity of people, a community, a family which is all for one and one for all (37).

But Quentin has made the discovery that this illusion of societal harmony is false, that social amenities and conventions hide an intricate system of betrayals among people everywhere.

---

[5]Robert A. Martin, "Arthur Miller and the Meaning of Tragedy," *Modern Drama*, 13 (May 1970), 34–39. Further citations are by page number in the text.

Few of the early critics of *After the Fall* saw the play as anything but a self-vindicating confession of Miller's failure in his marriage to Marilyn Monroe, and the lurid accounts in the press that advertised first the couple's divorce and then Monroe's suicide forced Miller fans and detractors alike to see the play in a narrowly personal sense. A broader, more detached view of the play was hard to come by. The reason for this is that in his earlier plays Miller had held an over-simplified view of man, which sensitive readers had come to look for and expect. The heroes of the early plays: Joe Keller in *All My Sons*, Willy Loman in *Death of a Salesman*, John Proctor in *The Crucible*, and Eddie Carbone in *A View from the Bridge* were, despite moral or psychological limitations or their lack of self-knowledge, basically good men; Miller has always believed in the "gift of innocence" (the term is Martin's) inborn in humans that would be corrupted by society or betrayed by the illusion that society was a friendly, co-operative community where a person could be successful by simply being well liked. In *After the Fall* Miller rejects optimism; he is concerned rather with guilt, the impulse toward evil in all people.

One of the few critics to recognize the new Arthur Miller was Arthur Ganz, whose two articles, "The Silence of Arthur Miller" and "Arthur Miller: After the Silence," were published a year apart.[6] The first of these essays deals mostly with *Death of a Salesman* and Willy Loman, who, according to Ganz, is the chief spokesman for Miller's optimistic view of man. Willy's error is his failure to understand the harshness of the world he has tried to conquer; he never has learned to cope with the system: the law of the jungle. He is guilty of no really immoral behavior; his shallow philosophy of being well liked is not seen as dangerous or widespread; although he represents a deterioration of the pioneer code of the sturdy, simple man, he is not to blame for this either. He is simply a victim of forces beyond his control; he fails to understand that one can get on, despite the ruthless competition, through ability and hard work.

Ganz's second essay deals exclusively with *After the Fall* and shows Quentin as gaining knowledge of his own guilt. He has betrayed his parents, his friends, and his two wives, just as they have betrayed him. He is aware of a total lack of human brotherhood. Miller gives the reader "a glimpse of that guilt that one discovers not in deeds but in the ultimate depths of the self" (530). Presenting subtle states of

[6]*Drama Survey*, 3 (October 1963), 224–37; *Drama Survey*, 3 (Spring-Fall 1964), 520–30. Further citations are by page number in the text.

mind, though, has never been Miller's forte. Still, "his vision is now beginning to encompass the complexities of guilt" (530) that it never did before. Although Ganz agrees with the early critics when he asserts that "the least attractive aspect of *After the Fall* is undoubtedly its nagging tone of self-exculpation" (523), he nevertheless takes note of the new Miller: "the play remains an earnest point of view" (523). In his final speech Quentin "is attempting to reject that element of romantic optimism that has up to now underlain even the grimmest of Miller's plays. As he contemplates his past, Quentin comes to believe that he has felt in his own mind the impulse to genuine evil and that he has come to understand the nature of universal human guilt" (523). Professor Ganz, then, like Professor Schwarz, is taking *After the Fall* on its own terms, rather than trying to make it fit a preconceived pattern derived from the earlier plays.

New point of view, man's kinship with evil, and landmark in Miller's career notwithstanding, Ganz reminds us that *After the Fall* is not without its faults. Indeed, critics have not been slow to point them out. But there are strengths too; whether these outweigh the weaknesses will be left to the reader (or better still the viewer—for a play as nonrepresentational as this should be seen). These flaws and strengths can profitably be considered in relation to four main aspects of the play: structure, language and speech, characterization, and theme.

I
Structure

That Miller chose to write *After the Fall* in the expressionistic style clearly indicates that he visualized Quentin's discovery of the evil that he shares with all men as a moral issue of universal proportions. In the theater of this century, issues of such magnitude have often been cast in the mold of the expressionistic play, which uses symbolic images and generalized characters who embody ideas; hence they are presented as being larger than life. Miller had demonstrated his mastery of this dramatic style in *Death of a Salesman*. In 1956 he published an important essay, "The Family in Modern Drama," in which he wrote: "Expressionism . . . is a form of play which manifestly seeks to dramatize the conflict of either social, religious, ethical, or moral forces *per se*, and in their own naked roles, rather than to present psychologically realistic human characters in a more or less realistic environment."[7] To dramatize the conflict of forces, expressionistic plays—especially those of Strindberg—employ a loose structure consisting of a succession of abrupt transitions in time, space, and mood, rather than the traditional act structure of realistic plays. The protagonist often undergoes a symbolic journey in search of his identity in a hostile and bizarre world. The point of view is subjective and some if not all scenes are characterized by nightmare distortion, as they would appear to the disoriented central character (or the author). Classic examples of such characters are Willy Loman in *Death of a Salesman* and Blanche DuBois in Tennessee Williams' *A Streetcar Named Desire*. Expressionistic plays probe an irrational, inner reality at the unconscious level.

Ganz demonstrates that the expressionistic technique of *After the Fall* is not consistently maintained. After the early scenes, which evoke Miller's intended effect of "the surging, flitting, instantaneousness of a mind questing over its own surfaces and into its depths" (opening stage direction), the play ceases to mingle scenes from Quentin's adult life in free association with memories of his childhood and increasingly becomes an orderly, chronological presentation of the events of his more recent life. There is little sense of a controlling dramatic structure, and the play, like a chronicle history, presents an extensive series of scenes of varying effectiveness, but without a cohesive driving force behind them. Further, the faulty balance between the two acts of the play makes the reader endure a static first act, alternating between monologues and instances of painful experiences, before being caught up in the much more inherently dramatic action of Act Two, which focuses on Quentin's deteriorating marriage to Maggie. Another structural weakness, according to Ganz, is the positioning of Holga's long and important speech about the need to accept one's past. Her dream of an idiot child receiving a kiss of love, although movingly told, comes too early in the play and is immediately recognizable as a solution to the problem of Quentin's guilt. When he returns to this imagery at the end of the play, there is a sense of anticlimax rather than fulfillment.

This last point is emphasized by Edward Murray,[8] who agrees that the play fails to maintain rising tension. Murray finds that a faulty point of view traps Miller into needless repetition. Since "the action

---

[7]*The Atlantic Monthly*, 197 (April 1956). Reprinted in *The Theater Essays of Arthur Miller*, ed. Robert A. Martin (New York: Viking, 1978), p. 75.

[8]*Arthur Miller, Dramatist* (New York: Ungar, 1967), Chapter 6.

takes place in the mind, thought, and memory of Quentin," and the stage levels represent various levels of Quentin's consciousness, Miller's use of the monologue Listener device means that everything of importance is thus said twice, once in monologue and once in stage action. The method, according to Murray, is "not only repetitious but excessively abstract and didactic." In the first act Miller also uses foreshadowing in a clumsy and transparent way to create suspense over the forthcoming Quentin-Maggie marriage in Act Two. Twice an image of Maggie suddenly appears as though begging to be recognized by Quentin. He answers: "Maybe I can get to it later. I can't now . . ." (p. 12 in 1964 Viking ed.) and "I'll get to it, honey . . . I'll get to it" (p. 68). "Cutting" from one character or scene to another (cinematic juxtapositions, contrasts, and fadeouts are used throughout) suggests complexity, but in the final analysis results in superficial treatment of characters. Murray believes the play would have been more tightly constructed without the device of the Listener, which simply results in needless repetition. One eccentric variation of the expressionistic style used by Miller that Murray finds confusing is the materialization of Quentin from his own skull—that is to say, from among the representations that exist in his mind. One of the figures who move about on stage and exist in Quentin's consciousness is the one that addresses the audience.

Murray's objection to the domination of the stage action by one character is shared by Ruby Cohn, but whereas Murray finds Quentin's rational ordering of events excessively subjective, allowing the audience no critical detachment, Cohn's expectations of the protagonist's achieving self-awareness are disappointed by Miller's structural method. Although Quentin addresses the Listener "*consciously and explicitly*" and calls forth scenes in a controlled and deliberate way, he is for Cohn no more enlightened in the end than is Willy Loman in *Death of a Salesman*; yet Willy is more "mental" than Quentin in the sense that he "is at the mercy of his own random associations." Quentin simply becomes the victim of an illusion of innocence; Willy, of an illusion of success predicated on being well liked. Both critics find the expressionistic structure that keeps the action of the play within the mind and memory of Quentin ultimately unsatisfying and self-defeating.

Gerald Weales' quarrel with the structure of *After the Fall* is not that one character dominates the play, but that one character's positive decision at the end of the play to commit himself to Holga is almost predetermined from the beginning and yet is not made inevitable by the play's action. Quentin is worried at the start of the play because he continues to feel hopeful even though his life has been miserable. Indeed, he has already partially involved himself with Holga before the play begins, and before he learns that all his life he has tried to establish his innocence; any guilt he has felt about the way he mistreated a member of his family, a wife, or a friend he has transferred to that other person. In the end he comes to see that there is no innocence, that the guilt is solely his. But "once the illusion of innocence is pushed aside, a man is free to act—even to act as a lover. . . ."[9] This positive act, however, is "simply the residue left by the burning away of the naïve belief in man implicit in the early plays. In *After the Fall* and *Incident at Vichy*, the heroes are not in a struggle; they are in analysis. The analysis is successful when they accept that they fit the love-hate stereotype of the psychological man" (140). So the play has taught a lesson that allows him to carry out what he'd already planned to do. In contrast to *Death of a Salesman*, where all the scenes serve the play's action, "the remembered scenes [in *After the Fall*] do not have the look of experiences being undergone, but of illustrations to prove a point. Even if we were to believe that Quentin is actually coming to conclusions as we watch him, those conclusions—his acceptance of himself—do not lead logically nor dramatically to Holga. It is as though he stepped to the front of the stage and said: 'I have a few hours to kill before I meet a plane. Let me spend it describing the human condition'" (142).

What is one to make of all these shortcomings in the structure of *After the Fall*? I generally agree with Ganz that the play lacks a driving force; also I find the second act, dealing with Quentin's marriage to Maggie, much more intense and interesting than the first, which tries to fuse too many glimpses of Quentin's abortive past relationships: those with Louise, his first wife, with his parents, with his friends Lou and Mickey, and even with Felice, the divorcée whom he had helped and who perpetually appears with her unwanted blessing. And I agree that Holga's speech about having to take one's disfigured life in one's arms (the idiot child) dulls the audience's anticipation of the remedy for the dilemma of Quentin's guilt. Murray's objection to the device of the Listener is also valid, as many otherwise needless or plainly undramatic repetitions occur as a result of its use. I believe,

---

[9]"Arthur Miller's Shifting Image of Man," in *The American Theatre Today*, ed. A. S. Downer (New York: Basic Books, 1967). Reprinted in *Arthur Miller: A Collection of Critical Essays*, ed. R. W. Corrigan (Englewood Cliffs, N.J.: Prentice-Hall, 1969), p. 140. Further citations are by page number in the text.

however, that Weales trenchantly explains the chief structural draw-
back of the play: the lack of motivation for Quentin's decision to
venture a third marriage with Holga at the end. More will be said on
this point in the discussion of the Nazi concentration camp tower in
the section on theme.

These shortcomings notwithstanding, Miller has created two of the
most absorbing expressionistic—or nonrepresentational—plays of
the American theater. *Death of a Salesman* is certainly one of the best
expressionistic plays in our theater, its rivals being, in my opinion,
O'Neill's *The Hairy Ape*, Williams' *A Streetcar Named Desire*, and
Wilder's *Our Town*. That *After the Fall* is inferior to its predecessor,
although disappointing, is certainly no catastrophe for either Miller
or the American theater. It is a bold and engaging experiment.
Several of its scenes—notably one in the middle of Act Two, in which
the deteriorating marriage of Quentin and Maggie is telescoped into
a continuous conversation, although in reality several years are
passing—are masterpieces. The skillful way in which the double time
scheme is sustained in this particular scene is a *tour de force* of effective
craftsmanship in the expressionistic style, which often presents life as
unfolding in a dreamlike manner, outside time and space.

II
Language and Speech

Probably the most universally criticized component of *After the Fall*
is the language used by the characters, especially in Quentin's
monologues. All the critics have commented adversely about his
tendency to talk endlessly (often with affected elegance of language)
and act little except as audience for the scenes his memory calls up.
Ruby Cohn, Arthur Ganz, Robert Heilman, and others pick out
examples of his abstractions and forced images, which often make
him appear self-righteous, pompous, and without humor. Here are a
few of them: *(1)* "I feel like a mirror in which [Felice] somehow saw
herself as . . . glorious" (p. 7 in Viking ed.); "That whole cemetery—I
saw it like a field of buried mirrors in which the living merely saw
themselves" (7). What do these mirror images mean? Both live *and*
dead people are compared to mirrors. The second image, in which
Quentin generalizes about his dead mother, is especially vague.
Often there is a confusion or an inappropriateness in the logic of
Miller's images. *(2)* "How few the days are that hold the mind in

place; like a tapestry hanging on four or five hooks. Especially the day you stop becoming; the day you merely are. I suppose it's when the principles dissolve, and instead of the general gray of what ought to be you begin to see what is. Even the bench by the park seems alive, having held so many actual men. The word 'Now' is like a bomb through the window, and it ticks" (47). This monologue seems empty—pretentious rather than sententious. The park bench is a kind of metaphor for Maggie who soon appears. Not only will she seem "alive, having held so many actual men," but the word "now" will be used several times to connote her nature. Yet, as foreshadowing the speech is inadequate; the buried allusions to Maggie go unnoticed. *(3)* Quentin tells Louise, "We are killing one another with abstractions" (61), and their endless bickering about whether or not one should be "a separate person" without resolving their temperamental differences attests to the rightness of the remark. *(4)* Another passage open to some question is Quentin's long concluding speech, which communicates the theme of the play. Realizing his capacity to kill, he moves toward the Nazi concentration camp tower "*as toward a terrible God*," and says, "Who can be innocent again on this mountain of skulls? I tell you what I know! My brothers died here . . . *He looks down at the fallen Maggie* . . . but my brothers built this place; our hearts have cut these stones!" (127). The knowledge "that we are very dangerous" finally gives him the courage to hope. He continues: "Is the knowing all? To know, and even happily that we meet unblessed; not in some garden of wax fruit and painted trees, that lie of Eden, but after, after the Fall, after many, many deaths. Is the knowing all? And the wish to kill is never killed, but with some gift of courage one may look into its face when it appears, and with a stroke of love—as to an idiot in the house—forgive it; again and again . . . forever?" (128).

Ruby Cohn does not find the union of the central verbal image "idiot" (used frequently in the play to signify betrayal), and the central visual image of the Nazi concentration camp tower dramatically functional. Whether one agrees or not, Quentin's calling Eden a "lie," as Robert Heilman points out,[10] creates a muddled metaphor because if that sanctuary to which we retreat to recover our lost innocence is only a mirage, then there has not been a Fall at all. Quentin is insisting that man's original sin did not take place in the

---

[10]*The Iceman, The Arsonist, and The Troubled Agent: Tragedy and Melodrama on the Modern Stage* (Seattle: Univ. of Washington Press, 1973), p. 155.

Garden of Eden, but has been present throughout history in man's propensity to evil. Perhaps Miller reconsidered the contradiction when he titled one of his more recent works *Up from Paradise.*

III
Characterization

If Quentin's cerebral confessions force the play to lose drive, Miller's dramatic instinct helped to offset this deficiency to some extent in his portrayal of minor characters. Although Quentin does not wish to be recognized as a Jew because he sees himself as having an affinity with the Nazi persecutors as well as the persecuted Jews, Mother and Father speak with Brooklyn Jewish zest; Mother is touchingly humorous in recalling her early romance with Strauss, the penniless medical student ("Who knew he'd end up so big in the gallstones?"), yet she is venomous toward Father, who displays a cynical humor before he is broken by the 1929 crash. Maggie is naïvely lovable with her grammatical slips and folksy Americanisms. Because of their abbreviated presentation, however, the reactions of minor characters are exaggerated or incomprehensible. Their abrupt appearances are incomplete and inadequately prepared. Why does Felice express effusive thanks to Quentin? Why does Holga show deep hurt? Maggie, mordant hatred? What does Mother's contempt of Father have to do with Quentin's malaise? Devoid of complexities and faults, Felice and Holga simply provide reassuring contrasts to Louise, Mother, and Maggie, all of whom betray and are betrayed by Quentin. As perpetual awarder of blessings, Felice simply serves to build Quentin's confidence. As constant bearer of flowers, Holga too easily symbolizes man's courage to face the full knowledge of his guilt.

IV
Theme

Faults *After the Fall* has then in plenty: lack of driving force; recollected moments scattered in time and space, which often cloud meaning; the hero's commitment to wife number three not inevitably motivated; universal complicity implying easy acceptance of one's psychological nature; remembered scenes serving as illustrations, not as felt experiences; affected language with strained images. Wherein lies the special distinction of this play?

According to Raymond H. Reno, "*After the Fall* . . . discloses twenty years of dramatic activity as taking the shape of a vast work dealing with the death of God."[11] Most of Miller's plays "fit together so as to constitute something of a corporate work" (1069) and an allegory. "From *All My Sons* to *After the Fall*, Miller has been dismantling the Christian myth" (1084). We are alerted to this ambitious theme (which began with Chris Keller in the first play destroying his father through exposure of his guilt) when Quentin voices his despair early in the play: "I think now that my disaster really began when I looked up one day . . . and the bench was empty. No judge in sight. And all that remained was the endless argument with oneself, this pointless litigation of existence before an empty bench" (p. 3 in Viking ed.). One of Quentin's most disillusioning memories is that of his father betraying his family by losing everything in the crash of 1929, thus proving himself an "idiot," to use Quentin's mother's term. "If projected on a larger screen," Reno explains, "a son's discovery that his father is a fraud takes on the shape of a worshiper's discovery that his deity is a fraud" (1073). Just after the early speech quoted above, Quentin expresses a vague hope about the future, a hope that is articulated only at the end of the play. Holga "hopes, because she knows? What burning cities taught her and the death of love taught me—that we are very dangerous!" (128). Our salvation lies in the knowledge that we meet unblessed. "We can conquer the wish to kill only with some gift of courage . . . and with a stroke of love . . . forgive it." *After the Fall* makes explicit what has been implicit in Miller's previous plays, that when the father is destroyed, God is destroyed; that *we alone* can judge ourselves because the bench is empty. "There is no Christ, only potential Cains who must each be his own Christ and forgive himself" (1086).

The sinister Nazi watch tower, which lights up whenever Quentin experiences guilt over his failures and betrayals of loved ones, is Miller's way of communicating this theme of Cain playing Christ. Allaying the demon of Cain in man is man's only hope of salvation. Yet, "human love cannot in itself overcome this demon because when human love strives to imitate God's infinite love, it is corrupted

---

[11]"Arthur Miller and the Death of God," *Texas Studies in Literature and Language*, 11 (Summer 1969), 1069–1087. Further citations are by page number in the text.

into power, and the resulting egocentricity only serves to arouse the Cain within us. Whoever goes to save another person with the lie of limitless love throws a shadow on the face of God" (p. 119 in Viking ed.). The tower as metaphor for Miller's secular version of "original sin"—the acknowledgement of continuous evil in *all* men—has been judged farfetched by many critics. "Miller . . . postulates in Quentin, and in us all, depths of aggression in some degree analogous to those that led to the horrors of Nazism. That such depths exist is at least a tenable contention; that Miller has demonstrated them in Quentin is, however, doubtful" (Ganz). Only in his relationship with Maggie does Quentin reveal destructive hostility to any great degree, but after all, Maggie is a very psychotic person. "Quentin, a lawyer, fails to promote a convincing case for his own incrimination in the slaughter of Jews during the war. . . . Can common self-interest be equated with genocide? If everyone possesses the urge to kill, is everyone equally guilty for actual murders? . . . Quentin does not accumulate enough data to answer these questions" (Moss).[12] "The concentration-camp tower that broods over the whole play . . . is the element in the play that is most difficult to take, but it is a necessary part of the idea Miller has imposed on his play" (Weales).

Unconvincing as the stage symbol of the tower may be to suggest extension of guilt from the personal to the social, Miller tries to emphasize it after Quentin's love for Maggie has given way to hate in his attempt to kill her. To show that Quentin is beginning to link his own awareness of guilt with the most heinous social betrayal in history, Miller has the Nazi tower light, "fierce, implacable," as Quentin says, "My innocence, you see? To get that back you kill most easily" (p. 126 in Viking ed.). Holga's repetition of "no one they didn't kill can be innocent again" (23, 127) bridges national and linguistic boundaries. Quentin's big speech, which concludes the play, incorporates Holga's words: "Who can be innocent again on this mountain of skulls?" Even if Quentin's acceptance of himself does not lead dramatically to Holga, Miller tries hard to make it lead in that direction, although the circumstances of Holga's involvement in wartime political activities are not made very clear or plausible.

If the conclusion of the play seems too pat, it is worth speculating how else it might have ended. In two interviews Miller has outlined two possible endings: (1) "[Quentin sees] that unless . . . he creates

---

[12]Leonard Moss, *Arthur Miller* (New York: Twayne, 1967), pp. 85–86. Further citations are by page number in the text.

good faith . . . , it will never exist. He has got to will it into existence. . . . otherwise we're doomed" (in Martin, "Tragedy," 37); (2) "Look, *After the Fall* would have been altogether different if by some means the hero was killed, or shot himself. Then we would have been in business" (Carlisle and Styron, in Martin, *Essays* 287). The public, in other words, saw no resemblance between Quentin's experience and their own, and wished Quentin (surrogate for Arthur Miller) to die, defeated by his death of love. But Miller wants his hero to offer a hesitant, skeptical alternative to life without hope, "life without conviction, without real feeling of any kind. . . . simply a life surviving within this scheme of mutual destruction" (in Martin, "Tragedy," 38). Life is more than a game of this kind because of man's ability to use free will in a world without God. As Quentin struggles with his memories of betrayal and failure, he gains a sudden awareness of a truth that he denied earlier: "we are all separate people" (p. 119 in Viking ed.). Each of us has a unique identity that is not merely an extension of someone else's needs and concerns; each of us must try to see how his actions will affect others; each of us has a responsibility not only to himself but also to others.[13] In the face of new knowledge that ego directs all our motives, Quentin determines to attempt to pacify his own destructive impulse. Since Miller has acknowledged a debt to Albert Camus' *The Fall* (Moss 130, footnote 23), he undoubtedly sees the union of Quentin and Holga as the commencement of a lonely existential quest for man's moral stability and redemption through an awareness of his complicity with Cain. If they (and all people) undertake the journey with hope, courage, love, and forgiveness, there is just a chance that we may transcend mere survival within a "scheme of mutual destruction"—"the main thing is not to be afraid."

---

[13]See Robert W. Corrigan's article on Miller in *Contemporary Dramatists*, ed. James Vinson (New York: St. Martin's, 1973), pp. 540–44.

Arthur Miller's *Incident at Vichy*:
A Sartrean Interpretation

by Lawrence D. Lowenthal

In 1944, just after Paris was liberated from the Nazi occupation, Jean Paul Sartre sat at the Café de Flore on the Left Bank and wrote *Anti Semite and Jew (Reflexions sur la Question Juive)*, a fascinating and controversial analysis of Europe's most terrifying problem. Twenty years later, America's leading dramatist, Arthur Miller, wrote a long, one-act play about the holocaust, called *Incident at Vichy*. Although Ronald Hayman, an English critic, recently suggested that "a good case could be made for calling Arthur Miller the most Sartrean of living playwrights,"[1] no critic has yet pointed out that *Vichy* is an explicit dramatic rendition of Sartre's treatise on Jews, as well as a clear structural example of Sartre's definition of the existential "theatre of situation."

This affinity between Sartre and Miller is understandable when one considers the existential development of Miller's later plays. Beginning with *The Misfits*, Miller's works begin to shift the tragic perspective from man's remediable alienation from society to man's hopeless alienation from the universe and from himself. *After the Fall*, *Incident at Vichy*, and *The Price* are all organized around "absurdist" themes of metaphysical anxiety, personal solitude, and moral ambivalence. Quite clearly, one presumes, the accumulated impact of international and personal tragedies has strained Miller's faith in man's ability to overcome social and spiritual diseases. Miller no longer has any illusion about a "Grand Design" whose revelation will enable man to live harmoniously as a social being. His characters now grope alone for values to sustain their dissipating lives and each

"Arthur Miller's *Incident at Vichy*: A Sartrean Interpretation" by Lawrence D. Lowenthal. From *Modern Drama*, 18 (March 1975), 29–41. Copyright © 1975 by the University of Toronto, Graduate Centre for Study of Drama. Reprinted by permission of the editor of *Modern Drama*, Jill Levenson.
[1]"Arthur Miller," *Encounter*, November 1970, p. 73.

value, once discovered, slips again into ambiguity. Most frightening of all is the realization that human corruption, once attributed to conscious deviation from recognizable moral norms, is now seen as an irresistible impulse in the heart of man. The theme of universal guilt becomes increasingly and despairingly affirmed. But Miller's belief in original sin in a world without God does not preclude the possibility of personal redemption, for Miller shares Sartre's insistence on free will and the possibility of "transcendence" or the recreation of self through a succession of choices.

Miller's existential concerns are clearly delineated in *Vichy*, a play that reminds us immediately of Sartre's "The Wall" and *The Victors*. In all these works a fundamental Sartrean thesis is dramatized: "A man's secret, the very frontier of his freedom is his power of resistance to torture and death."[2]

Structurally, *Vichy* answers Sartre's call for "situational drama" which, he hoped, would replace the outmoded drama of "character" so prevalent in the contemporary bourgeois theatre. In a famous article, "Forgers of Myth," written in 1946, Sartre described situational drama as "short and violent, sometimes reduced to the dimensions of a single long act"[3] "A single set, a few entrances, a few exits, intense arguments among the characters who defend their individual rights with passion. . . ."[4]

Each character is displayed as a free being, entirely indeterminate, who must choose his own being when confronted with certain necessities."[5] Men do not have "ready made" natures, consistent throughout alternating circumstances—a primary assumption in the theatre of character—but are rather naked wills, pure, free choices whose passion unites with action.

The characters in *Vichy* are not simply "types" or "public speakers with a symbolic role" as one critic maintains;[6] on the contrary they are dynamic, fluid, undetermined beings, "freedoms caught in a trap," to use a Sartrean phrase. We know nothing about them, aside from their professions, until they reveal themselves through their choices of behavior, and their choices often prove to be surprising. They are all faced with undeniable limits to these choices, but within

[2]Quoted ibid., p. 74.

[3]"Forgers of Myth," in *Playwrights on Playwriting*, ed. Toby Cole, New York, 1960, p. 123.

[4]Ibid., p. 122.

[5]Ibid., p. 117.

[6]Robert Brustein, *Seasons of Discontent*, New York, 1967, p. 260.

these limits they are always free to act. The Jew can resist or submit; the German can murder or rebel. The structural movement of the play is existential in that individual possibilities for evading choice are methodically decreased. As each Jew is taken into the dreaded office, the option to revolt becomes more difficult. The traditional palliatives of reason, civilization, political ideology, and culture which ordinarily stand between man and the absurd are dispelled, one by one, until each character is made to face the realities of torture and irrational deaths.

Miller's play, though existentialist in theme, is rationalistic in structure. Like Sartre, Miller writes about the absurd in coherent terms. Miller's intention is still to explore "sheer process itself. How things connected,"[7] and although his discovery of cause and effect patterns no longer reveals "the hidden laws of the gods" with any certainty, the disasters in the play do not spring from a mysterious void as they do in the absurdist plays of Beckett and Ionesco. The central crisis is, of course, precipitated by Nazism, but Miller's analysis of the cause of this evil is more existential than political or sociological, and is expressed in terms of the Sartrean concepts of Nothingness and Dread.

Sartrean "dread" is a state-of-being arising from one's confrontation with "contingency," or the inherent meaninglessness of the physical world. Sartre's vision of ontological chaos or the absurd is most graphically described in *Nausea,* his first novel. As Roquentin, the narrator, sits idly on a park bench, he sees the root of a chestnut tree suddenly ooze into viscosity before his eyes. Flowing obscenely beyond its bounds, its shape, its position amidst other physical objects, the tree suddenly loses its essence as a tree and becomes merely substance, *there*, without reason or justification. The tree's abandonment of its *a priori* essence compels Roquentin to acknowledge the general fact of the world's contingency: "I mean that one cannot define existence as necessity. . . . Everything is gratuitous. . . . When you realize this, your heart turns upside down and everything begins to float."[8] Roquentin's awareness that "existence comes before essence" is the starting point of Sartre's philosophy. Beginning as an undefinable consciousness in a world of innately undefinable objects, man finds himself responsible for imposing himself on the

[7]"The Shadows of the Gods," in *American Playwrights on Drama*, ed. Horst Frenz, New York, 1965, p. 139.
[8]*Nausea*, Norfolk, Conn., undated, p. 176.

world and creating a reason for his existence. The realization of his superfluity leaves man forlorn because "neither within him nor without does he find anything to cling to. He can't start making excuses for himself."[9]

Roquentin's psychic epiphany in *Nausea* is paralleled in *Incident at Vichy* by the phenomenon of Nazism. Both events undermine all assumptions about the necessity of human existence. The Nazis are the fulfillment of Ivan Karamazov's cry, "everything is permitted." Their boundless evil is like Roquentin's oozing tree. Like the tree's outrageous proliferation which shatters the theory that essence precedes existence, the Nazis' refusal to abide by the rules of civilization makes a mockery of all illusions about moral behavior, social order, and humanist conceptions of man. If civilized people like the Germans can suddenly become uncivilized monsters, then one's belief in the continuity of human essence is destroyed. As Von Berg says, "What one used to conceive a human being to be will have no room on this earth."[10] The effect of this transformation stuns those who retain the civilized codes, now seen as absurdly fragile artifices, and arouses the sense of "nausea" that afflicts Roquentin. Von Berg is the first to recognize the implication of the Nazi power. When told of the death camps in Poland, he says, "I find it the most believable atrocity I have heard." When asked why, he replies: "Because it is so inconceivably vile. That is their power, to do the inconceivable; it paralyzes the rest of us" (p. 61). The Nazis are like Camus' "plague" which falls upon our safe and ordered lives and alienates us from all harmonious connections with the universe. In the wake of their attack on civilization lies the void, the disintegrated wreckage of all human constructs against the threat of chaos. "Who can ever save us," cries Von Berg after his awakening (p. 107).

But Von Berg's plea is, of course, the starting point for existential ethics, for if man can no longer find refuge in external deities and beliefs, he must look for sanctions within himself. Since existence is neither inherently necessary or predefined, man is free in that he is permanently in flux; his capacity for self definition is therefore illimitable: "Man is nothing but that which he makes of himself," Sartre writes, "that is the first principle of existentialism."[11] The only

[9]"Existentialism," in *A Casebook on Existentialism*, ed. William Spanos, New York, 1964, p. 282.

[10]*Incident at Vichy*, New York, 1967, p. 61. Subsequent references are cited in the text.

[11]"Existentialism," p. 278.

solution to the devastation wrecked upon human security by the plague is a responsible and free human action, an end in itself, which will momentarily solidify the relentless flow of our inner and outer being. But it is precisely this obligation that causes dread in man. As Sartre says, "Man is condemned to be free." The constant necessity to reassert and redefine values, projects, and commitments—the perpetual challenge to justify one's life—produces anguish, the feeling that results when we confront "the absolute openness of our future, the nothingness in the center of which we live."[12] Rather than commit himself to responsible actions without recourse to outside justification, man clings instead to "bad faith," that "lie in the soul," as Sartre calls it, which enables him to flee from responsibility into determinism.

Bad faith appears in a variety of forms: the coward abandons freedom by fabricating excuses for his condition; the masochist accepts the congealed image imposed upon him by the Other; the "salaud" claims special rights to existence in accord with a fabricated, a priori system of values and assumptions. The persecutors and victims in Miller's play clearly illustrate one or more of these types.

The Nazi, to begin with, is the most violent example of Sartre's concept of the anti-Semite—the most dangerous man of "bad faith." If the phenomenon of Nazism illuminates the horror of contingency to the naive civilized man, Nazism itself can be seen as a flight from the same Nothingness. The Nazi is incapable of accepting his condition of freedom. He flees from consciousness which reveals to him the contingency of the human condition, the openness of all truth, the limitless and elusive possibilities of his self image, and chooses instead "impenetrability," the durability of a stone.[13] He cannot tolerate the continual suspension of his existence but wishes "to exist all at once and right away" (p. 19). Sartre's concept is clearly expressed by Von Berg's analysis of the Germans, who assiduously "despise everything that is not German": "They do these things not because they are Germans but because they are nothing. It is the hallmark of our age—the less you exist the more important it is to make a clear impression" (p. 61).

Fleeing from Nothingness, the Germans find refuge in the "durable stone" of Nazi ideology. Their lives, as a result, far from being gratuitous, become absolutely necessary: they have "rights," like

[12]Maurice Cranston, *Jean Paul Sartre*, New York, 1962, p. 49.
[13]*Anti-Semite and Jew*, trans. George J. Becker, New York, 1962, p. 18. Subsequent references are cited in the text.

Lucien, the anti-Semite in Sartre's short story "The Childhood of a Leader," but these "rights" can only be affirmed by denying them to other people. Like the actors in Genet's *The Balcony* who need the cooperation of the Other in order for the game of illusion to be maintained, the Nazi needs the Jew to affirm his illusion of personal necessity. "If the Jew did not exist," Sartre says, "the anti-Semite would have to invent him" (p. 13).

Anti-Semitism, therefore, is an ontological phenomena in that it reveals a yearning for a cohesive sense of being, a passion for essence. Because one's essence, however, is continuously nihilated by the Nothingness that separates man from what he was and what he wants to be, the anti-Semite must repress his consciousness and thereby convert a false assumption into a sacred belief. To achieve this aim, the anti-Semite divides the world into a Manichean duality of good and evil—gentiles and Jews—and to sustain this duality he must be constantly alert, wary of any sudden, rational intrusion into his fabrication.

Anti-Semitism is thus a freely chosen project which crystalizes the world and the individual anti-Semite's place in it. He no longer fears isolation, ego deflation, or purposelessness; he belongs not only to his country, a condition forever barred to the alien Jew, but also to the community of anti-Semites to which he clings. His essence is clearly defined, tangible, and, in his own mind, empirically defensible.

The Professor in *Vichy* is the clearest example of the Nazis' "bad faith." Armed with the scientific conclusions of the "Race Institute," the Professor's function is to separate "inferiors" like Jews and gypsies from the superior race. His "rights" as a superior person, sanctioned to live whereas other people are not, are never questioned: "Science is not capricious," he tells the Major. "My degree is in racial anthropology" (p. 65). The Professor is a "salaud" and he fits Sartre's description of the anti-Semite as a "destroyer in function, a sadist with a pure heart. . . . He knows that he is wicked, but since he does evil for the sake of Good, since a whole people waits for deliverance at his hands, he looks upon himself as a sanctified evildoer" (p. 50). The Professor's "bad faith" extends beyond his scientific assertion of "rights and duties" to a disavowal of personal responsibility for the acts he performs: "I will not continue without you, Major. The Army's responsibility is quite as great as mine here (p. 67). By diffusing all responsibility, the Professor hopes to de-individualize himself; he seeks facelessness in the collective unit of the Nazi apparatus because, even though he is scientifically convinced of his "rights" as a German, he is unwilling to stand alone and assume the consequences of his assertion.

The Jews themselves all face an existential crisis: "The Jew remains the stranger, the intruder, the unassimilated at the heart of our society," Sartre writes (p. 83). As Sartre says: "To be a Jew is to be thrown into—to be abandoned to—the situation of a Jew" (p. 88). The particular situation of the Jew is to be looked at by the anti-Semite. This "look" of the other is the essence of Sartre's concept of Being-for-Others—a mode of existence clearly illustrated by the Jew's relationship with his enemy. "Conflict," Sartre says, "is the original meaning of Being-for-Others."[14] One's consciousness, Sartre says, is unreflective of itself and needs the presence not only of objects but of the Other's subjectivity to realize its structure of being. We determine ourselves according to the other's image of us. But the confrontation between two individuals results in a struggle to undermine the freedom of each since the Other's look is unfortunately negative and enslaving.

The presence of the Other is Sartre's version of the fall, since the Other cuts off man's freedom and renders him vulnerable to feelings of shame and ossification. The loss of innocence is the consciousness of being seen and the consequent guilt one feels in the "look" of the Other. The Other freezes our possibilities for transcendence by imposing on us a "Nature," an outside, an objective identity. We are no longer in process but are fixed in the jelled image of the Other's gaze. Because the "look" is reciprocative, human relations become a relentless, see-saw battle of wills, each person attempting to wriggle out of the Medusa stare of the Other in a desperate effort to regain freedom. The antagonists often collapse into the bad faith of sadism and masochism in order to end the struggle.

In the Jew–anti-Semite confrontation, the anti-Semite sadistically objectifies the Jew in order to justify his own existence, while the Jew often submits to this manipulation in order to escape the struggle toward transcendence. But the masochistic Jew will always feel anguish because he knows that within his violently narrow sphere he is free to make choices. If nothing else, he is free to determine his attitude toward uncontrollable circumstances. In his situation, therefore, the Jew can either act authentically by maintaining a "lucid

---

[14]*Being and Nothingness*, trans. Hazel Barnes, New York, 1956, p. 367.

consciousness" of the situation and assuming the risks and responsibilities it involves (meaning, to defy the gaze of the anti-Semite), or
inauthentically by escaping into the "bad faith" of cowardice and
masochism.

Marchand, the wealthy merchant, acts inauthentically by removing
himself from his fellow Jews and indirectly denying his Jewishness.
Similar to Birenshatz in Sartre's novel, *The Reprieve*, Marchand is
disgusted by the Jewishness of others and considers himself to be
purely French. But, as Sartre says, "If the Jew has decided that his
race does not exist, it is up to him to prove it: for a Jew cannot choose
not to be a Jew" (p. 89). The Nazis release Marchand, presumably
because they still consider him useful, but once they choose to
manifest his "race" all his efforts to repudiate their "look" will be in
vain.

Both Miller and Sartre agree that a Jew cannot be defined by
religion, race, or national identity: one is a Jew if a gentile says one is
a Jew, a thesis Miller previously affirmed in his novel *Focus*. Quite
simply, Sartre says, "what makes the Jew is his concrete situation,
what unites him to other Jews is the identity of their situation"
(p. 145). The look of the gentile circumscribes the situation of a Jew
and defines the choices he is compelled to make. In *Vichy* the Jews are
thrust into their Jewishness. The victims in the play, aside from the
religious old man, are either indifferent or hostile to their Jewishness. Each considers himself French, and each identifies himself with
his profession or political ideology rather than his religion. There is
no feeling of unity in their mutual crisis and even their physical
movements on stage lead away from their fellow victims toward a
brooding isolation. What unites them technically into a "we" consciousness is simply the fact that the Nazi, or the "third" as Sartre
would call him, looks upon them hostilely as a collective unit. The
Jew experiences the "look" of the anti-Semite as a community
alienation, but his sense of "community" ironically arouses only fear
and antagonism.

The artist Lebeau, for example, is a masochist who feels a
Kafkaesque sense of guilt because he is a Jew and is driven by his
humiliation and despair into a death wish. He waits for slaughter like
a naughty child waits for parental punishment: "I don't know. Maybe
it's that they keep saying such terrible things about us, and you can't
answer. And after years of it you . . . I wouldn't say you believe it,
but . . . you do, a little" (p. 80). Sartre points out that this kind of
inferiority complex is not actually received from the outside, but that

the Jew "creates this complex when he chooses to live out his situation in an unauthentic manner. He has allowed himself to be persuaded by the anti-Semites; he is the first victim of their propaganda" (p. 94). Lebeau accepts the image of himself that he sees reflected in the eyes of the Other, and instead of transcending the Other's gaze, he allows himself to be paralyzed and destroyed. He relinquishes his freedom as a man in order to sink into the blissful passivity of a Thing. Like the Nazi, who solidifies himself in the role of "Superior One," Lebeau escapes his crisis by falling into the stone-like posture of "victim." His struggle ends in resigned submission.

Bayard, the communist, can suppress his panic only by depersonalizing himself. He is the Sartrean "man of seriousness," like Brunet, the dedicated party worker in *Roads to Freedom*, whose individual fate will be redeemed by the inevitable proletarian victory. Bayard, too, is guilty of "bad faith": like the Professor he abdicates his freedom by dissolving his individuality in a collective mass, and by turning back on the existential present for the theoretical proletarian revolt in the future. Von Berg's pointed assertion that most Nazis are from the working class damages Bayard's thesis, but he continues to delude himself in the absence of any other defense. Without his communistic idealism, Bayard explains, "I wouldn't have the strength to walk through that door" (p. 54). Like Sartre's Brunet, Bayard is an attractive character, strong, alert and ideologically sincere, but his absolute belief in historical determinism compromises his authenticity.

Monceau, an actor, puts the reality of the Absurd at a distance by fabricating an image for himself as he does on stage. He believes he can flee from his crisis into the illusion of a role. Believing that the Nazis are like dangerous animals who can sniff out the fear in their victims, he will *act* as if he is unafraid, for salvation lies simply in the ability to convince one's executioners that one is not a victim. Monceau refuses to acknowledge the absence of reason in their plight and chooses instead to delude himself into believing the Nazis cannot be as monstrous as people say and that civilization has not ended, despite all the evidence to the contrary: "I go on the assumption that if I obey the law with dignity I will live in peace" (p. 82). Pushed by Leduc to the extremity of his illusion, Monceau finally admits that if the world is mad, there is nothing he can do but submit to its madness, a conclusion which draws from Leduc the despairing remark: "Your heart is conquered territory, mister" (p. 83).

Like Lebeau, Monceau succumbs to the temptation of "impenetrability." He, too, is masochistic, an object to be casually destroyed by the hostile Other. His "bad faith" lies in his refusal to acknowledge the mutability of the world, its potentiality for alteration through human action. But action demands revolt, and, as in the case of Lebeau, the role of rebel proves more terrifying to him than the role of victim.

The dramatic core of the play is the moral debate between the psychiatrist Leduc, the German Major, and Von Berg. Their arguments revolve around Miller's central question: What is the nature and possibility of responsibility in a world acknowledged to be absurd? The German Major, according to his statements to Leduc, is a decent man who despises Nazi brutality and madness, but in order for him to protest against this evil he would have to sacrifice his life. Furthermore, his sacrifice would change absolutely nothing because, as he tells Leduc, "We would all be replaced by tomorrow morning, wouldn't we?" (p. 85). All that he would gain from helping Leduc escape would be Leduc's love and respect, but the Major cannot accept this reward as adequate compensation because, "Nothing of that kind is left, don't you understand that yet?" (p. 86).

The Major's "bad faith" is similar to Monceau's: Both men relinquish their freedom by submitting to what they insist is an overwhelming determinism. "There are no persons anymore, don't you see that? There will never be persons again," the Major shouts (p. 87). Responsibility and ethics in a fallen world become meaningless words to the Major, but his plea of helplessness is merely an evasion of his own tormenting moral impulses.

The Major, like Garcin in Sartre's *No Exit*, is guilty of essentialism. He tries to convince Leduc that he has an essence of decency which circumstances cannot violate. "Captain, I would only like to say that . . . this is all as inconceivable to me as it is to you. Can you believe that?" (p. 85). But Miller, like Sartre, insists on defining character through action. Since essence is never given but rather chosen and constantly renewed, a man *is* what he *does*, and all the Major's civilized instincts are nullified by his uncivilized acts. "I'd believe it if you shot yourself," Leduc replies. "And better yet, if you took a few of them with you" (p. 85).

Deprived of his decent "nature" by the scornful "Look" of Leduc, the Major now tries to ensnare a new being completely outside himself. Exploding with hysterical fury, he hurls himself into the role of anti-Semite by making the Jews cower under his pistol: "Like dogs, Jew-dogs—look at him—with his paws folded. Look what happens when I yell at him, Dog" (p. 87). Submitting to the lure of sadism, the

Major now decides to be nothing but the fear he inspires in others. By conforming his words and gestures to the disquieting image he sees in the eyes of his victim, he achieves a solid reality and momentarily dispels his anguish.

The Major's sadistic "bad faith" is further reinforced when he skillfully challenges Leduc's assumption of moral superiority. By forcing Leduc to admit that his innocence is coincident with his present role of victim, the Major makes clear the circumstantial nature of morality. When asked by the Major if he would refuse to be released while his fellow Jews were kept prisoners, Leduc is forced to answer "no." It becomes clear that the foundation for moral stability is precarious, and even decent men like Leduc would rather survive in disgrace than die with honor. Under these circumstances, the efficacy of individual moral action becomes buried in an infinite chain of destructive power: an executioner like the Major is himself a victim, acting in response to a gun pointing at his head. In a crisis situation, when individual moral action can only be equated with self destruction and when evil is seen as a constant in human relations, all rational motives for decency decay and the world collapses into moral anarchy.

Up to this point, Miller seems to have presented a nihilistic vision. Von Berg, however, is Miller's answer to despair. Like Sartre's Orestes in *The Flies*, he is the existential hero who wrenches himself from passivity to engagement by freely committing a sacrificial act. Von Berg's act is absurd in that it has no rational basis, but it elevates him to moral authenticity. His rebellion annihilates the nausea brought on by his understanding of the Nazi plague and his realization of his personal complicity in the holocaust, a realization unknown to him until his conversation with Leduc toward the end of the play. Leduc convinces the apparently innocent Von Berg that he harbors in his heart, unknown to himself, "a dislike, if not hatred of Jews," not like an ordinary anti-Semite, but simply as a human being who must somehow objectify his need to despise "that stranger, that agony we cannot feel, that death we look at like a cold abstraction" (p. 105). For Von Berg, the Jew fulfills Heidegger's concept of "the one" upon whom we thrust off the threat of death: "one dies," we say, never imagining the statement to apply to ourselves. "Each man has his Jew; it is the other," Leduc says. "And the Jews have their Jews" (p. 105). The hunger for survival makes accomplices of us all.

Von Berg's sacrifice, however, eradicates his guilt as victimizer and confirms his previously untested assertion that "there are people who would find it easier to die than stain one finger with this murder" (p. 104). Von Berg's present action throws Leduc's accusation of complicity into the irrelevant past. Von Berg, in effect, becomes what he does: by dying in Leduc's place he translates his guilt into active responsibility and becomes Leduc's "Jew."

Leduc is now stained by Von Berg's gift of life and must carry on the existential cycle of transmuting his guilt into redemptive action. He is free, like all men, to transcend his present action by choosing a new and redeeming project. If Leduc fights in the Resistance, he will modify the guilt brought on by Von Berg's sacrifice: the death of the weak aristocrat will then be justified by the services of the strong combat officer. Until he performs that action, however, Leduc will feel as morally debased as the Major who also saves his life at the expense of the Other.

Von Berg is the only triumphant character in the play since death will cut him off at his highest point and permanently fix his essence as martyr. His act frees him from alienation and imposes a moral coherence upon his previously contingent world.

The varied threads of the intellectual and emotional debate finally crystallize around the concrete act of Von Berg. A moral norm is unequivocally established: One's life must submit to one's conscience, despite the absence of any external moral criteria. All the characters in the play, particularly the Major, are judged by Von Berg's "Look," and since Von Berg will die, his look becomes uneradicable. Of course the possibility of the Major's moral transcendence in the eyes of others continues to exist, but under the implacable gaze of Von Berg the Major can never alter his constitution as a degraded object.

The play thus represents in its total action the essence of Sartre's philosophy, which was, and still is, the demand for authenticity, or the moral awakening to individual responsibility. But if Miller follows Sartre in the general theme, structure, and dynamics of his play, his implied conclusion to the threat of anti-Semitism differs radically from Sartre's *Anti-Semite and Jew*. Ironically, Sartre offers an optimistic proposal to the problem while Miller remains doubtful and pessimistic. In the twenty-one years between the publication of *Being and Nothingness* and the production of *Incident at Vichy* the two writers have exchanged philosophic positions—Miller subscribing to Sartre's corrosive analysis of human relations in *Being and Nothingness* and Sartre affirming Miller's former belief in human solidarity.

Despite Sartre's analysis of anti-Semitism as a cowardly search for being and, therefore, an ontological problem, he nevertheless concludes that the Jew's dilemma is social and consequently remediable.

Sartre's ordinarily complex and tough-minded Marxism seems simplistic and contradictory in *Anti-Semite and Jew*. While allowing for the freedom of the anti-Semite, Sartre nevertheless believes that an alteration of the anti-Semite's situation will consequently alter his choice of being. Existential free will and socialist determinism are unsatisfactorily mixed. With the advent of the Marxist state, Sartre predicts, all members would feel a mutual bond of solidarity because they would all be engaged in a common enterprise, and anti-Semitism would naturally disappear. Man's fear of being would be overcome by the benevolent leadership of the unbiased proletarian, the abolition of private ownership of land, and the consequent elimination of class struggles.

As Sartre's political activism increased, Miller's early leftist enthusiasm diminished. Leduc undoubtedly speaks for the playwright when he insists that "man is not reasonable, that he is full of murder, that his ideals are only the little tax he pays for the right to hate and kill with a clear conscience" (p. 104). Leduc's description might well fit the brutal characters in Sartre's early play *No Exit*, that grim dramatization of human interaction as outlined in *Being and Nothingnes*. Since the void at the heart of being is a static condition, man's attempts to escape it through sadism and masochism cannot be expected to change.

Understandably, *Incident at Vichy* has been attacked by left wing critics. Eric Mottram has accused Miller of expounding nihilistic despair: "Miller can only see the present repeated endlessly as the future . . . Miller can suggest no argument for the future based on social change, through economic legislation, education and sexual understanding."[15] Miller would answer that he is still a liberal, but his faith in the efficacy of social reform has diminished since man's evil, he now feels, is directly related to his fear of existence, an unalterable condition even in the Marxist "utopia."

Tom F. Driver, writing from a theological perspective, criticizes Miller's loss of faith in a "universal moral sanction" and his subsequent failure to discover a conceivable basis for a new one.[16] Miller

---

[15]"Arthur Miller: The Development of a Political Dramatist in America," in *Arthur Miller: A Collection of Critical Essays*, ed. Robert W. Corrigan, Englewood Cliffs, New Jersey, 1969, pp. 55–6.

[16]"Strength and Weakness in Arthur Miller," *Arthur Miller*, ed. Robert Corrigan, p. 65.

does offer a "lesson" in *Incident at Vichy* however: If man can awaken to his complicity in evil, he can exchange his guilt for responsibility, as does Von Berg. But Miller admits that "it is immensely difficult to be human precisely because we cannot detect our own hostility in our own actions. It is tragic, fatal blindness. . . ."[17] Driver describes the existential nature of Miller's conclusions:

> There being no objective good and evil, and no imperative other than conscience, man himself must be made to bear the full burden of creating his values and living up to them. The immensity of this task is beyond human capacity . . . to insist upon it without reference to ultimate truth is to create a situation productive of despair.[18]

Obviously, however, this moral task is not "beyond human capacity" since Von Berg succeeds in fulfilling it. It is well to remember that Miller based his play on a true story.

Undeniably, Miller's moral imperative is difficult. His attack on Jewish victims like Lebeau and Monceau, who willingly submit to their destruction, may seem callous, especially since Miller concedes the terrible plight of the escaped Jew in occupied Europe. But in the claustrophobic intensity of the drama, Miller succeeds in turning us against these inauthentic characters. He strips away all extenuating circumstances and brings each man into an irreducible conflict with his fate. There is no mitigation of the harsh necessity to choose ourselves, especially since Miller seems to agree with the Sartrean ethic that what one chooses for oneself, one chooses for all men. Miller is, in essence, dramatizing Sartre's famous account of the freedom one felt in France during the Occupation, "When the choice each of us made with our life was an authentic choice because it was made face to face with death."[19] Man is always capable of saying "no," even to his torturer.

Von Berg chooses to say "no" to the men and circumstances that threaten to degrade him, and he therefore fits Miller's definition of the tragic hero in his early essay, "Tragedy and the Common Man." Although the play is grim, it is not "productive of despair" since the heroic action of a frightened and delicate man sets the norm for all the characters. If Miller now seems pessimistic about Mankind, he is

---

[17]"Our Guilt for the World's Evil," quoted by Leonard Moss, *Arthur Miller*, New Haven, 1967, p. 97.

[18]Driver, p. 66.

[19]Quoted by William Barrett, "Jean Paul Sartre," in *On Contemporary Literature*, ed. Richard Kostelanetz, New York, 1964, p. 557.

still optimistic about individual man. Solidarity between two individuals is achieved; a gentile has broken through the ontological barrier that makes an enemy or an object of the Jew; and guilt has been eradicated through heroic action. If it is clear at the end that Evil is unredeemable and that the horror just witnessed will be repeated after the arrival of new prisoners, the cycle of complicity has been momentarily broken and the human reaffirmed.

Eric Mottram has negatively described the climax of *Vichy* as "an act of courage and love within the context of nihilism."[20] But is this statement not an apt description of some of the most powerful of modern tragedies?

[20]Mottram, p. 54

All About Talk: Arthur Miller's *The Price*

by Gerald Weales

When Arthur Miller's *The Price* opened in New York on February 7, 1968, most of the daily reviewers, whether they praised or damned the play, responded to the talkiness of it. Clive Barnes, condescending to Miller in an essentially favorable review in the New York *Times* (February 8), said, "The action has ended before the play starts, and we the audience have been brought here to listen to the explanations." Richard Watts Jr. complained in the New York *Post* (February 8) that "discussion goes on and on," and an even more disgruntled Martin Gottfried (*Women's Wear Daily*, February 8) insisted that "discussion . . . kills the play." The magazine critics echoed their daily colleagues. Robert Brustein, in one of his typical attacks on Miller (*New Republic*, February 24), reduced the talk to "jabbering and jawing," and my own reluctantly favorable review in *The Reporter* (March 21) noted that "like *Incident at Vichy*, it is little more than a round-table discussion, however emotionally charged." The oddest and in some ways the most interesting reaction to all that talk came from the reviewer on Riverside Radio WRVR—Dr. Walter Shepard, as his titular billing has it. He likened the play to Bernard Shaw's *Don Juan in Hell*, but having stumbled on that happy comparison, he failed to use it in terms of the set discussion piece, nodded at the four-character similarity and waded into such an addled comment on the play that it is impossible to imagine that he knew what he had with the *Don Juan* reference. For that matter, none of us really knew what we had. Some of us used words like *discussion* as weapons to chastise the play; others (I like to think I am in this group) at least suggested that we were trying to define Miller's method; but none of us really recognized the implications of our responses. Talk, it turns out, is one of the things *The Price* is about. Such a realization need not make either the talk or the play more attractive to the playgoer/reader who is suspicious of Miller's wedding of psychoanalysis with Ibsenite revelation, but at least it gives *The Price* its due. A close look at the play indicates that Miller is using and questioning the dramatic, social, and therapeutic uses of talk and that our understanding of the play, particularly of the ending, hinges on the degree to which the author—and the audience—is willing to admit that there may be efficacy in conversation.

This reading of the play is not intended as a substitute for the standard one. *The Price* is still the story of two brothers who meet again for the first time in sixteen years to dispose of an attic full of discarded furniture—that is, to face the past. Victor is in a kind of spiritual stasis, haunted by the suspicion that his life and his marriage with Esther have no meaning and that there must be someone, something back there to blame for his being a police sergeant instead of a successful scientist, for his having sacrificed career and comfort perhaps unnecessarily to a father, broken by the crash and the depression. Walter, the surgeon brother, who thinks he has accounted for all his losses, is in need of dispensation, forgiveness for the wrong he may or may not have done in letting Victor assume the burden of their father. Miller, as his title indicates, is primarily interested in the recognition that acts, decisions, choices have consequences, often unforeseeable, and that a man, if he is to live,[1] has to accept that he is a product of those consequences, has to pay the price of those acts. If his bills are truly paid—if he has rid himself of guilt for his own past and the need to transfer that guilt to someone else—then the present becomes possible. Although the central thrust of the play is psychological, there is the inevitable social undertone, the suggestion that the choices that both brothers made were dictated by their responses to received attitudes (about success, about the family) just as the situation that called for the decisions was a

---

[1] There is an interesting "dead" pattern running through the play, a reflection of the paralysis that afflicts Victor and Esther. Very early, recalling a man who once lived in the building, Victor assumes he must be dead, only to realize that at the remembered time the man was "my age now. Huh!" "You're worse than my daughter!" Solomon says, attacking Victor's failure to go beyond his disbelief. "And if you can't do that, my friend—you're a dead man!" Later, when we learn that the daughter committed suicide, the earlier speech comes back, enriched. "Come on, we'll all be dead soon," cajoles Walter, shortly before the recriminative revelations begin, and, as they unfold, Esther says, "We are dying, that's what's true." By contrast, Solomon, who is almost ninety, holds onto the present with "if I'm there tomorrow" or "if I'll live," not with a phrase like "unless I'm dead."

societal as well as a personal one. This sense of things does not surface, as it does in *After the Fall*, to become an excuse, a rationalization, a family-of-man credit card to absorb the price for the individual.

Although Miller's theme is a major one, both in his work and in twentieth-century literature in general, the fascination of *The Price*, at least for me, lies in the way that theme emerges in a work in which talk is both tool and subject. That is the facet of *The Price* that I want to give my attention to in this essay. The curtain opens on an attic room, cluttered with old furniture, a closed in playing area, with little space for any but verbal action. A policeman (Victor) enters, in uniform, suggesting to an audience which knows popular plays, but not this one, that a mystery story is about to begin—and, indeed, there is a secret to be unearthed but it has more to do with *Ghosts* than ghost stories. The policeman takes off his jacket, relieving himself of his label, and domesticates the scene as he moves about reintroducing himself to the props. The first sound we hear comes from the harp which he plucks in passing, but the first voices come from a record that he finds on the victrola. It is "Mr. Gallagher and Mr. Shean," the most famous question-and-answer act of the 1920's, and the play gets underway with a conversation routine, a vaudeville ritual.[2] A hint of things to come. There will be questions and answers enough before the play ends—and questions without answers. The point made, Victor takes the record off the phonograph and replaces it with a laughing record, preparation for the end of the play. He is laughing with the performers on the record when Esther enters and the talk begins.

At least, the speeches begin. "What in the world is that?" asks Esther and Victor answers, "Hi!" She asks again and he answers, having kissed her lightly, "Where'd you get a drink?" She replies, "I told you. I went for my checkup." Eventually, after we are well into the scene, Victor does explain what the record is, but by that time the

[2]The text of the play does not identify the specific Gallagher and Shean record and I confess that I never thought to make a note of it either time I saw the play. Clive Barnes quotes, "Now Mr. Gallagher, now Mr. Gallagher, will you tell me what that question really means, I just wanted to find out . . ." and Stefan Kander (*Life*, March 8, 1968), who found the device "a too obvious billboard for the evening to follow," heard, "Won't you tell me just exactly what you mean?" The Gallagher and Shean exchanges I know, the ones that have been re-pressed in recent years, have no such lines in them, but somewhere in the Gallagher and Shean canon such lyrics may exist. It is possible for a reviewer, wanting to make the implicit explicit, to edit his memory. Barnes and Kanfer may have heard the lines they report, but . . . . Absotively, Mr. Gallagher? Possilutely, Mr. Shean?

initial exchange has done its job. These two people answer questions with questions, send out words that pass other word clusters en route without even a nod of recognition. In the world of conventional Broadway drama, where indicators are obvious and superficial, that opening could be taken as a standard Failure-of-Communication scene. Miller is not all that simple-minded. There is tension in this marriage, uncertainty on both sides, reflected in Victor's inability to decide about retirement and in Esther's drinking, but there is also closeness, an understanding that hardly knows any longer that it still understands. There are moments in their long first scene together in which one of them purposely deflects an incipient conversation, as when Esther, not wanting to talk about her sense of disconnection now that their child is grown and out of the house, switches abruptly to Victor's failure to reach his brother. There are moments when one of them answers an unasked question, perhaps an imaginary one, as when Victor, nagged by Esther's moody silence, blurts out, "Esther, I said I would bargain!" For much of the time, however, their apparently fragmented talk is the shorthand of two people who know each other well, who can indicate affection or annoyance without having to make a formal presentation. By the time the furniture dealer comes coughing up the stairs to interrupt them,[3] it should be clear that this is a marriage that is under strain, perhaps really in danger of breaking up, but it should also be obvious that there is a solidity here that prepares for the almost unspoken reconciliation at the end of the play.

What grows out of this opening scene is a sense of the way words are used not so much to say something as to suggest it or, just as often, purposely to avoid saying it. There is, however, another sense

[3]In this play entrances and exits are handled very clumsily if the play is taken as unremittingly realistic. I do not think it should be. The verbal encounters are almost like set pieces and for Solomon to signal his coming with a cough or to pull Walter offstage with "Please, Doctor, if you wouldn't mind . . ." is an admission by Miller of the basic artificiality of his form. Given an attic full of symbolic furniture and a life figure that is also a Yiddish comedy turn, the play is reasonably divorced from the realism that many commentators read into it and found wanting. Much of the incidental, presumably factual material in the play will not hold up under rigid scrutiny. Even the dates and ages are suspect; by my count, Victor would have had to become a policeman around 1940 which would have played havoc with the whole concept of the great Depression sacrifice. So far as I am concerned, these things are unimportant since the play is in the talk not in what it uncovers, but anyone who dotes on the minor inconsistencies of art might look at Nathan Cohen's acidulous review of the road company production (Toronto *Star*, November 11, 1969) for his is surely the most complete collection of instances of the play's sloppy way with facts.

of talk established, if not practiced, as Victor and Esther fill the time before Solomon's arrival. It is through Esther that this idea of talk emerges. Out of her exasperation comes a need for solutions and, product of her environment that she is, she assumes that solutions lie just beyond the proper gathering of words. If Victor and Walter could talk to one another—*really* talk, to use the soap opera intensive—communicate, to use the jargon—then everything would somehow be solved. This is not a peculiarly American attitude, of course. Nora Helmer, just before she slammed that door to *A Doll's House*, confronted Torvald with "We've been married now eight years. Doesn't it occur to you that this is the first time we two, you and I, man and wife, have ever talked seriously together?" Not that Ibsen necessarily assumed that a few more serious conversations would have kept the Helmers together, but I think that dear, dull Nora half suspects that talk might have done the trick. That suspicion is almost an article of faith in the United States and has been for several decades. While I was working on this essay, to catch my breath between paragraphs, I picked up an old copy of *McCall's* (September, 1970) that happened to be lying around the house and read a confessional article by an ex-priest explaining how difficult it is for him to relate to his new wife and her children. The word *talk* runs though the article, an insistent imperative, and it also turns up in a piece by Mary Jo Kopechne's mother in which she explains that Mary Jo was a good girl because she always talked over everything with her parents. Solutions, solutions. This was not an unusual issue of *McCall's*, nor is there anything particularly special about that magazine. All the ladies' magazines, all the newspaper psychologists, all the advice-to-the-lovelorners, licensed and unlicensed, have been telling us for years that holes in marriages, generation gaps, social chasms can be filled with words. The social attitude implicit in this easy adherence to talk operates not only around the dining room table, but in the pages of the presumably serious magazines and in the offices and conference rooms of all our institutions from the federal government down. A symposium in the pages of *Commentary* or *Partisan Review*, a Women's Lib rap, a group therapy session, "dialogue" kept open on the campus, a national conference on poverty or pollution, a peace conference in Paris—all these are part of a pattern. The assumption is that if enough words are spoken, the magic word will cross someone's lips and the heavens will open. "Baby, Talk to Me," sang the hero in the whiniest song in Charles Strouse's *Bye Bye Birdie*.

This amorphous but very pervasive faith in the spoken word had an inevitable effect on the American theater. Playwrights at their best—from Shakespeare to Chekhov—have always been preoccupied with the strategies of language, the way people use words to confuse, to manipulate, to obscure. Popular drama has never been really comfortable with that degree of ambiguity, but it was only during the late 1940s and the 1950s that the Broadway theater developed the drama of the therapeutic conversation. If *A Doll's House* were rewritten in that genre, Torvald would pick up the clue in Nora's speech and turn confessional; after a rapid exchange of "but-don't-you-sees," they both would, and, joining hands, they would go off to face the dark at the top of the stairs. If that air-clearing conversation could have been taken simply as a theatrical device, a means to a happy curtain, it might have taken its place along with the ritual joining of couples at the end of comedy and the mandatory unmasking of the villain in melodrama, but its creators had greater claims to make for it. The plays were supposed to—and in fact did—deal with real problems and, hence, presumably, real solutions, and an alert couple in the audience might take a message out of the theater with them, might probe their own problems on the train home and thus arrive snarling in Rye and not speak to one another for a week. The more serious playwrights were never comfortable with the device. Tennessee Williams wrote such a scene for *Cat on a Hot Tin Roof*, but when he published the play, he offered both his original and the Broadway versions of the last act, commenting on the latter: ". . . I don't believe that a conversation, however revelatory, ever effects so immediate a change in the heart or even conduct of a person in Brick's state of spiritual disrepair." In *Death of a Salesman*, it is Biff's tears not his words that get through to Willy, who never does understand what the words are saying.

In *The Price*, then, we have a character who believes, with much of her society, in the therapy of talk, and a playwright who has his doubts. Aside from the Esther-Victor opening, Miller provides two conversations—one between Victor and Solomon, the other between Victor and Walter—and both of them have consequences within the play. Both are successful theatrical constructions, taking their form from the characters and the demands of the dramatic action, not from some extratheatrical idea about the curative power of talk. It is almost as though Miller is using his play not only to question Esther's attitude toward talk, but by implication and example to criticize the audience expectations on that score and the genre that once fed them.

Miller's complicated approach to talk as subject and device is apparent in his treatment of Esther. In my discussion I have simply assigned her the prevailing societal faith in words, but—although she acts and reacts out of that faith in Act II[4]—she is never simply a vehicle for the idea. Although she harps on "talk," she is as defensive as any of the other characters when the occasion demands, ready to retreat into hurt silence or deflect the conversation to a subject on which she is less vulnerable. Even in her *talk* talk there is no clear line for us to follow. "I mean we ought to start talking the way people talk!" she says at one point, meaning that they should face facts, that Victor should confront Walter and get what the past says Walter owes him. Even if we avoid the obvious ambiguity—that the facts are hers, the past her version of Victor's version—we are faced with her unrecognized doubt about the power of speech. A few lines after the sentence quoted above, she becomes exasperated at Victor's refusal to face the problem of retirement. "It's all I've been talking about since you became eligible—I've been saying the same thing for three years!" she snaps, never hearing how those years of nagging words contradict the point she has just been making. A few seconds later, she is pleading, "Well, why not talk about what you don't understand?" For Victor, although he has certainly tried to call Walter, there is not even Esther's on-again-off-again confidence about talk. When he tries, disbelievingly, to conjure up what went on between him and his father in the attic all those years ago, Esther offers him the reluctant comfort of "Well . . . you loved him." Victor answers, "I know, but it's all words."

It is clear before we are very far into the play that Walter will have to turn up, that he and Victor will have to have some kind of confrontation, but the expectations that hang on that scene are obviously different for Esther, for Victor, and for the audience. Miller, however, has no intention of giving us that scene until we have listened to another conversation, one of a very different character and one that will help shape the Victor-Walter scene when it comes. Solomon arrives to buy the furniture and Esther exits, clearing the stage for him and Victor, leaving a warning hanging in the air, "Well, you give him a good price now, you hear?" The implications of her line—that Victor is a natural sucker, that Solomon is necessarily a

---

[4]*The Price* opened its Philadelphia try-out in January as a two-act play, but when the production reached New York, it was performed without intermission. Both the first published version (*Saturday Evening Post*, February 10, 1968) and the editions in print (Viking, 1968; Bantam, 1969) are in two acts.

crook—are not greatly softened by the old man's "I like her, she's suspicious." The two men are left alone, wearing labels not of their own choosing, and a pattern of approach and retreat begins in which Solomon tries to win Victor over. Solomon is the character that drew the warmest praise from critics, even from those who disliked the play, but a great many reviewers persisted in seeing his scene as a comic interlude, irrelevant to the rest of the play. An old man, pushing ninety, willing to start all over again, to use this roomful of Victor's past as a new beginning, Solomon is obviously a major character in the play's structure of ideas. More important, he has a central dramatic function to perform as well. In New York, he was played in a broadly comic way, achieving his humanity only within the bounds of Yiddish theater stereotypes—a reading that the play allows but does not demand. On the page, he is sadder, tougher, less funny, and, according to Howard Taubman (New York *Times*, October 19, 1968), he was played in Tel Aviv so that his entrance and first line were greeted with a sigh rather than a laugh. In either case, he is a professional dealer, a man who understands the verbal rituals of his own trade. Early in the act, Esther warns Victor that "you're going to have to bargain." Victor insists that he can, that he will, but he has no talent for it. To him, however, bargaining is simply a way for one man to best another, to screw the most profitable deal out of him, and what Solomon is doing, if that is bargaining, is the means by which the second-hand furniture business remains a human endeavor. No one should expect him—particularly at his age—to come crashing into the attic, set a price, pay the money and storm out again. Buying the furniture is not a simple act, it is an event and it demands its mystery. "What're you in such a hurry?" he says. "Talk a little bit, we'll see what happens." So he pokes around the attic, admires the furniture, discusses the state of the world, offers bits of his autobiography, asks Victor questions about himself, philosophizes, jokes, cajoles, badgers, gets politely angry when the deal falters. The effectiveness of the scene depends on an implicit analogy between it and any swindling scene, for the audience, like Victor, begins to love the old man without being completely convinced that he is anything but a very talented *goniff*. George Oppenheimer was apparently so taken by Solomon's appearance of chicanery that he never got beyond that aspect of the scene, for he wrote in his otherwise enthusiastic review (*Newsday*, February 8, 1968), "We realize that the talk is partially a device to soften Vic . . . for the kill—the offer of a price far below what the furniture is worth."

A device, yes; to soften Victor, yes; but beyond that. . . . All during the first part of his scene with Solomon, Victor fights his interest in, his admiration for, finally his fondness for the old man. He keeps insisting: "I'm not sociable." "I'm not good at conversations." He wants Solomon to "talk money," to be direct, blunt, quick; yet he cannot help, even at the beginning, responding to some of Solomon's statements, feeding the old man straight lines that send him down conversational byways. When, at last, Solomon has played the game as far as it will go, has topped his verbal performance with a last pantomimic postponement, the eating of a hard-boiled egg, he sets to work in apparent earnest, jotting down figures, making his appraisal, "I'm going to go here like an IBM." At this point, it is Victor who interrupts, who reinstates the conversation, "You really got married at seventy-five?" By the time Walter arrives, interrupting them in the middle of the payment, the two men have achieved an unspoken understanding more important than the agreement on a price for the furniture. Talk has turned out to be efficacious after all, but not in the way that Esther imagines, nor even as Solomon intended when he went into his routine. Talk can create something, Miller says, but he does so not by insisting but by putting the creation on stage, by doing the job dramatically. The relationship between Victor and Solomon, whatever it is (at the end of the play, Solomon sits down in the father's chair), is an alliance that is used all during the second act. Banished from the stage by the brothers, Solomon emerges from the bedroom from time to time, interruptions that are intrusive in a more basic way than the original reviewers seemed to think. He tends to come back on the scene, to create a diversion, when Walter has Victor on the defensive, when Esther and Walter have too obviously ganged up on Victor.[5] Even when he is not on stage, he manages to be a presence. Victor's final self-realization does not spring full-blown from his argument with Walter; the seeds are planted in the conversation with Solomon.

Walter and Victor begin their conversation as strangers with a "how's-the-wife" exchange that commits neither to anything. "Relax,

[5]The television production made clear what has to be assumed in the theater, that the offstage Solomon is an eavesdropper, willing or not. One shot shows Solomon lying on the bed, eating a candy bar, while the voices of the other three can be heard from outside. That was practically the only thing made clear on television. Produced by the Hallmark Hall of Fame, broadcast over NBC, February 3, 1971, this version of *The Price* was so badly, so stupidly cut that Solomon had no existence as character or symbol and the heart of the play was cut out with him.

we're only talking," says Walter, trying to put Solomon in his place (or the place that Walter thinks ought to be his, for he keeps being surprised that Victor did not know the old man before today). More than a sixteen-year separation lies between the two brothers. There are those unanswered telephone calls, those attempts to reach Walter that Victor so resents, having failed to communicate at third hand, stymied by the machine and the machine-like nurse. Whatever his reason for not answering the phone (he says he was afraid to), Walter is now trying to reach Victor. His scene, at least in the beginning, might be taken as a deadly serious parody of Solomon's but he is not a professional persuader, his need is too naked, his power to give too limited, finally only material. The reminiscence remains sentimental. His revelations about himself (his divorce, his breakdown, his estrangement from his children) suggest a self-awareness more solid than his picking at Victor implies. He quickly begins to make offers (*cf.*, Solomon's reluctance to reach that point)—that he deny any claim to the furniture, that he take a tax write-off on the furniture and give Victor the money, that he find Victor a job in the hospital. Too much, too soon, and Victor remains unconvinced. All Walter's talk seems to him a way of not talking, of avoiding the questions in their mutual past, and Victor, the man who doesn't believe in talk, decides "I feel I have to say something." At this point, it is Esther, of all people, who tries to stop the incipient conversation. Not surprising, really; from the beginning her call for talk has hinged on the hope of practical results, material consequences. Yet, when Victor indicates that he will not "just take the money and shut up," she falls back to one of her *talk* defenses: "You throw this away, you've got to explain it to me."

Walter is offstage seeing to Solomon when the exchange between Esther and Victor takes places. When he returns, when the possibility of the hospital job is broached, the three streams that will feed the final flood of words begin to bubble. Walter, who wishes "we could talk for weeks," who is "still unused to talking about anything that matters," wants Victor to absolve him for the past, to admit that he chose failure. Victor, not yet ready to give up the cast of characters—helpless father, selfless Victor, villainous Walter—who inhabit his past wants Walter's *mea culpa*. Esther wants a reconciliation between the two brothers and the sentimental and material rewards that would grow out of it; and she wants it so badly that she is almost willing to sacrifice Victor for it. She is the one who stops Walter, when, stung by Victor's ingratitude (noble doctor brother rejected), he starts to storm out: "Vic, listen—maybe you *ought* to talk about it." She insists, over Solomon's protests ("so what's the good you'll tear him to pieces"), that "what's so dreadful about telling the truth," that "We're giving this furniture away because nobody's able to say the simplest things." Walter agrees that "maybe it's just as well to talk now," and in a conventional play this would be the signal for the therapeutic conversation, the truth-telling that would lead to the brotherly embrace. Conversation there is and therapeutic it may be for Victor, but it is not conventional. As revelation follows revelation, as first one brother then the other takes the floor, each tries to score points against the other. Recrimination, accusation, but no understanding. Now one, now another of the participants, Esther included, tries to stop the flow of words when he sees himself endangered, but there is no retaining the flood once it is released. When, finally, Victor emerges from the talk with a new sense of self, it is no thanks to Walter, and it is a self that has no absolution to offer his brother. Earlier in the play, Walter picks up one of their mother's evening gowns, thinking to give it to his dress-designing daughter. Now, in a final wordless fury, he scoops it up and throws it at Victor and then, embarrassed, leaves the stage for good. "After all these years you can't expect to settle everything in one conversation, can you?" Walter had asked earlier. Even now, poor Esther cannot quite let it go, "So many times I thought—the one thing he wanted most was to talk to his brother. . . . It always seems to me that one little step more and some crazy kind of forgiveness will come and lift up everyone." But Esther, as she herself says several times in the play, "can never believe anything I see."

If the mandatory cure-all scene has come and gone and the brothers have not fallen into one another's arms, where does that leave the play? In black despair, some reviewers thought, empty lives displayed in all their emptiness. Brendan Gill, for instance, thought the play ended with "three of the four characters. . . even more miserable than they were before" (*New Yorker*, February 17, 1968). Thierry Maulnier, who adapted Miller's play into French, seems to agree. In a note in the program for the French production (*Théâtre Montparnasse*, March 5, 1969), Maulnier, who saw the play's end in its beginning, wrote, "But in the course of that conversation, a man lays himself bare for us and discovers for himself the failure of his life, the absurdity of his failure, and the impossibility for him, even when the occasion arises, to find a reason other than that failure for which to live" (my translation). In a way, Maulnier is right. What emerges from the long talk is the fact that Victor's sacrifice was unnecessary on practical grounds and indefensible in terms of societal values (Walter is persuasive when he denies that their family ever embodied the virtues of loyalty and love). Victor recognizes this and goes beyond it. Maulnier's description is too narrow, the easy label-making of the outsider. Victor does not concede that he is a failure. He acknowledges the consequences of his acts. As Miller said, testifying before the House Un-American Activities Committee in June 1956, "I accept my life." The talk has been effective, but not as a revelatory conversation between the two men. "The confrontation is with each other," Ernest Schier wrote in his review of the Philadelphia try-out (Philadelphia *Bulletin*, January 18, 1968), "but it actually turns out to be . . . a confrontation of each man with himself." Presumably, from Victor's self-confrontation comes a release from the paralysis that has held him, but this is indicated only in small ways, which may explain why some reviewers failed to see it. It would have been impossible for Miller to give Victor a final positive speech—like the one he gave John Proctor in the *The Crucible*—for it would have violated the character and, at the same time, have muddied the play's concern with the uses of speech, on and off stage. So we have to catch those small things. The moment when Esther comes over to Victor's side as wife and ally: "Nothing was sacrificed." The acceptance of the present in her willingness that he should wear his uniform when they go out to the movie. His decision to return for the mask and foil of his college fencing days, an acceptance of the past which must be contrasted to Walter's throwing the dress back. Finally, after Esther and Victor leave, Solomon's last non-verbal testimony to life. He puts the laughing record on the victrola. It begins, tinnily, as only an old record can, and then Solomon starts laughing with the record, finally swallowing the mechanical in the human. As at the beginning, laughter has replaced the voices. Being has stilled discussion.

Chronology of Important Dates

1915   Arthur Asher Miller born in New York City.

1929   Family moves to Brooklyn.

1934   Enrolls in journalism at the University of Michigan.

1936   Writes first play, *No Villain*, in six days during spring vacation. In May, *No Villain* wins Hopwood Award in Drama from Hopwood Writing Awards Contest. Revises *No Villain* for the Theatre Guild's Bureau of New Plays Contest with new title, *They Too Arise*. Begins work on a new play, *Honors At Dawn*.

1937   Enrolls in Professor Kenneth T. Rowe's playwriting class. *They Too Arise* is awarded $1,250 from Bureau of New Plays, and is produced. *Honors At Dawn* receives a Hopwood Award in June. Begins work on a new play, *The Great Disobedience*, for the 1938 Hopwood Contest.

1938   Begins revision of *They Too Arise* with new title, *The Grass Still Grows*. *The Great Disobedience* does not receive a Hopwood Award, but is given a laboratory production by the University of Michigan Theatre Department. Graduates in June with Bachelor of Arts degree in English. Joins Federal Theatre Project in New York City; writes radio plays and scripts as well as stage plays.

1940   Marries Mary Grace Slattery.

1944   *The Man Who Had All the Luck* is produced on Broadway. *Situation Normal* published.

1945   *Focus*, a novel, is published.

1947   *All My Sons* is produced and published.

1949   *Death of a Salesman* is produced and published; wins Pulitzer Prize.

1950   *An Enemy of the People* is produced (an adaptation of Ibsen's play) and published in 1951.

1953	*The Crucible* is produced and published.
1955	*A View from the Bridge* and *A Memory of Two Mondays* (one-act plays) are produced and published.
1956	Appears before House Un-American Activities Committee, receives honorary doctorate from the University of Michigan, divorces Mary Slattery, and marries Marilyn Monroe. Two-act version of *A View from the Bridge* premieres in London.
1957	*Arthur Miller's Collected Plays* published.
1960	Divorces Marilyn Monroe.
1961	*The Misfits*, a film, is produced.
1962	Marries Inge Morath.
1964	*After the Fall* is produced and published. *Incident at Vichy* also produced (1964) and published in 1965.
1967	*I Don't Need You Anymore*, a collection of short stories, is published.
1968	*The Price* is produced and published.
1969	*In Russia* (with photographs by Inge Morath) is published.
1972	*The Creation of the World and Other Business* is produced and published.
1974	*Up From Paradise* is produced in Ann Arbor, Michigan.
1977	*In the Country* (with photographs by Inge Morath) is published. *The Archbishop's Ceiling* is produced in Washington, D.C.
1978	*The Theater Essays of Arthur Miller* is published.
1979	*Chinese Encounters* (with photographs by Inge Morath) is published.
1980	*Playing For Time*, a film adapted from a book by Fania Fenelon, is produced for television and published. *The American Clock* is produced and published.
1981	*Arthur Miller's Collected Plays, Volume II*, is published. Two one-act plays, *Elegy for a Lady* and *Some Kind of Love Story*, are scheduled for production and publication.

Notes on the Editor and Contributors

ROBERT A. MARTIN is Professor of English in the Department of Humanities at the University of Michigan in Ann Arbor. He has published reviews, poetry, and essays on Arthur Miller, F. Scott Fitzgerald, Willa Cather, and Sherwood Anderson in numerous scholarly journals. He is the editor of *The Theater Essays of Arthur Miller.*

PAUL BLUMBERG is Associate Professor of Sociology at Queens College of the City University of New York. His articles have appeared in *Dissent, The Nation, The New Republic,* and *Midstream*, in addition to *The American Quarterly.* He is the author of *Industrial Democracy: the Sociology of Participation* and *The Future of Inequality in an Age of Decline.*

ENOCH BRATER, whose published works on Beckett, Pinter, Stoppard, and other contemporary playwrights have appeared in journals, reviews, and collections, is Associate Professor of English Language and Literature at the University of Michigan in Ann Arbor.

CHARLES A. CARPENTER is Professor of English at the State University of New York at Binghamton. He has compiled the Annual Bibliography for *Modern Drama* since 1974, and has published articles on Shaw and Pinter, in addition to numerous bibliographies in journals. He is the author of *Bernard Shaw & The Art of Destroying Ideals: The Early Plays*, and has published *Modern British Drama,* a book-length bibliography.

RUBY COHN is Professor of Comparative Drama at the University of California (Davis). She has published three books and edited two others on the works of Samuel Beckett, as well as *Currents in Contemporary Drama, Dialogue in American Drama,* and *Modern Shakespeare Offshoots*. She is an Associate Editor of *Modern Drama* and *Theatre Journal.*

LAWRENCE D. LOWENTHAL was a lecturer in the Department of English and American Literature at Tel Aviv University when his article was originally published. His present location is unknown.

WALTER J. MESERVE is Professor of Theatre and Drama at Indiana University. He is the editor of *Studies in Death of a Salesman, Discussions of Modern American Drama*, and compiler of *American Drama to 1900*, a book-length bibliography. He is the author of *An Outline History of American Drama, Robert*

E. Sherwood: Reluctant Moralist, An Emerging Entertainment: The Drama of the American People to 1828, and has been on the editorial board of *Modern Drama* since 1960.

LEONARD MOSS is Professor of Comparative Literature at the State University of New York at Geneseo, and has recently completed the second edition of his *Arthur Miller*. His main scholarly interest is the theory and practice of tragedy. He has published studies on Greek tragedy, Plato and Aristotle, Milton, Hegel, and Nietzsche.

BENJAMIN NELSON is Professor of English and Comparative Literature at Fairleigh Dickinson University, New Jersey. He is the author of *Tennessee Williams: the Man and His Work* and *Arthur Miller: Portrait of a Playwright*. He is currently writing a series of essays on American-Jewish literature.

ORM ÖVERLAND is Professor of American Literature at the University of Bergen, Norway, and is the editor of *American Studies in Scandinavia*. He is the author of *The Making of an American Classic: James Fenimore Cooper's The Prairie* and *America Perceived: A View from Abroad in the 20th Century*. His articles have been published in numerous journals and collections in the United States and Europe.

THOMAS E. PORTER is Professor of English and Dean of Liberal Arts at the University of Texas at Arlington. As administrative duties permit, he teaches modern and world drama. He is the author of *Myth and Modern American Drama*.

KENNETH T. ROWE is Professor-Emeritus of English at the University of Michigan in Ann Arbor, where he originated and taught the courses in playwriting. He was head of the play department of the Theater Guild in 1945–1946 and was Chairman of Production of New Plays for the American Educational Theatre Association. He is the editor of three volumes of *University of Michigan Plays* and the author of *Write That Play* and *A Theatre in Your Head*.

STEPHEN S. STANTON is Professor of English in the Department of Humanities at the University of Michigan in Ann Arbor. A former bibliographer for *The Shaw Review*, he has published articles on American and European drama in numerous journals such as *PMLA* and *Modern Drama*, and is the editor of *Camille and Other Plays*, *A Casebook on Candida*, and *Tennessee Williams: A Collection of Critical Essays*. He is the founder and editor of *The Tennessee Williams Newsletter*.

J. L. STYAN was born in London and educated at Cambridge. He is Franklyn Bliss Snyder Professor of English Literature at Northwestern University, and is the author of several books on drama, including *The Elements of Drama*, *The Dark Comedy*, *Chekhov in Performance*, and *Drama, Stage, and Audience*.

GERALD WEALES is Professor of English at the University of Pennsylvania. He is the author of *American Drama Since World War II* and *The Jumping-Off Place*; editor of critical editions of *Death of a Salesman* and *The Crucible*; and contributor of the drama section of *The Harvard Guide to Contemporary American Writing*. Winner of the George Jean Nathan Award for Dramatic Criticism, 1964–1965, he is currently reviewing theater for *Commonweal*.

Studies of Arthur Miller's Drama:
A Selective International Bibliography, 1966–1979

by Charles A. Carpenter

The following bibliography of criticism on Arthur Miller's drama lists about 200 selected books, parts of books, and articles published since 1966 in all Roman-alphabet languages. It is restricted to the more substantial and useful commentary; besides excluding items valuable primarily for statements by Miller,* it omits biographical summaries, most reviews of performances, and unpublished dissertations. The checklist is drawn from my work in progress, an international bibliography of modern drama studies, 1966–1980, and thus derives from personally examining over 1,400 journals and thousands of books. As the first list of Miller commentary based on such a wide-ranging search, it considerably supplements the book-length secondary bibliography by John H. Ferres (see below). The present list includes about 90 items not in Ferres, half of them foreign-language, half English. Ferres's compilation remains indispensable, however, not only for its pre-1966 material and cogent annotations, but also for the hundreds of more ephemeral English-language items it lists. Students of Miller's plays can keep informed of current scholarship by consulting my annual checklists of modern drama studies in the journal *Modern Drama*.

A. Bibliographies

Ferres, John H., *Arthur Miller: A Reference Guide*. Boston: Hall, 1979, 225 pp. Annotated bibliography of English-language essays, reviews, and interviews.

Charles A. Carpenter's bibliography appears in print for the first time in this volume, with the author's permission.

*For a convenient list of interviews with Miller, see *The Theater Essays of Arthur Miller*, Robert A. Martin, ed. (New York: Viking, 1978), pp. 388–90.

Hayashi, Tetsumaro, *An Index to Arthur Miller Criticism* (2nd ed.). Metuchen, N.J.: Scarecrow Press, 1976, 151 pp. Not annotated.

Jensen, George H., *Arthur Miller: A Bibliographical Checklist*. Columbia, S.C.: Faust, 1976, 145 pp. Lists writings, speeches, interviews, testimony, recordings, etc.

Ungar, Harriet, "The Writings of and About Arthur Miller: A Check List 1936–1967," *Bulletin of the New York Public Library*, 74 (1970), 107–34. No longer useful.

B. *Collections of Essays*

Corrigan, Robert W., ed., *Arthur Miller: A Collection of Critical Essays*. Englewood Cliffs, N.J.: Prentice-Hall, Inc., 1969, 176 pp.

Ferres, John H., ed., *Twentieth Century Interpretations of The Crucible*. Englewood Cliffs, N.J.: Prentice-Hall, Inc., 1972, 122 pp.

Martine, James J., ed., *Critical Essays on Arthur Miller*. Boston: Hall, 1979, 211 pp.

Meserve, Walter J., ed., *The Merrill Studies in Death of a Salesman*. Columbus, Ohio: Merrill, 1972, 99 pp.

Weales, Gerald, ed., *Arthur Miller: The Crucible: Text and Criticism*. New York: Viking, 1971, 484 pp. (Introduction, pp. ix–xvii).

————, *Arthur Miller: Death of a Salesman: Text and Criticism*. New York: Viking, 1967, 426 pp. (Introduction, pp. vii–xx).

C. *Criticism*

Altena, I., and A. M. Aylwin, *Notes on Arthur Miller's Death of a Salesman*. London: Methuen, 1976, 42 pp.

Aswad, Betsy B., "*The Crucible*," in *Insight IV: Analyses of Modern British and American Drama,* ed. Hermann J. Weiand. Frankfurt: Hirschgraben, 1975, pp. 230–38.

Baker, Isadore L., *Notes on Arthur Miller, The Crucible*. Bath, Eng.: Brodie, 1976, 68 pp.

Bates, Barclay W., "The Lost Past in *Death of a Salesman*," *Modern Drama*, 11 (1968), 164–72.

Baxandall, Lee, "Arthur Miller: Still the Innocent," in *Salesman*, Weales (B).; from 1964 *Encore*, pp. 352–58.

Bear Nicol, Bernard de, ed., *Varieties of Dramatic Experience: Discussions on Dramatic Forms and Themes Between Stanley Evernden, Roger Hubank, Thora Burnley Jones and Bernard de Bear Nicol.* London: Univ. of London Press, 1969, pp. 235–47.

Bécsy, Tamás, *"Az ügynök halála" A drámamodellek és a mai dráma.* Budapest: Akadémiai, 1974, pp. 305–10. On *Death of a Salesman.*

Bell, Robert F., "Perspectives on Witch Hunts: Lion Feuchtwanger and Arthur Miller," in *Deutsches Exildrama und Exiltheater*, ed. Wolfgang Elfe et al. Bern: Lang, 1977, pp. 112–18. *The Crucible* and *Wahn oder Der Teufel in Boston.*

Bergeron, David M., "Arthur Miller's *The Crucible* and Nathaniel Hawthorne: Some Parallels." *English Journal*, 58 (1969), 47–55.

Bergman, Herbert, "The Interior of a Heart: *The Crucible* and *The Scarlet Letter.*" *Univ. College Quarterly*, 15 (1970), 27–32.

Bettina, Sister M., "Willy Loman's Brother Ben: Tragic Insight in *Death of a Salesman*," in Meserve (B) pp. 80–83; from 1962 *Modern Drama.*

Bhatia, S. K., "Father and Son Relationship in *All My Sons* and *Death of a Salesman*," *Rajasthan Journal of English Studies*, 4–5 (1976–77), 101–12.

Bigsby, C. W. E., *Confrontation and Commitment: A Study of Contemporary American Drama, 1959–66.* Columbia: Univ. of Missouri Press, 1968, pp. 26–49.

———, "What Price Arthur Miller? An Analysis of *The Price*," *Twentieth Century Literature*, 16 (1970), 16–25; reprinted in Martine (B), pp. 161–71.

Bleich, David, "Psychological Bases of Learning from Literature: Arthur Miller's *Death of a Salesman*," *College English*, 33 (October 1971), 32–45.

Bliquez, Guerin. "Linda's Role in *Death of a Salesman*," *Modern Drama*, 10 (1968), 383–86; reprinted in Meserve (B), pp. 77–79.

Blumberg, Paul. "Sociology and Social Literature: Work Alienation in the Plays of Arthur Miller," *American Quarterly*, 21 (1969), 291–310.

Bonnet, Jean-Marie, "Nom et renom dans *The Crucible.*" *Études Anglaises*, 30 (1977), 179–83.

Bottman, Philip N., "Quentin's Quest: Arthur Miller's Move into Expressionism," *Wisconsin Studies in Contemporary Literature*, 5 (1968), 41–52.

Brashear, William R., "The Empty Bench: Arthur Miller and Social Drama," *The Gorgon's Head: A Study in Tragedy and Despair.* Athens: Univ. of Georgia Press, 1977, pp. 134–49; rev. from *Michigan Quarterly Review*, 5 (1966), 270–78. On *After the Fall* and tragedy.

Bredella, Lothar, "Arthur Millers Stück *All My Sons* im Unterricht und die

Frage nach seiner didaktischen Begründung," *Neueren Sprachen*, 21 (1972), 595–600.

Bronson, David, *"An Enemy of the People:* A Key to Arthur Miller's Art and Ethics," *Comparative Drama*, 2 (1968–69), 229–47; reprinted in Martine (B), pp. 55–71.

Brüning, Eberhard, "Arthur Miller: Spätbürgerlicher Humanist und Gesellschaftskritiker," in *Studien zum amerikanischen Drama nach dem Zweiten Weltkrieg*, ed. Brüning et al. Berlin: Rütten & Loening, 1977, pp. 40–53.

Buitenhuis, Peter, "Arthur Miller: The Fall from the Bridge," *Canadian Assn. for American Studies Bulletin*, 3 (1967), 55–71.

Burhans, Clinton S., "Eden and the Idiot Child: Arthur Miller's *After the Fall*," *Ball State Univ. Forum*, 20 (Spring 1979), 3–16.

Calarco, N. Joseph, "Production as Criticism: Miller's *The Crucible*," *Educational Theatre Journal*, 29 (1977), 354–61.

Callahan, Elizabeth A., "The Tragic Hero in Contemporary Secular and Religious Drama," *Literary Half-Yearly*, 8 (1967), 42–49. Part on *The Crucible*.

Casty, Alan, "Post-Loverly Love: A Comparative Report," *Antioch Review*, 26 (1966), 399–411. Compares *After the Fall* with Saul Bellow's *Herzog* and Federico Fellini's *8½*.

Cismaru, Alfred, "Before and *After the Fall*," *Forum* (Houston), 11 (Winter 1974), 67–71. The play's similarities to Camus's *The Fall*.

Clurman, Harold, "Director's Notes for *Incident at Vichy*" and "Letter to Boris Aronson Apropos of *The Creation of the World and Other Business*," *On Directing*. New York: Macmillan, 1972, pp. 242–53 (from 1965 *Tulane Drama Review*), 292–99.

——, "Editor's Introduction," *The Portable Arthur Miller*. New York: Viking, 1971, pp. xi–xxv.

Codignola, Luciano, "Il dramma a soggetto in America," *Il teatro della guerra fredda e altre cose*. Urbino: Argalia, 1969, pp. 123–40. Reprinted discussions of Miller, Williams, and Wilder.

Coen, Frank, "Teaching the Drama," *English Journal*, 56 (1967), 1136–39. On *All My Sons* and Ibsen's *Master Builder*.

Cohn, Ruby, "The Articulate Victims of Arthur Miller," *Dialogue in American Drama*. Bloomington: Indiana Univ. Press, 1971, pp. 68–96.

Cook, Larry W., "The Function of Ben and Dave Singleman in *Death of a Salesman*," *Notes on Contemporary Literature*, 5 (January 1975), 7–9.

Corrigan, Robert W., "The Achievement of Arthur Miller," *The Theatre in Search of a Fix*. New York: Delacorte, 1973, pp. 325–47; reprinted in Corrigan (B), pp. 1–22; from *Comparative Drama*, 2 (1968), 141–60.

Couchman, Gordon W., "Arthur Miller's Tragedy of Babbitt," in Meserve (B), pp. 68–75; from 1955 *Educational Theatre Journal*.

Coy, Javier, "Arthur Miller: Notas para una interpretación sociológica," *Filología Moderna*, 23–24 (1966), 299–312.

——, and Juan J. Coy, *Teatro norteamericano actual: Miller, Inge, Albee*. Madrid: Prensa Española, 1967, pp. 11–145.

Curtis, Penelope, "Setting, Language, and the Force of Evil in *The Crucible*," in Ferres (B), pp. 67–76, and *Crucible*, Weales (B), pp. 255–71; from 1965 *Critical Review* (Sydney).

Czanerle, Maria, *Twarze i maski: Szkice teatralne*. Krakow: Wydawn. Literackie, 1970, pp. 257–308. Reprinted reviews.

Dillingham, William B., "Arthur Miller and the Loss of Conscience," in *Salesman*, Weales (B), pp. 339–49; from 1960 *Emory Univ. Quarterly*.

Ditsky, John M., "All Irish Here: The 'Irishman' in Modern Drama," *Dalhousie Review*, 54 (1974), 94–102. Part on *A Memory of Two Mondays*.

——, "Stone, Fire and Light: Approaches to *The Crucible*," *North Dakota Quarterly*, 46 (Spring 1978), 65–72.

Doménech, Ricardo, "Miller: Una crisis personal y representativa [*After the Fall*]," *El teatro, hoy (Doce crónicas)*. Madrid: Cuadernos para el Diálogo, 1966, pp. 39–48.

Dommergues, Pierre, "Le théâtre entre deux aliénations," *Les U.S.A. à la recherche de leur identité: Rencontres avec 40 écrivains américains*. Paris: Grasset, 1967, pp. 329–76. Part on Miller.

Donahue, Francis, "Arthur Miller: Las dos moralidades," *Cuadernos Americanos*, 38, v (1979), 157–68.

Driver, Tom F., "Strength and Weakness in Arthur Miller," in Corrigan (B), pp. 59–67, and in *Discussions of American Drama*, ed. Walter J. Meserve. Boston: Heath, 1966, pp. 105–13; from 1960 *Tulane Drama Review*.

Eisinger, Chester E., "Focus on Arthur Miller's *Death of a Salesman:* The Wrong Dreams," in *American Dreams, American Nightmares*, ed. David Madden. Carbondale: Southern Illinois Univ. Press, 1970, pp. 165–74.

Elvin, Bernstein, *Teatrul şi interogaţia tragică*. Bucharest: Pentru Literatură Universală, 1969, pp. 272–83.

Epstein, Arthur D., "A Look at *A View from the Bridge*," in Martine (B), pp. 107–18; from 1965 *Texas Studies in Literature and Language*.

Evans, Gareth L., "American Connections: O'Neill, Miller, Williams and Albee," *The Language of Modern Drama*. London: Dent, 1977, pp. 177–204.

Falb, Lewis W., *American Drama in Paris, 1945–1970: A Study of Its Critical Reception*. Chapel Hill: Univ. of North Carolina Press, 1973, pp. 37–50.

Fender, Stephen, "Precision and Pseudo Precision in *The Crucible*," *Journal of American Studies*, 1 (1967), 87–98; reprinted in *Crucible*, Weales (B), pp. 272–89.

Ferguson, Alfred R., "The Tragedy of the American Dream in *Death of a Salesman*," *Thought*, 53 (1978), 82–98.

Ferres, John H., "Still in the Present Tense: *The Crucible* Today," *Univ. College Quarterly*, 17 (May 1972), 8–18; reprinted in Ferres (B), pp. 1–19.

Field, B. S., "[Hamartia in] *Death of a Salesman*," *Twentieth Century Literature*, 18 (1972), 19–24.

Filipič, Lojze, "Arthur Miller in njegova dramska dela," *Živa dramaturgija 1952–1975*. Ljubljana: Cankarjeva, 1977, pp. 423–37.

Foulkes, Peter A., "Arthur Miller's *The Crucible:* Contexts of Understanding and Misunderstanding," in *Theater und Drama in Amerika,* ed. Edgar Lohner and Rudolf Haas. Berlin: Schmidt, 1978, pp. 295–309.

Freedman, Morris, "Bertolt Brecht and American Social Drama," *The Moral Impulse: Modern Drama from Ibsen to the Present*. Carbondale: Southern Illinois Univ. Press, 1967, pp. 99–114. Part on Miller.

———, "The Jewishness of Arthur Miller: His Family Epic," *American Drama in Social Context*. Carbondale: Southern Illinois Univ. Press, 1971, pp. 43–58.

García Pavón, Francisco, "Las secretas galerías de Arthur Miller," *Textos y escenarios*. Barcelona: Plaza y Janés, 1971, pp. 119–30.

Gianakaris, C. J., "Theatre of the Mind in Miller, Osborne and Shaffer," *Renascence,* 30 (Autumn 1977), 33–42. Part on *After the Fall*.

Goetsch, Paul, "Arthur Millers Zeitkritik in *Death of a Salesman*," *Neueren Sprachen*, 66 (1967), 105–17.

———, *"Death of a Salesman,"* in *Das amerikanische Drama*, ed. Paul Goetsch. Düsseldorf: Bagel, 1974, pp. 208–33.

Golden, Joseph, *The Death of Tinker Bell: The American Theatre in the 20th Century*. Syracuse, N.Y.: Syracuse Univ. Press, 1967, pp. 130–37.

Gordon, Lois, "*Death of a Salesman:* An Appreciation," in *The Forties: Fiction, Poetry, Drama*, ed. Warren French. Deland, Fla.: Everett/Edwards, 1969, pp. 273–83.

Gottfried, Martin, *A Theater Divided: The Postwar American Stage*. Boston: Little, Brown, 1968, pp. 149–54, 241–48.

Gould, Jean, "Arthur Miller," *Modern American Playwrights*. New York: Dodd, Mead, 1966, pp. 247–63.

Grandel, Hartmut, "*Death of a Salesman:* Tragödie oder soziales Drama?", in *Amerikanisches Drama und Theater im 20. Jahrhundert*, ed. Alfred Weber and Siegfried Neuweiler. Göttingen: Vandenhoeck & Ruprecht, 1975, pp. 204–17.

Groene, Horst, "*Death of a Salesman:* Beispielhafte amerikanische Dramenkunst," *Literatur in Wissenschaft und Unterricht*, 4 (1971), 177–86.

Gross, Barry E., "*All My Sons* and the Larger Context," *Modern Drama*, 18 (1975), 15–27; reprinted in Martine (B), pp. 10–20.

———, "Peddler and Pioneer in *Death of a Salesman*," in Meserve (B), pp. 29–34; from 1965 *Modern Drama*.

Gruber, Christian P., "*The Price*," in *Insight IV* (see under Aswad), pp. 225–30.

Guardia, Alfredo de la, "Invención y crítica en el teatro," *Temas dramáticos y otros ensayos*. Buenos Aires: Academia Argentina de Letras, 1978, pp. 151–61; 1965 essay.

Guerrero Zamora, Juan, "Arthur Miller, humanista," *Historia del teatro contemporáneo*, IV. Barcelona: Flors, 1967, pp. 65–77.

Hagopian, John V., "Arthur Miller: The *Salesman*'s Two Cases," in Meserve (B), pp. 34–42; from 1963 *Modern Drama*; rev. version in *Insight I: Analyses of American Literature*, eds. John V. Hagopian and Martin Dolch, 2nd ed. rev. Frankfurt: Hirschgraben, 1971, pp. 174–86.

Hallett, Charles A., "The Retrospective Technique and Its Implications for Tragedy," *Comparative Drama*, 12 (1978), 3–21. Stresses Miller and Ibsen.

Hansen, Chadwick, "The Metamorphosis of Tituba, or Why American Intellectuals Can't Tell an Indian Witch from a Negro." *New England Quarterly*, 47 (1974), 3–12.

Harshbarger, Karl, *The Burning Jungle: An Analysis of Arthur Miller's Death of a Salesman*. Washington, D.C.: Univ. Press of America, 1978, 104 pp.

Haugen, Einar, "Ibsen as Fellow Traveler: Arthur Miller's Adaptation of *An Enemy of the People*," *Scandinavian Studies*, 51 (1979), 343–53.

Hayman, Ronald, *Arthur Miller.* London: Heinemann Educational, 1970, 141 pp. Includes interview, pp. 3–21.

Hays, Peter L., "Arthur Miller and Tennessee Williams," *Essays in Literature* (Western Illinois Univ.), 4 (1977), 239–49. Influence of *The Glass Menagerie* on *Death of a Salesman.*

Hegedüs, Géza, "Pillantás egy nagy drámaíróra," *A kentaur és az angyal.* Budapest: Szépirodalmi, 1968, pp. 538–46.

Heilman, Robert B., *The Iceman, the Arsonist, and the Troubled Agent: Tragedy and Melodrama on the Modern Stage.* Seattle: Univ. of Washington Press, 1973, pp. 142–61.

———, "Salesmen's Deaths: Documentary and Myth." *Shenandoah,* 20 (Spring 1969), 20–28. Miller's play and Eudora Welty's "The Death of a Traveling Salesman."

———, *Tragedy and Melodrama: Versions of Experience.* Seattle: Univ. of Washington Press, 1968, pp. 233–37 and passim. On *Salesman.*

Helwig, Karin, "Die komparative Strategie der Charaktere, die Grammatik der Handlung im Stück *A View from the Bridge* von Arthur Miller und dem entsprechenden Librett von Renzo Rossellini," *Cahiers de Linguistique Théorique et Appliquée,* 11 (1974), 247–70.

Hermann, István, "Az emberség tartalékai: Arthur Miller, *A salemi boszorkányok,*" *A személyiség nyomában: Drámai kalauz.* Budapest: Magvetö, 1972, pp. 495–504.

Herron, Ima H., *The Small Town in American Drama.* Dallas: Southern Methodist Univ. Press, 1969, pp. 30–35. On *The Crucible.*

Heyen, William, "Arthur Miller's *Death of a Salesman* and the American Dream," in *Amerikanisches Drama* (see under Grandel), pp. 190–201.

Higgins, David, "Arthur Miller's *The Price:* The Wisdom of Solomon," in *Itinerary 3: Criticism,* ed. Frank Baldanza. Bowling Green, Ohio: Bowling Green Univ. Press, 1977, pp. 85–94.

Hill, Philip G. "*The Crucible:* A Structural View." *Modern Drama,* 10 (1967), 312–17; reprinted in Ferres (B), pp. 86–92.

Högel, Rolf K., "Arthur Miller: *A Memory of Two Mondays:* Versuch einer dramatischen Darstellung der industriellen Arbeitswelt," *Neueren Sprachen,* 5 (1975), 419–29.

———, "*The Creation of the World and Other Business:* Arthur Millers Spekulationen über die Ursprünge des Bösen," *Literatur in Wissenchaft und Unterricht,* 12 (1974), 37–48.

———, "The Manipulation of Time in Miller's *After the Fall*," *Literatur in Wissenschaft und Unterricht*, 7 (1974), 115–21.

Hoeveler, D. L., "*Death of a Salesman* as Psychomachia," *Journal of American Culture*, 1 (1978), 632–37.

Hogan, Robert, "Arthur Miller," in *American Writers: A Collection of Literary Biographies*, III, ed. Leonard Unger. New York: Scribner, 1974, pp. 145–69; reprint of 1964 pamphlet.

Hombitzer, Eleonore, "Die Selbstentfremdung des modernen Menschen im dramatischen Werk Arthur Millers," *Neueren Sprachen*, 69 (1970), 409–16.

Hughes, Catherine, "*The Crucible*," *Plays, Politics, and Polemics*. New York: Drama Book Specialists, 1973, pp. 15–25.

Hunt, Albert, "Realism and Intelligence: Some Notes on Arthur Miller," in *Crucible*, Weales (B), pp. 324–32; from 1960 *Encore*.

Hynes, Joseph A., "Attention Must Be Paid...," in *Salesman*, Weales (B), pp. 280–89; from 1962 *College English*. On *Salesman*.

Innes, Christopher, "The Salesman on the Stage: A Study in the Social Influence of Drama," *English Studies in Canada*, 3 (1977), 336–50.

Isoldo, Ludovico, "La vera morte di Willy Loman: La radici economiche di *Death of a Salesman* di A. Miller." *Annali Istituto Universitario Orientale, Napoli: Sezione Germanica: Anglistica*, 18, iii (1975), 85–107.

Itschert, Hans, "Amerikanische Dramaturgie: Theater als Dichtung," *Literatur—Kultur—Gesellschaft in England und Amerika*, ed. Gerhard Müller-Schwefe and Konrad Tuzinski. Frankfurt: Diesterweg, 1966, pp. 349–65; reprinted in *Das amerikanische Drama von den Anfängen bis zur Gegenwart*, ed. Itschert. Darmstadt: Wissenschaftliche Buchgesellschaft, 1972, pp. 77–97.

———, "*The Price*," *Das amerikanische Drama*, ed. Paul Goetsch. Düsseldorf: Bagel, 1974, pp. 234–51.

Jackson, Esther M., "*Death of a Salesman*: Tragic Myth in the Modern Theatre," in Meserve (B), pp. 57–68; from 1963 *College Language Assn. Journal*.

Jacobson, Irving F., "The Child as Guilty Witness [in Miller's stories and plays]," *Literature & Psychology*, 24, i (1974), 12–23. Stresses "I Don't Need You Any More."

———, "Christ, Pygmalion, and Hitler in *After the Fall*," *Essays in Literature* (Univ. of Denver), 2 (August 1974), 12–27.

——, "Family Dreams in *Death of a Salesman*," *American Literature*, 47 (1975), 247–58; reprinted in Martine (B), pp. 44–52.

Jacquot, Jean, and Catherine Mounier, "*Mort d'un commis voyageur* d'Arthur Miller et ses réalisations à Broadway et au Théâtre de la Commune d'Aubervilliers," in *Les voies de la création théâtrale*, IV, ed. Denis Bablet and Jean Jacquot. Paris: Centre National de la Recherche Scientifique, 1975, pp. 13–62.

James, Stuart B., "Pastoral Dreamer in an Urban World," *Univ. of Denver Quarterly*, 1 (Autumn 1966), 45–57.

Jensen, Carsten, *Salg, klasse og død: En analyse af Arthur Millers Death of a Salesman.* Copenhagen: SIL, 1975, 44 pp.

Jochems, Helmut, "*Death of a Salesman*—eine Nachlese," *Literatur in Wissenschaft und Unterricht*, 1 (1968), 77–97.

Köhler, Klaus, "Bewusstseinsanalyse und Gesellschaftskrise im Dramenwerk Arthur Millers," *Zeitschrift für Anglistik und Amerikanistik*, 22 (1974), 18–40.

Kónya, Judit, "*Az ügynök halála*," in *Kalandozás a dramaturgia világában*, ed. Géza Hegedüs and Judit Kónya. Budapest: Gondolat, 1973, pp. 271–85. On *Death of a Salesman*.

Koppenhaver, Allen J., "*The Fall* and After: Albert Camus and Arthur Miller," *Modern Drama*, 9 (1966), 206–9.

Lengeler, Rainer, "*After the Fall*," in *Das amerikanische Drama der Gegenwart*, ed. Herbert Grabes. Kronberg: Athenäum, 1976, pp. 12–28.

Levin, David, "Salem Witchcraft in Recent Fiction and Drama," in *Crucible*, Weales (B), pp. 248–54; from 1955 *New England Quarterly*.

Lewis, Allan, "Arthur Miller: Return to the Self," *American Plays and Playwrights of the Contemporary Theatre*, rev. ed. New York: Crown, 1970, pp. 35–52. Stresses *After the Fall*.

Liston, William T., "John Proctor's Playing in *The Crucible*," *Midwest Quarterly*, 20 (1979), 394–403.

Lowenthal, Lawrence D., "Arthur Miller's *Incident at Vichy*: A Sartrean Interpretation," *Modern Drama*, 18 (1975), 29–41; reprinted in Martine (B), pp. 143–54.

Lübbren, Rainer, *Arthur Miller.* Velber: Friedrich, 1966, 155 pp.

Lumley, Frederick, *New Trends in 20th Century Drama*, 4th ed. New York: Oxford Univ. Press, 1972, pp. 194–99.

Macey, Samuel L., "Nonheroic Tragedy: A Pedigree for American Tragic Drama," *Comparative Literature Studies*, 6 (1969), 1–19.

McMahon, Helen, "Arthur Miller's Common Man: The Problem of the Realistic and the Mythic," *Drama & Theatre*, 10 (Spring 1972), 128–33.

Malhotra, M. L., "Triumph and Tragedy: An Examination of Arthur Miller's *The Crucible*," *Bridges of Literature*. Ajmer: Sunanda, 1971, pp. 63–78.

Manocchio, Tony, and William Petitt, "The Loman Family," *Families Under Stress: A Psychological Interpretation*. London: Routledge & Paul, 1975, pp. 129–68. *Death of a Salesman* treated as a case study.

Martin, Robert A., "Arthur Miller's *The Crucible*: Background and Sources," *Modern Drama*, 20 (1977), 279–92; reprinted in Martine (B), pp. 93–104.

———, "Introduction," in Arthur Miller, *The Theater Essays*, ed. Robert A. Martin. New York: Viking, 1978, pp. xv–xxxix.

Mennemeier, Franz N., *Das moderne Drama des Auslandes*, 3rd ed. Düsseldorf: Bagel, 1976, pp. 81–93.

Moss, Leonard, *Arthur Miller*. New York: Twayne, 1967, 160 pp.

———, "Arthur Miller and the Common Man's Language," in Meserve (B), pp. 85–92; from 1964 *Modern Drama*.

Mottram, Eric, "Arthur Miller: The Development of a Political Dramatist in America," in *American Theatre*, ed. John R. Brown and Bernard Harris. London: Arnold, 1967, pp. 127–61; reprinted in Corrigan (B), 23–57.

Mukerji, Nirmal, "John Proctor's Tragic Predicament," *Panjab Univ. Research Bulletin*, 4 (April 1973), 75–79.

Murray, Edward, "Arthur Miller: *Death of a Salesman, The Misfits,* and *After the Fall*," *The Cinematic Imagination: Writers and the Motion Pictures*. New York: Ungar, 1972, pp. 69–85.

———, *Arthur Miller, Dramatist*. New York: Ungar, 1967, 186 pp.

Nelson, Benjamin, *Arthur Miller: Portrait of a Playwright*. New York: McKay, 1970, 336 pp.

Nolan, Paul T., "Two Memory Plays: *The Glass Menagerie* and *After the Fall*," *McNeese Review*, 17 (1966), 27–38.

Oberg, Arthur K., "*Death of a Salesman* and Arthur Miller's Search for Style," *Criticism*, 9 (1967), 303–11; reprinted in Meserve (B), pp. 92–99.

Överland, Orm, "The Action and Its Significance: Arthur Miller's Struggle with Dramatic Form," *Modern Drama*, 18 (1975), 1–14.

Parker, Brian, "Point of View in Arthur Miller's *Death of a Salesman*." *University of Toronto Quarterly*, 35 (1966), 144–57; reprinted in Corrigan (B), pp. 95–109.

Partridge, C. J., *The Crucible*. Oxford: Blackwell, 1971, 87 pp.

——, *Death of a Salesman*. Oxford: Blackwell, 1969, 58 pp.

Paul, Rajinder, "*Death of a Salesman* in India," in Meserve (B), pp. 23–27.

Popkin, Henry, "Historical Analogy and *The Crucible*," in Ferres (B), pp. 77–85; from 1964 *College English*.

Porter, Thomas E., "Acres of Diamonds: *Death of a Salesman*" and "The Long Shadow of the Law: *The Crucible*," *Myth and Modern American Drama*. Detroit: Wayne State Univ. Press, 1969, pp. 127–52, 177–99; reprinted in Martine (B), pp. 24–43, 75–92.

Pradhan, Narindar S., "Arthur Miller and the Pursuit of Guilt," in *Studies in American Literature*, ed. Jagdish Chander and N. S. Pradhan. Delhi: Oxford Univ. Press, 1976, pp. 28–42.

Prudhoe, John, "Arthur Miller and the Tradition of Tragedy," in *Das amerikanische Drama von den Anfängen bis zur Gegenwart*, ed. Hans Itschert. Darmstadt: Wissenschaftliche Buchgesellschaft, 1972, pp. 341–52; from 1962 *English Studies*.

Przybylska, Krystyna, "Nowe sztuki Arthura Millera [*After the Fall*]," *Dialog* (Warsaw), 11, x (1966), 105–10.

Rahv, Philip, "Arthur Miller and the Fallacy of Profundity," *Literature and the Sixth Sense*. Boston: Houghton Mifflin, 1970, pp. 385–91. 1964 essay on *Incident at Vichy*.

Rama Murthy, V., *American Expressionistic Drama; Containing Analyses of Three Outstanding American Plays: O'Neill, The Hairy Ape; Williams, The Glass Menagerie; Miller, Death of a Salesman*. Delhi: Doaba House, 1970, pp. 73–96.

Razum, Hannes, "Schuld und Verantwortung im Werk Arthur Millers," in *Theater und Drama in Amerika*, ed. Edgar Lohner and Rudolf Haas. Berlin: Schmidt, 1978, pp. 310–20.

Reno, Raymond H., "Arthur Miller and the Death of God," *Texas Studies in Literature and Language*, 11 (1969), 1069–87.

Riese, Teut A., "Der Konflikt zwischen Individuum und Gesellschaft im amerikanischen Drama," in *Amerika: Vision und Wirklichkeit*, ed. Franz H. Link. Frankfurt: Athenäum, 1968, pp. 64–84. Pp. 79–84 on *The Crucible*.

Rössle, Wolfgang, *Die soziale Wirklichkeit in Arthur Millers Death of a Salesman*. Freiburg: Universitätsverlag, 1970, 129 pp.

Rothenberg, Albert, and Eugene D. Shapiro, "The Defense of Psycho-analysis in Literature: *Long Day's Journey Into Night* and *A View from the Bridge*," *Comparative Drama*, 7 (1973), 51–67.

Rutnin, M. M., *"Death of a Salesman:* A Myth or Reality in a Developing Country," in *Asian Response to American Literature,* ed. C. D. Narasimhaiah. Delhi: Vikas, 1972, pp. 171–80.

Saisselin, Remy G., "Is Tragic Drama Possible in the Twentieth Century?" in Meserve (B), pp. 44–51; from 1960 *Theatre Annual.*

Scanlan, Tom, ". . . Family and Society in Arthur Miller," *Family, Drama, and American Dreams.* Westport, Conn.: Greenwood, 1978, pp. 126–55.

Scheller, Bernhard, "Zur Gestaltung des Arbeiters im Drama," *Weimarer Beiträge,* 19, i (1973), 47–70. Stresses Miller and Arnold Wesker.

Schwarz, Alfred, *From Büchner to Beckett: Dramatic Theory and the Modes of Tragic Drama.* Athens: Ohio Univ. Press, 1978, pp. 87–93 (on *The Crucible*), 116–22, 161–78 (stresses *After the Fall*).

Schweckendiek, Adolf, "Willy Loman in Arthur Millers *Der Tod des Handlungsreisenden* [Hunger—Angst—Schmerz—Trauerneurose]," *Könnt ich Magie von meinem Pfad entfernen: Neurodenkundliche Studien über Gestalten der Dichtung.* Berlin: Lungwitz-Stiftung, 1970, pp. 246–54.

Schweinitz, George de, *"Death of a Salesman:* A Note on Epic and Tragedy," in *Salesman,* Weales (B), pp. 272–79, and Meserve (B), pp. 52–57; from 1960 *Western Humanities Review.*

Sharma, P. P., "Search for Self-Identity in *Death of a Salesman," Literary Criterion,* 11 (Summer 1974), 74–79.

Shatzky, Joel, "Arthur Miller's 'Jewish' Salesman," *Studies in American Jewish Literature,* 2 (Winter 1976), 1–9.

———, "The 'Reactive Image' and Miller's *Death of a Salesman," Players,* 48 (1973), 104–10.

Shelton, Frank W., "Sports and the Competitive Ethic: *Death of a Salesman* and [Jason Miller's] *That Championship Season," Ball State Univ. Forum,* 20, ii (1979), 17–21.

Silkenat, Anne L., *"Death of a Salesman,"* in *Zeitgenössische amerikanische Dichtung,* 3rd ed, ed. Werner Hüllen et al. Frankfurt: Hirschgraben, 1969, pp. 158–64.

Singh, Ram S., "Arthur Miller and the American Psyche," *Kurukshetra Univ. Research Journal: Arts and Humanities,* 3 (1969), 154–64.

Singh Maini, Darshan, "The Moral Vision of Arthur Miller," in *Indian Essays in American Literature,* eds. Sujit Mukherjee and D. V. K. Raghavacharyulu. Bombay: Popular Prakashan, 1969, pp. 85–96.

Sontag, Susan, *Against Interpretation, and Other Essays.* New York: Delta, 1966, pp. 140–45. Reprinted essay on *After the Fall.*

Stambusky, Alan A., "Arthur Miller: Aristotelian Canons in the Twentieth Century Drama," in *Modern American Drama: Essays in Criticism*, ed. William E. Taylor. DeLand, Fla.: Everett/Edwards, 1968, pp. 91–115.

Standley, Fred L., "An Echo of Milton in *The Crucible*," *Notes & Queries*, 15 (1968), 303; rejoinder by Oliver H. P. Ferris, *Notes & Queries*, 16 (1969), 268. Corey's "More weight!"

Steinberg, M. W., "Arthur Miller and the Idea of Modern Tragedy," in Corrigan (B), pp. 81–93; from 1960 *Dalhousie Review*.

Stinson, John J., "Structure in *After the Fall:* The Relevance of the Maggie Episodes to the Main Themes and the Christian Symbolism," *Modern Drama*, 10 (1967), 233–40.

Toschi, Gastone, *Angoscia e solitudine nel teatro contemporaneo.* Fossano: Esperienze, 1970, pp. 129–39.

Trowbridge, Clinton W., "Arthur Miller: Between Pathos and Tragedy," *Modern Drama*, 10 (1967), 221–32; reprinted in Martine (B), pp. 125–35.

Tuhela, Marián, "Problémy americkej tragédie (Zamyslenie nad otázkami etiky v dramatike)," *Slovenské Divadlo*, 16 (1968), 89–111. On Robinson Jeffers, Maxwell Anderson, and Miller.

Vajda, Miklós, "Arthur Miller: Moralist as Playwright," *New Hungarian Quarterly*, 16 (1975), 171–80.

Vogel, Dan, "Willy Tyrannos," *The Three Masks of American Tragedy*. Baton Rouge: Louisiana State Univ. Press, 1974, pp. 91–102.

Von Szeliski, John, *Tragedy and Fear: Why Modern Tragic Drama Fails.* Chapel Hill: Univ. of North Carolina Press, 1971, 257 pp. See index under play titles.

Walden, Daniel, "Miller's Roots and His Moral Dilemma; or, Continuity from Brooklyn to *Salesman*," in Martine (B), pp. 189–96.

Warshow, Robert, "The Liberal Conscience in *The Crucible*," in *Crucible*, Weales (B), pp. 210–26; from 1953 *Commentary*.

Weales, Gerald, "All About Talk: Arthur Miller's *The Price*," *Ohio Review*, 13 (Winter 1972), 74–84.

———, "Arthur Miller's Shifting Image of Man," in Corrigan (B), pp. 131–42; reprinted from *The American Theater Today*, ed. Alan Downer. New York: Basic Books, 1967, pp. 85–98.

———, *The Jumping-Off Place: American Drama in the 1960's.* New York: Macmillan, 1969, pp. 14–23.

Welland, Dennis, "*Death of a Salesman* in England," in Meserve (B), pp. 8–17.

Wells, Arvin R., *"All My Sons,"* in *Insight I: Analyses of American Literature*, 2nd rev. ed., ed. John V. Hagopian and Martin Dolch. Frankfurt: Hirschgraben, 1971; reprinted as "The Living and the Dead in *All My Sons*" in Martine (B), p. 5–9, and in *Das amerikanische Drama von den Anfängen bis zur Gegenwart*, ed. Hans Itschert. Darmstadt: Wissenschaftliche Buchgesellschaft, 1972, pp. 367–77; from 1964 *Modern Drama*.

———, "Arthur Miller: The Dramatist as Social Critic?", in *Das amerikanische Drama* (see preceding entry), pp. 353–66.

White, Sidney H., *The Merrill Guide to Arthur Miller*. Columbus, Ohio: Merrill, 1970, 47 pp. (Cover-title: *Guide to Arthur Miller*).

Wiegand, William, "Arthur Miller and the Man Who Knows," in *Salesman*, Weales (B), pp. 290–312; also *Crucible*, Weales (B), pp. 290–314; from 1957 *Western Review*. Overview of Miller's work to 1955.

Willett, Ralph W., "The Ideas of Miller and Williams," *Theatre Annual*, 22 (1965–66), 31–40.

———, "A note on Arthur Miller's *The Price*," *Journal of American Studies*, 5 (1971), 307–10.

Williams, Raymond, *Drama from Ibsen to Brecht*. Harmondsworth: Penguin Books, 1973 (c. 1968), pp. 304–15; reprinted in Corrigan (B), pp. 69–79; version from 1959 *Critical Quarterly*, "The Realism of Arthur Miller," reprinted in *Salesman*, Weales (B), pp. 313–25.

Wilson, Robert N., "Arthur Miller: The Salesman and Society," *The Writer as Social Seer*. Chapel Hill: Univ. of North Carolina Press, 1979, pp. 56–71.

Winegarten, Renee, "The World of Arthur Miller," *Jewish Quarterly*, 17 (Summer 1969), 48–53. On *The Price*.

Wood, E. R. (Introduction), in Miller, *A View from the Bridge*. London: Heinemann Educational, 1975 (not examined).

Index